BRITISH ENGLIS

MW00327094

ENGLISH PERSIAN

THEME-BASED DICTIONARY

Contains over 9000 commonly used words

Theme-based dictionary British English-Persian - 9000 words
British English collection

By Andrey Taranov

T&P Books vocabularies are intended for helping you learn, memorize and review foreign words. The dictionary is divided into themes, covering all major spheres of everyday activities, business, science, culture, etc.

The process of learning words using T&P Books' theme-based dictionaries gives you the following advantages:

- Correctly grouped source information predetermines success at subsequent stages of word memorization
- Availability of words derived from the same root allowing memorization of word units (rather than separate words)
- Small units of words facilitate the process of establishing associative links needed for consolidation of vocabulary
- Level of language knowledge can be estimated by the number of learned words

T&P Books Publishing
www.tpbooks.com

ISBN: 978-1-78716-710-0

This book is also available in E-book formats.
Please visit www.tpbooks.com or the major online bookstores.

PERSIAN THEME-BASED DICTIONARY
British English collection

T&P Books vocabularies are intended to help you learn, memorize, and review foreign words. The vocabulary contains over 9000 commonly used words arranged thematically.

- Vocabulary contains the most commonly used words
- Recommended as an addition to any language course
- Meets the needs of beginners and advanced learners of foreign languages
- Convenient for daily use, revision sessions, and self-testing activities
- Allows you to assess your vocabulary

Special features of the vocabulary

- Words are organized according to their meaning, not alphabetically
- Words are presented in three columns to facilitate the reviewing and self-testing processes
- Words in groups are divided into small blocks to facilitate the learning process
- The vocabulary offers a convenient and simple transcription of each foreign word

The vocabulary has 256 topics including:

Basic Concepts, Numbers, Colors, Months, Seasons, Units of Measurement, Clothing & Accessories, Food & Nutrition, Restaurant, Family Members, Relatives, Character, Feelings, Emotions, Diseases, City, Town, Sightseeing, Shopping, Money, House, Home, Office, Working in the Office, Import & Export, Marketing, Job Search, Sports, Education, Computer, Internet, Tools, Nature, Countries, Nationalities and more ...

TABLE OF CONTENTS

PRONUNCIATION GUIDE

T&P phonetic alphabet	Persian example	English example
['] (ayn)	دعوا [da'vā]	voiced pharyngeal fricative
['] (hamza)	تایید [ta'id]	glottal stop
[a]	رود [ravad]	shorter than in ask
[ā]	آتش [ātaš]	calf, palm
[b]	بانک [bānk]	baby, book
[č]	چند [čand]	church, French
[d]	هشتاد [haštād]	day, doctor
[e]	عشق [ešq]	elm, medal
[f]	فندک [fandak]	face, food
[g]	لوگو [logo]	game, gold
[h]	گیاه [giyāh]	home, have
[i]	جزیره [jazire]	shorter than in feet
[j]	جشن [jašn]	joke, general
[k]	کاج [kāj]	clock, kiss
[l]	لیمو [limu]	lace, people
[m]	ماجرا [mājarā]	magic, milk
[n]	نروژ [norvež]	sang, thing
[o]	گلف [golf]	pod, John
[p]	اپرا [operā]	pencil, private
[q]	لاغر [lāqar]	between [g] and [h]
[r]	رقم [raqam]	rice, radio
[s]	سوپ [sup]	city, boss
[š]	دوش [duš]	machine, shark
[t]	ترجمه [tarjome]	tourist, trip
[u]	نیرو [niru]	book
[v]	ورشو [varšow]	very, river
[w]	روشن [rowšan]	vase, winter
[x]	کاخ [kāx]	as in Scots 'loch'
[y]	بیابان [biyābān]	yes, New York
[z]	زنجیر [zanjir]	zebra, please
[ž]	ژوئن [žuan]	forge, pleasure

ABBREVIATIONS
used in the dictionary

English abbreviations

ab.	-	about
adj	-	adjective
adv	-	adverb
anim.	-	animate
as adj	-	attributive noun used as adjective
e.g.	-	for example
etc.	-	et cetera
fam.	-	familiar
fem.	-	feminine
form.	-	formal
inanim.	-	inanimate
masc.	-	masculine
math	-	mathematics
mil.	-	military
n	-	noun
pl	-	plural
pron.	-	pronoun
sb	-	somebody
sing.	-	singular
sth	-	something
v aux	-	auxiliary verb
vi	-	intransitive verb
vi, vt	-	intransitive, transitive verb
vt	-	transitive verb

BASIC CONCEPTS

Basic concepts. Part 1

1. Pronouns

I, me	man	من
you	to	تو
he, she, it	u	او
we	mā	ما
you (to a group)	šomā	شما
they	ān-hā	آنها

2. Greetings. Salutations. Farewells

Hello! (form.)	salām	سلام
Good morning!	sobh bexeyr	صبح بخیر
Good afternoon!	ruz bexeyr!	روز بخیر!
Good evening!	asr bexeyr	عصربخیر
to say hello	salām kardan	سلام کردن
Hi! (hello)	salām	سلام
greeting (n)	salām	سلام
to greet (vt)	salām kardan	سلام کردن
How are you? (form.)	haletān četowr ast?	حالتان چطور است؟
How are you? (fam.)	četorid?	چطورید؟
What's new?	če xabar?	چه خبر؟
Goodbye!	xodāhāfez	خداحافظ
Bye!	bāy bāy	بای بای
See you soon!	be omid-e didār!	به امید دیدار!
Farewell!	xodāhāfez!	خداحافظ!
to say goodbye	xodāhāfezi kardan	خداحافظی کردن
Cheers!	tā bezudi!	تا بزودی!
Thank you! Cheers!	motešakker-am!	متشکرم!
Thank you very much!	besyār motešakker-am!	بسیار متشکرم!
My pleasure!	xāheš mikonam	خواهش می کنم
Don't mention it!	tašakkor lāzem nist	تشکر لازم نیست
It was nothing	qābel-i nadārad	قابلی ندارد
Excuse me! (fam.)	bebaxšid!	ببخشید!
to excuse (forgive)	baxšidan	بخشیدن
to apologize (vi)	ozr xāstan	عذر خواستن
My apologies	ozr mixāham	عذرمی خواهم

I'm sorry!	bebaxšid!	ببخشید!
to forgive (vt)	baxšidan	بخشیدن
It's okay! (that's all right)	mohem nist	مهم نیست
please (adv)	lotfan	لطفأ

Don't forget!	farāmuš nakonid!	فراموش نکنید!
Certainly!	albate!	البته!
Of course not!	albate ke neh!	البته که نه!
Okay! (I agree)	besyār xob!	بسیارخوب!
That's enough!	bas ast!	بس است!

3. How to address

Excuse me, ...	bebaxšid!	ببخشید!
mister, sir	āqā	آقا
madam	xānom	خانم
miss	xānom	خانم
young man	mard-e javān	مرد جوان
young man (little boy)	pesar bače	پسر بچه
miss (little girl)	doxtar bačče	دختربچه

4. Cardinal numbers. Part 1

0 zero	sefr	صفر
1 one	yek	یک
2 two	do	دو
3 three	se	سه
4 four	čāhār	چهار

5 five	panj	پنج
6 six	šeš	شش
7 seven	haft	هفت
8 eight	hašt	هشت
9 nine	neh	نه

10 ten	dah	ده
11 eleven	yāzdah	یازده
12 twelve	davāzdah	دوازده
13 thirteen	sizdah	سیزده
14 fourteen	čāhārdah	چهارده

15 fifteen	pānzdah	پانزده
16 sixteen	šānzdah	شانزده
17 seventeen	hefdah	هفده
18 eighteen	hijdah	هیجده
19 nineteen	nuzdah	نوزده

20 twenty	bist	بیست
21 twenty-one	bist-o yek	بیست ویک
22 twenty-two	bist-o do	بیست ودو
23 twenty-three	bist-o se	بیست وسه
30 thirty	si	سی

31 thirty-one	si-yo yek	سی ویک
32 thirty-two	si-yo do	سی ودو
33 thirty-three	si-yo se	سی وسه

40 forty	čehel	چهل
41 forty-one	čehel-o yek	چهل ویک
42 forty-two	čehel-o do	چهل ودو
43 forty-three	čehel-o se	چهل وسه

50 fifty	panjāh	پنجاه
51 fifty-one	panjāh-o yek	پنجاه ویک
52 fifty-two	panjāh-o do	پنجاه ودو
53 fifty-three	panjāh-o se	پنجاه وسه

60 sixty	šast	شصت
61 sixty-one	šast-o yek	شصت ویک
62 sixty-two	šast-o do	شصت ودو
63 sixty-three	šast-o se	شصت وسه

70 seventy	haftād	هفتاد
71 seventy-one	haftād-o yek	هفتاد ویک
72 seventy-two	haftād-o do	هفتاد ودو
73 seventy-three	haftād-o se	هفتاد وسه

80 eighty	haštād	هشتاد
81 eighty-one	haštād-o yek	هشتاد ویک
82 eighty-two	haštād-o do	هشتاد ودو
83 eighty-three	haštād-o se	هشتاد وسه

90 ninety	navad	نود
91 ninety-one	navad-o yek	نود ویک
92 ninety-two	navad-o do	نود ودو
93 ninety-three	navad-o se	نود وسه

5. Cardinal numbers. Part 2

100 one hundred	sad	صد
200 two hundred	devist	دویست
300 three hundred	sisad	سیصد
400 four hundred	čāhārsad	چهارصد
500 five hundred	pānsad	پانصد

600 six hundred	šeššad	ششصد
700 seven hundred	haftsad	هفتصد
800 eight hundred	haštsad	هشتصد
900 nine hundred	nohsad	نهصد

1000 one thousand	hezār	هزار
2000 two thousand	dohezār	دوهزار
3000 three thousand	se hezār	سه هزار
10000 ten thousand	dah hezār	ده هزار
one hundred thousand	sad hezār	صد هزار
million	milyun	میلیون
billion	milyārd	میلیارد

6. Ordinal numbers

first (adj)	avvalin	اولین
second (adj)	dovvomin	دومین
third (adj)	sevvomin	سومین
fourth (adj)	čāhāromin	چهارمین
fifth (adj)	panjomin	پنجمین
sixth (adj)	šešomin	ششمین
seventh (adj)	haftomin	هفتمین
eighth (adj)	haštomin	هشتمین
ninth (adj)	nohomin	نهمین
tenth (adj)	dahomin	دهمین

7. Numbers. Fractions

fraction	kasr	کسر
one half	yek dovvom	یک دوم
one third	yek sevvom	یک سوم
one quarter	yek čāhārom	یک چهارم
one eighth	yek panjom	یک هشتم
one tenth	yek dahom	یک دهم
two thirds	do sevvom	دو سوم
three quarters	se čāhārrom	سه چهارم

8. Numbers. Basic operations

subtraction	tafriq	تفریق
to subtract (vi, vt)	tafriq kardan	تفریق کردن
division	taqsim	تقسیم
to divide (vt)	taqsim kardan	تقسیم کردن
addition	jam'	جمع
to add up (vt)	jam' kardan	جمع کردن
to add (vi)	ezāfe kardan	اضافه کردن
multiplication	zarb	ضرب
to multiply (vt)	zarb kardan	ضرب کردن

9. Numbers. Miscellaneous

digit, figure	raqam	رقم
number	adad	عدد
numeral	adadi	عددی
minus sign	manfi	منفی
plus sign	mosbat	مثبت
formula	formul	فرمول
calculation	mohāsebe	محاسبه
to count (vi, vt)	šemordan	شمردن

| to count up | mohāsebe kardan | محاسبه کردن |
| to compare (vt) | moqāyse kardan | مقایسه کردن |

How much?	čeqadr?	چقدر؟
sum, total	jam'-e kol	جمع کل
result	natije	نتیجه
remainder	bāqimānde	باقیمانده

a few (e.g., ~ years ago)	čand	چند
little (I had ~ time)	kami	کمی
the rest	baqiye	بقیه
one and a half	yek-o nim	یک و نیم
dozen	dojin	دوجین

in half (adv)	be do qesmat	به دو قسمت
equally (evenly)	be tāsavi	به تساوی
half	nim	نیم
time (three ~s)	daf'e	دفعه

10. The most important verbs. Part 1

to advise (vt)	nasihat kardan	نصیحت کردن
to agree (say yes)	movāfeqat kardan	موافقت کردن
to answer (vi, vt)	javāb dādan	جواب دادن
to apologize (vi)	ozr xāstan	عذر خواستن
to arrive (vi)	residan	رسیدن

to ask (~ oneself)	porsidan	پرسیدن
to ask (~ sb to do sth)	xāstan	خواستن
to be (vi)	budan	بودن

to be afraid	tarsidan	ترسیدن
to be hungry	gorosne budan	گرسنه بودن
to be interested in ...	alāqe dāštan	علاقه داشتن
to be needed	hāmi budan	حامی بودن
to be surprised	mote'ajjeb šodan	متعجب شدن

to be thirsty	tešne budan	تشنه بودن
to begin (vt)	šoru' kardan	شروع کردن
to belong to ...	ta'alloq dāštan	تعلق داشتن
to boast (vi)	be rox kešidan	به رخ کشیدن
to break (split into pieces)	šekastan	شکستن
to call (~ for help)	komak xāstan	کمک خواستن

can (v aux)	tavānestan	توانستن
to catch (vt)	gereftan	گرفتن
to change (vt)	avaz kardan	عوض کردن
to choose (select)	entexāb kardan	انتخاب کردن
to come down (the stairs)	pāyin āmadan	پایین آمدن

to compare (vt)	moqāyse kardan	مقایسه کردن
to complain (vi, vt)	šekāyat kardan	شکایت کردن
to confuse (mix up)	qāti kardan	قاطی کردن
to continue (vt)	edāme dādan	ادامه دادن

| to control (vt) | kontorol kardan | کنترل کردن |
| to cook (dinner) | poxtan | پختن |

to cost (vt)	qeymat dāštan	قیمت داشتن
to count (add up)	šemordan	شمردن
to count on …	hesāb kardan	حساب کردن
to create (vt)	ijād kardan	ایجاد کردن
to cry (weep)	gerye kardan	گریه کردن

11. The most important verbs. Part 2

to deceive (vi, vt)	farib dādan	فریب دادن
to decorate (tree, street)	tazyin kardan	تزیین کردن
to defend (a country, etc.)	defā' kardan	دفاع کردن
to demand (request firmly)	darxāst kardan	درخواست کردن
to dig (vt)	kandan	کندن

to discuss (vt)	bahs kardan	بحث کردن
to do (vt)	anjām dādan	انجام دادن
to doubt (have doubts)	šok dāštan	شک داشتن
to drop (let fall)	andāxtan	انداختن
to enter (room, house, etc.)	vāred šodan	وارد شدن

to excuse (forgive)	baxšidan	بخشیدن
to exist (vi)	vojud dāštan	وجود داشتن
to expect (foresee)	pišbini kardan	پیش بینی کردن
to explain (vt)	touzih dādan	توضیح دادن
to fall (vi)	oftādan	افتادن

to fancy (vt)	dust dāštan	دوست داشتن
to find (vt)	peydā kardan	پیدا کردن
to finish (vt)	be pāyān resāndan	به پایان رساندن
to fly (vi)	parvāz kardan	پرواز کردن
to follow … (come after)	donbāl kardan	دنبال کردن

to forget (vi, vt)	farāmuš kardan	فراموش کردن
to forgive (vt)	baxšidan	بخشیدن
to give (vt)	dādan	دادن
to give a hint	sarnax dādan	سرنخ دادن
to go (on foot)	raftan	رفتن

to go for a swim	ābtani kardan	آبتنی کردن
to go out (for dinner, etc.)	birun raftan	بیرون رفتن
to guess (the answer)	hads zadan	حدس زدن

to have (vt)	dāštan	داشتن
to have breakfast	sobhāne xordan	صبحانه خوردن
to have dinner	šām xordan	شام خوردن
to have lunch	nāhār xordan	ناهار خوردن
to hear (vt)	šenidan	شنیدن

to help (vt)	komak kardan	کمک کردن
to hide (vt)	penhān kardan	پنهان کردن
to hope (vi, vt)	omid dāštan	امید داشتن

| to hunt (vi, vt) | šekār kardan | شکار کردن |
| to hurry (vi) | ajale kardan | عجله کردن |

12. The most important verbs. Part 3

to inform (vt)	āgah kardan	آگاه کردن
to insist (vi, vt)	esrār kardan	اصرار کردن
to insult (vt)	towhin kardan	توهین کردن
to invite (vt)	da'vat kardan	دعوت کردن
to joke (vi)	šuxi kardan	شوخی کردن

to keep (vt)	hefz kardan	حفظ کردن
to keep silent	sāket māndan	ساکت ماندن
to kill (vt)	koštan	کشتن
to know (sb)	šenāxtan	شناختن
to know (sth)	dānestan	دانستن
to laugh (vi)	xandidan	خندیدن

to liberate (city, etc.)	āzād kardan	آزاد کردن
to look for ... (search)	jostoju kardan	جستجو کردن
to love (sb)	dust dāštan	دوست داشتن
to make a mistake	eštebāh kardan	اشتباه کردن
to manage, to run	edāre kardan	اداره کردن

to mean (signify)	ma'ni dāštan	معنی داشتن
to mention (talk about)	zekr kardan	ذکر کردن
to miss (school, etc.)	qāyeb budan	غایب بودن
to notice (see)	motevajjeh šodan	متوجه شدن
to object (vi, vt)	moxalefat kardan	مخالفت کردن
to observe (see)	mošāhede kardan	مشاهده کردن
to open (vt)	bāz kardan	باز کردن
to order (meal, etc.)	sefāreš dādan	سفارش دادن
to order (mil.)	farmān dādan	فرمان دادن
to own (possess)	sāheb budan	صاحب بودن

to participate (vi)	šerekat kardan	شرکت کردن
to pay (vi, vt)	pardāxtan	پرداختن
to permit (vt)	ejāze dādan	اجازه دادن
to plan (vt)	barnāmerizi kardan	برنامه ریزی کردن
to play (children)	bāzi kardan	بازی کردن

to pray (vi, vt)	do'ā kardan	دعا کردن
to prefer (vt)	tarjih dādan	ترجیح دادن
to promise (vt)	qowl dādan	قول دادن
to pronounce (vt)	talaffoz kardan	تلفظ کردن
to propose (vt)	pišnahād dādan	پیشنهاد دادن
to punish (vt)	tanbih kardan	تنبیه کردن

13. The most important verbs. Part 4

| to read (vi, vt) | xāndan | خواندن |
| to recommend (vt) | towsie kardan | توصیه کردن |

to refuse (vi, vt)	rad kardan	رد کردن
to regret (be sorry)	afsus xordan	افسوس خوردن
to rent (sth from sb)	ejāre kardan	اجاره کردن

to repeat (say again)	tekrār kardan	تکرار کردن
to reserve, to book	rezerv kardan	رزرو کردن
to run (vi)	davidan	دویدن
to save (rescue)	najāt dādan	نجات دادن

to say (~ thank you)	goftan	گفتن
to scold (vt)	da'vā kardan	دعوا کردن
to see (vt)	didan	دیدن
to sell (vt)	foruxtan	فروختن

to send (vt)	ferestādan	فرستادن
to shoot (vi)	tirandāzi kardan	تیراندازی کردن
to shout (vi)	faryād zadan	فریاد زدن
to show (vt)	nešān dādan	نشان دادن
to sign (document)	emzā kardan	امضا کردن

to sit down (vi)	nešastan	نشستن
to smile (vi)	labxand zadan	لبخند زدن
to speak (vi, vt)	harf zadan	حرف زدن
to steal (money, etc.)	dozdidan	دزدیدن
to stop (for pause, etc.)	motevaghef šhodan	متوقف شدن

to stop (please ~ calling me)	bas kardan	بس کردن
to study (vt)	dars xāndan	درس خواندن
to swim (vi)	šenā kardan	شنا کردن
to take (vt)	bardāštan	برداشتن
to think (vi, vt)	fekr kardan	فکر کردن

to threaten (vt)	tahdid kardan	تهدید کردن
to touch (with hands)	lams kardan	لمس کردن
to translate (vt)	tarjome kardan	ترجمه کردن
to trust (vt)	etminān kardan	اطمینان کردن
to try (attempt)	talāš kardan	تلاش کردن

to turn (e.g., ~ left)	pičidan	پیچیدن
to underestimate (vt)	dast-e kam gereftan	دست کم گرفتن
to understand (vt)	fahmidan	فهمیدن
to unite (vt)	mottahed kardan	متحد کردن
to wait (vt)	montazer budan	منتظر بودن

to want (wish, desire)	xāstan	خواستن
to warn (vt)	hošdār dādan	هشدار دادن
to work (vi)	kār kardan	کار کردن
to write (vt)	neveštan	نوشتن
to write down	neveštan	نوشتن

14. Colours

colour	rang	رنگ
shade (tint)	teyf-e rang	طیف رنگ

| hue | rangmaye | رنگمایه |
| rainbow | rangin kamān | رنگین کمان |

white (adj)	sefid	سفید
black (adj)	siyāh	سیاه
grey (adj)	xākestari	خاکستری

green (adj)	sabz	سبز
yellow (adj)	zard	زرد
red (adj)	sorx	سرخ

blue (adj)	abi	آبی
light blue (adj)	ābi rowšan	آبی روشن
pink (adj)	surati	صورتی
orange (adj)	nārenji	نارنجی
violet (adj)	banafš	بنفش
brown (adj)	qahve i	قهوه ای

| golden (adj) | talāyi | طلایی |
| silvery (adj) | noqre i | نقره ای |

beige (adj)	baž	بژ
cream (adj)	kerem	کرم
turquoise (adj)	firuze i	فیروزه ای
cherry red (adj)	ālbāluyi	آلبالویی
lilac (adj)	banafš yasi	بنفش یاسی
crimson (adj)	zereški	زرشکی

light (adj)	rowšan	روشن
dark (adj)	tire	تیره
bright, vivid (adj)	rowšan	روشن

coloured (pencils)	rangi	رنگی
colour (e.g. ~ film)	rangi	رنگی
black-and-white (adj)	siyāh-o sefid	سیاه و سفید
plain (one-coloured)	yek rang	یک رنگ
multicoloured (adj)	rangārang	رنگارنگ

15. Questions

Who?	če kas-i?	چه کسی؟
What?	če čiz-i?	چه چیزی؟
Where? (at, in)	kojā?	کجا؟
Where (to)?	kojā?	کجا؟
From where?	az kojā?	از کجا؟
When?	če vaqt?	چه وقت؟
Why? (What for?)	čerā?	چرا؟
Why? (~ are you crying?)	čerā?	چرا؟

What for?	barā-ye če?	برای چه؟
How? (in what way)	četor?	چطور؟
What? (What kind of ...?)	kodām?	کدام؟
Which?	kodām?	کدام؟
To whom?	barā-ye ki?	برای کی؟

About whom?	dar bāre-ye ki?	درباره کی؟
About what?	darbāre-ye či?	درباره چی؟
With whom?	bā ki?	با کی؟

| How many? How much? | čeqadr? | چقدر؟ |
| Whose? | māl-e ki? | مال کی؟ |

16. Prepositions

with (accompanied by)	bā	با
without	bedune	بدون
to (indicating direction)	be	به
about (talking ~ ...)	rāje' be	راجع به
before (in time)	piš az	پیش از
in front of ...	dar moqābel	در مقابل

under (beneath, below)	zir	زیر
above (over)	bālā-ye	بالای
on (atop)	ruy	روی
from (off, out of)	az	از
of (made from)	az	از

| in (e.g. ~ ten minutes) | tā | تا |
| over (across the top of) | az bālāye | از بالای |

17. Function words. Adverbs. Part 1

Where? (at, in)	kojā?	کجا؟
here (adv)	in jā	این جا
there (adv)	ānjā	آنجا

| somewhere (to be) | jā-yi | جایی |
| nowhere (not anywhere) | hič kojā | هیچ کجا |

| by (near, beside) | nazdik | نزدیک |
| by the window | nazdik panjere | نزدیک پنجره |

Where (to)?	kojā?	کجا؟
here (e.g. come ~!)	in jā	این جا
there (e.g. to go ~)	ānjā	آنجا
from here (adv)	az injā	از اینجا
from there (adv)	az ānjā	از آنجا

| close (adv) | nazdik | نزدیک |
| far (adv) | dur | دور |

near (e.g. ~ Paris)	nazdik	نزدیک
nearby (adv)	nazdik	نزدیک
not far (adv)	nazdik	نزدیک

| left (adj) | čap | چپ |
| on the left | dast-e čap | دست چپ |

to the left	be čap	به چپ
right (adj)	rāst	راست
on the right	dast-e rāst	دست راست
to the right	be rāst	به راست
in front (adv)	jelo	جلو
front (as adj)	jelo	جلو
ahead (the kids ran ~)	jelo	جلو
behind (adv)	aqab	عقب
from behind	az aqab	از عقب
back (towards the rear)	aqab	عقب
middle	vasat	وسط
in the middle	dar vasat	در وسط
at the side	pahlu	پهلو
everywhere (adv)	hame jā	همه جا
around (in all directions)	atrāf	اطراف
from inside	az daxel	از داخل
somewhere (to go)	jā-yi	جایی
straight (directly)	mostaqim	مستقیم
back (e.g. come ~)	aqab	عقب
from anywhere	az har jā	از هر جا
from somewhere	az yek jā-yi	از یک جایی
firstly (adv)	avvalan	اولاً
secondly (adv)	dumā	دوما
thirdly (adv)	sālesan	ثالثاً
suddenly (adv)	nāgahān	ناگهان
at first (in the beginning)	dar avval	در اول
for the first time	barā-ye avvalin bār	برای اولین بار
long before ...	xeyli vaqt piš	خیلی وقت پیش
anew (over again)	az now	از نو
for good (adv)	barā-ye hamiše	برای همیشه
never (adv)	hič vaqt	هیچ وقت
again (adv)	dobāre	دوباره
now (adv)	alān	الان
often (adv)	aqlab	اغلب
then (adv)	ān vaqt	آن وقت
urgently (quickly)	foran	فوراً
usually (adv)	ma'mulan	معمولاً
by the way, ...	rāst-i	راستی
possible (that is ~)	momken ast	ممکن است
probably (adv)	ehtemālan	احتمالاً
maybe (adv)	šāyad	شاید
besides ...	bealāve	بعلاوه
that's why ...	be hamin xāter	به همین خاطر
in spite of ...	alāraqm	علیرغم
thanks to ...	be lotf	به لطف
what (pron.)	če?	چه؟

that (conj.)	ke	که
something	yek čiz-i	یک چیزی
anything (something)	yek kāri	یک کاری
nothing	hič čiz	هیچ چیز

who (pron.)	ki	کی
someone	yek kas-i	یک کسی
somebody	yek kas-i	یک کسی

nobody	hič kas	هیچ کس
nowhere (a voyage to ~)	hič kojā	هیچ کجا
nobody's	māl-e hičkas	مال هیچ کس
somebody's	har kas-i	هر کسی

so (I'm ~ glad)	xeyli	خیلی
also (as well)	ham	هم
too (as well)	ham	هم

18. Function words. Adverbs. Part 2

Why?	čerā?	چرا؟
for some reason	be dalil-i	به دلیلی
because ...	čon	چون
for some purpose	barā-ye maqsudi	برای مقصودی

and	va	و
or	yā	یا
but	ammā	اما
for (e.g. ~ me)	barā-ye	برای

too (excessively)	besyār	بسیار
only (exclusively)	faqat	فقط
exactly (adv)	daqiqan	دقیقا
about (more or less)	taqriban	تقریباً

approximately (adv)	taqriban	تقریباً
approximate (adj)	taqribi	تقریبی
almost (adv)	taqriban	تقریباً
the rest	baqiye	بقیه

the other (second)	digar	دیگر
other (different)	digar	دیگر
each (adj)	har	هر
any (no matter which)	har	هر
many, much (a lot of)	ziyād	زیاد
many people	besyāri	بسیاری
all (everyone)	hame	همه

in return for ...	dar avaz	در عوض
in exchange (adv)	dar barābar	در برابر
by hand (made)	dasti	دستی
hardly (negative opinion)	baid ast	بعید است
probably (adv)	ehtemālan	احتمالاً
on purpose (intentionally)	amdan	عمداً

by accident (adv)	tasādofi	تصادفى
very (adv)	besyār	بسيار
for example (adv)	masalan	مثلاً
between	beyn	بين
among	miyān	ميان
so much (such a lot)	in qadr	اين قدر
especially (adv)	maxsusan	مخصوصاً

Basic concepts. Part 2

19. Weekdays

Monday	došanbe	دوشنبه
Tuesday	se šanbe	سه شنبه
Wednesday	čāhāršanbe	چهارشنبه
Thursday	panj šanbe	پنج شنبه
Friday	jom'e	جمعه
Saturday	šanbe	شنبه
Sunday	yek šanbe	یک شنبه
today (adv)	emruz	امروز
tomorrow (adv)	fardā	فردا
the day after tomorrow	pas fardā	پس فردا
yesterday (adv)	diruz	دیروز
the day before yesterday	pariruz	پریروز
day	ruz	روز
working day	ruz-e kāri	روز کاری
public holiday	ruz-e jašn	روز جشن
day off	ruz-e ta'til	روز تعطیل
weekend	āxar-e hafte	آخر هفته
all day long	tamām-e ruz	تمام روز
the next day (adv)	ruz-e ba'd	روز بعد
two days ago	do ruz-e piš	دو روز پیش
the day before	ruz-e qabl	روز قبل
daily (adj)	ruzāne	روزانه
every day (adv)	har ruz	هر روز
week	hafte	هفته
last week (adv)	hafte-ye gozašte	هفته گذشته
next week (adv)	hafte-ye āyande	هفته آینده
weekly (adj)	haftegi	هفتگی
every week (adv)	har hafte	هر هفته
twice a week	do bār dar hafte	دو بار درهفته
every Tuesday	har sešanbe	هر سه شنبه

20. Hours. Day and night

morning	sobh	صبح
in the morning	sobh	صبح
noon, midday	zohr	ظهر
in the afternoon	ba'd az zohr	بعد ازظهر
evening	asr	عصر
in the evening	asr	عصر

night	šab	شب
at night	šab	شب
midnight	nesfe šab	نصفه شب

second	sānie	ثانیه
minute	daqiqe	دقیقه
hour	sā'at	ساعت
half an hour	nim sā'at	نیم ساعت
a quarter-hour	yek rob'	یک ربع
fifteen minutes	pānzdah daqiqe	پانزده دقیقه
24 hours	šabāne ruz	شبانه روز

sunrise	tolu-'e āftāb	طلوع آفتاب
dawn	sahar	سحر
early morning	sobh-e zud	صبح زود
sunset	qorub	غروب

early in the morning	sobh-e zud	صبح زود
this morning	emruz sobh	امروز صبح
tomorrow morning	fardā sobh	فردا صبح
this afternoon	emruz zohr	امروز ظهر
in the afternoon	ba'd az zohr	بعد ازظهر
tomorrow afternoon	fardā ba'd az zohr	فردا بعد ازظهر
tonight (this evening)	emšab	امشب
tomorrow night	fardā šab	فردا شب

at 3 o'clock sharp	sar-e sā'at-e se	سر ساعت ۳
about 4 o'clock	nazdik-e sā'at-e čāhār	نزدیک ساعت ۴
by 12 o'clock	nazdik zohr	نزدیک ظهر

in 20 minutes	bist daqiqe-ye digar	۲۰ دقیقه دیگر
in an hour	yek sā'at-e digar	یک ساعت دیگر
on time (adv)	be moqe'	به موقع

a quarter to ...	yek rob' be	یک ربع به
within an hour	yek sā'at-e digar	یک ساعت دیگر
every 15 minutes	har pānzdah daqiqe	هر ۱۵ دقیقه
round the clock	šabāne ruz	شبانه روز

21. Months. Seasons

January	žānvie	ژانویه
February	fevriye	فوریه
March	mārs	مارس
April	āvril	آوریل
May	meh	مه
June	žuan	ژوئن

July	žuiye	ژوئیه
August	owt	اوت
September	septāmbr	سپتامبر
October	oktobr	اکتبر
November	novāmbr	نوامبر
December	desāmr	دسامبر

spring	bahār	بهار
in spring	dar bahār	در بهار
spring (as adj)	bahāri	بهاری

summer	tābestān	تابستان
in summer	dar tābestān	در تابستان
summer (as adj)	tābestāni	تابستانی

autumn	pāyiz	پاییز
in autumn	dar pāyiz	در پاییز
autumn (as adj)	pāyizi	پاییزی

winter	zemestān	زمستان
in winter	dar zemestān	در زمستان
winter (as adj)	zemestāni	زمستانی

month	māh	ماه
this month	in māh	این ماه
next month	māh-e āyande	ماه آینده
last month	māh-e gozašte	ماه گذشته

a month ago	yek māh qabl	یک ماه قبل
in a month (a month later)	yek māh digar	یک ماه دیگر
in 2 months (2 months later)	do māh-e digar	۲ ماه دیگر
the whole month	tamām-e māh	تمام ماه
all month long	tamām-e māh	تمام ماه

monthly (~ magazine)	māhāne	ماهانه
monthly (adv)	māhāne	ماهانه
every month	har māh	هر ماه
twice a month	do bār dar māh	دو بار درماه

year	sāl	سال
this year	emsāl	امسال
next year	sāl-e āyande	سال آینده
last year	sāl-e gozašte	سال گذشته

a year ago	yek sāl qabl	یک سال قبل
in a year	yek sāl-e digar	یک سال دیگر
in two years	do sāl-e digar	۲ سال دیگر
the whole year	tamām-e sāl	تمام سال
all year long	tamām-e sāl	تمام سال

every year	har sāl	هر سال
annual (adj)	sālāne	سالانه
annually (adv)	sālāne	سالانه
4 times a year	čāhār bār dar sāl	چهار بار در سال

date (e.g. today's ~)	tārix	تاریخ
date (e.g. ~ of birth)	tārix	تاریخ
calendar	taqvim	تقویم

half a year	nim sāl	نیم سال
six months	nim sāl	نیم سال
season (summer, etc.)	fasl	فصل
century	qarn	قرن

22. Time. Miscellaneous

time	zamān	زمان
moment	lahze	لحظه
instant (n)	lahze	لحظه
instant (adj)	āni	آنی
lapse (of time)	baxši az zamān	بخشی از زمان
life	zendegi	زندگی
eternity	abadiyat	ابدیت

epoch	asr	عصر
era	dowre	دوره
cycle	čarxe	چرخه
period	dowre	دوره
term (short-~)	mohlat	مهلت

the future	āyande	آینده
future (as adj)	āyande	آینده
next time	daf'e-ye ba'd	دفعه بعد
the past	gozašte	گذشته
past (recent)	gozašte	گذشته
last time	daf'e-ye gozašte	دفعه گذشته

later (adv)	ba'dan	بعداً
after (prep.)	ba'd az	بعد از
nowadays (adv)	aknun	اکنون
now (adv)	alān	الان
immediately (adv)	foran	فوراً
soon (adv)	be zudi	به زودی
in advance (beforehand)	az qabl	از قبل

a long time ago	moddathā piš	مدت ها پیش
recently (adv)	axiran	اخیراً
destiny	sarnevešt	سرنوشت
memories (childhood ~)	xāterāt	خاطرات
archives	āršiv	آرشیو

during ...	dar zamān	در زمان
long, a long time (adv)	tulāni	طولانی
not long (adv)	kutāh	کوتاه
early (in the morning)	zud	زود
late (not early)	dir	دیر

forever (for good)	barā-ye hamiše	برای همیشه
to start (begin)	šoru' kardan	شروع کردن
to postpone (vt)	mowkul kardan	موکول کردن

at the same time	ham zamān	هم زمان
permanently (adv)	dāemi	دائمی
constant (noise, pain)	dāemi	دائمی
temporary (adj)	movaqqati	موقتی

sometimes (adv)	gāh-i	گاهی
rarely (adv)	be nodrat	به ندرت
often (adv)	aqlab	اغلب

23. Opposites

rich (adj)	servatmand	ثروتمند
poor (adj)	faqir	فقیر
ill, sick (adj)	bimār	بیمار
well (not sick)	sālem	سالم
big (adj)	bozorg	بزرگ
small (adj)	kučak	کوچک
quickly (adv)	sari'	سریع
slowly (adv)	āheste	آهسته
fast (adj)	sari'	سریع
slow (adj)	āheste	آهسته
glad (adj)	xošhāl	خوشحال
sad (adj)	qamgin	غمگین
together (adv)	bāham	باهم
separately (adv)	jodāgāne	جداگانه
aloud (to read)	boland	بلند
silently (to oneself)	be ārāmi	به آرامی
tall (adj)	boland	بلند
low (adj)	kutāh	کوتاه
deep (adj)	amiq	عمیق
shallow (adj)	sathi	سطحی
yes	bale	بله
no	neh	نه
distant (in space)	dur	دور
nearby (adj)	nazdik	نزدیک
far (adv)	dur	دور
nearby (adv)	nazdik	نزدیک
long (adj)	derāz	دراز
short (adj)	kutāh	کوتاه
good (kindhearted)	mehrbān	مهربان
evil (adj)	badjens	بدجنس
married (adj)	mote'ahhel	متاهل
single (adj)	mojarrad	مجرد
to forbid (vt)	mamnu' kardan	ممنوع کردن
to permit (vt)	ejāze dādan	اجازه دادن
end	pāyān	پایان
beginning	šoru'	شروع

left (adj)	čap	چپ
right (adj)	rāst	راست
first (adj)	avvalin	اولین
last (adj)	āxarin	آخرین
crime	jenāyat	جنایت
punishment	mojāzāt	مجازات
to order (vt)	farmān dādan	فرمان دادن
to obey (vi, vt)	etā'at kardan	اطاعت کردن
straight (adj)	mostaqim	مستقیم
curved (adj)	monhani	منحنی
paradise	behešt	بهشت
hell	jahannam	جهنم
to be born	motevalled šodan	متولد شدن
to die (vi)	mordan	مردن
strong (adj)	nirumand	نیرومند
weak (adj)	za'if	ضعیف
old (adj)	kohne	کهنه
young (adj)	javān	جوان
old (adj)	qadimi	قدیمی
new (adj)	jadid	جدید
hard (adj)	soft	سفت
soft (adj)	narm	نرم
warm (tepid)	garm	گرم
cold (adj)	sard	سرد
fat (adj)	čāq	چاق
thin (adj)	lāqar	لاغر
narrow (adj)	bārik	باریک
wide (adj)	vasi'	وسیع
good (adj)	xub	خوب
bad (adj)	bad	بد
brave (adj)	šojā'	شجاع
cowardly (adj)	tarsu	ترسو

24. Lines and shapes

square	morabba'	مربع
square (as adj)	morabba'	مربع
circle	dāyere	دایره
round (adj)	gard	گرد

31

| triangle | mosallas | مثلث |
| triangular (adj) | mosallasi | مثلثی |

oval	beyzi	بیضی
oval (as adj)	beyzi	بیضی
rectangle	mostatil	مستطیل
rectangular (adj)	mostatil	مستطیل

pyramid	heram	هرم
rhombus	lowz-i	لوزی
trapezium	zuzanaqe	ذوزنقه
cube	moka'ab	مکعب
prism	manšur	منشور

circumference	mohit-e monhani	محیط منحنی
sphere	kare	کره
ball (solid sphere)	kare	کره

diameter	qotr	قطر
radius	šo'ā'	شعاع
perimeter (circle's ~)	mohit	محیط
centre	markaz	مرکز

horizontal (adj)	ofoqi	افقی
vertical (adj)	amudi	عمودی
parallel (n)	movāzi	موازی
parallel (as adj)	movāzi	موازی

line	xat	خط
stroke	xat	خط
straight line	xatt-e mostaqim	خط مستقیم
curve (curved line)	monhani	منحنی
thin (line, etc.)	nāzok	نازک
contour (outline)	borun namā	برون نما

intersection	taqāto'	تقاطع
right angle	zāvie-ye qāem	زاویه قائم
segment	qet'e	قطعه
sector	baxš	بخش
side (of triangle)	taraf	طرف
angle	zāvie	زاویه

25. Units of measurement

weight	vazn	وزن
length	tul	طول
width	arz	عرض
height	ertefā'	ارتفاع
depth	omq	عمق
volume	hajm	حجم
area	masāhat	مساحت

| gram | garm | گرم |
| milligram | mili geram | میلی گرم |

kilogram	kilugeram	کیلوگرم
ton	ton	تن
pound	pond	پوند
ounce	ons	اونس

metre	metr	متر
millimetre	mili metr	میلی متر
centimetre	sāntimetr	سانتیمتر
kilometre	kilumetr	کیلومتر
mile	māyel	مایل

inch	inč	اینچ
foot	fowt	فوت
yard	yārd	یارد

| square metre | metr morabba' | متر مربع |
| hectare | hektār | هکتار |

litre	litr	لیتر
degree	daraje	درجه
volt	volt	ولت
ampere	āmper	آمپر
horsepower	asb-e boxār	اسب بخار

quantity	meqdār	مقدار
a little bit of ...	kami	کمی
half	nim	نیم
dozen	dojin	دوجین
piece (item)	tā	تا

| size | andāze | اندازه |
| scale (map ~) | meqyās | مقیاس |

minimal (adj)	haddeaqal	حداقل
the smallest (adj)	kučaktarin	کوچکترین
medium (adj)	motevasset	متوسط
maximal (adj)	haddeaksar	حداکثر
the largest (adj)	bištarin	بیشترین

26. Containers

canning jar (glass ~)	šišeh konserv	شیشه کنسرو
tin, can	quti	قوطی
bucket	satl	سطل
barrel	boške	بشکه

wash basin (e.g., plastic ~)	tašt	تشت
tank (100L water ~)	maxzan	مخزن
hip flask	qomqome	قمقمه
jerrycan	dabbe	دبه
tank (e.g., tank car)	maxzan	مخزن

| mug | livān | لیوان |
| cup (of coffee, etc.) | fenjān | فنجان |

saucer	na'lbeki	نعلبکی
glass (tumbler)	estekān	استکان
wine glass	gilās-e šarāb	گیلاس شراب
stock pot (soup pot)	qāblame	قابلمه

| bottle (~ of wine) | botri | بطری |
| neck (of the bottle, etc.) | gardan-e botri | گردن بطری |

carafe (decanter)	tong	تنگ
pitcher	pārč	پارچ
vessel (container)	zarf	ظرف
pot (crock, stoneware ~)	sofāl	سفال
vase	goldān	گلدان

bottle (perfume ~)	botri	بطری
vial, small bottle	viyāl	ویال
tube (of toothpaste)	tiyub	تیوب

sack (bag)	kise	کیسه
bag (paper ~, plastic ~)	pākat	پاکت
packet (of cigarettes, etc.)	baste	بسته

box (e.g. shoebox)	ja'be	جعبه
crate	sanduq	صندوق
basket	sabad	سبد

27. Materials

material	mādde	ماده
wood (n)	deraxt	درخت
wood-, wooden (adj)	čubi	چوبی

| glass (n) | šiše | شیشه |
| glass (as adj) | šiše i | شیشه ای |

| stone (n) | sang | سنگ |
| stone (as adj) | sangi | سنگی |

| plastic (n) | pelāstik | پلاستیک |
| plastic (as adj) | pelāstiki | پلاستیکی |

| rubber (n) | lāstik | لاستیک |
| rubber (as adj) | lāstiki | لاستیکی |

| cloth, fabric (n) | pārče | پارچه |
| fabric (as adj) | pārče-i | پارچه ی |

| paper (n) | kāqaz | کاغذ |
| paper (as adj) | kāqazi | کاغذی |

cardboard (n)	kārton	کارتن
cardboard (as adj)	kārtoni	کارتونی
polyethylene	polietilen	پلیاتیلن
cellophane	solofān	سلوفان

| linoleum | linoleom | لینولئوم |
| plywood | taxte-ye čand lāyi | تخته چند لایی |

porcelain (n)	čini	چینی
porcelain (as adj)	čini	چینی
clay (n)	xāk-e ros	خاک رس
clay (as adj)	sofāli	سفالی
ceramic (n)	serāmik	سرامیک
ceramic (as adj)	serāmiki	سرامیکی

28. Metals

metal (n)	felez	فلز
metal (as adj)	felezi	فلزی
alloy (n)	āiyāž	آلیاژ

gold (n)	talā	طلا
gold, golden (adj)	talā	طلا
silver (n)	noqre	نقره
silver (as adj)	noqre	نقره

iron (n)	āhan	آهن
iron-, made of iron (adj)	āhani	آهنی
steel (n)	fulād	فولاد
steel (as adj)	fulādi	فولادی
copper (n)	mes	مس
copper (as adj)	mesi	مسی

aluminium (n)	ālominiyom	آلومینیوم
aluminium (as adj)	ālominiyomi	آلومینیومی
bronze (n)	boronz	برنز
bronze (as adj)	boronzi	برنزی

brass	berenj	برنج
nickel	nikel	نیکل
platinum	pelātin	پلاتین
mercury	jive	جیوه
tin	qal'	قلع
lead	sorb	سرب
zinc	ruy	روی

HUMAN BEING

Human being. The body

29. Humans. Basic concepts

human being	ensān	انسان
man (adult male)	mard	مرد
woman	zan	زن
child	kudak	کودک

girl	doxtar	دختر
boy	pesar bače	پسر بچه
teenager	nowjavān	نوجوان
old man	pirmard	پیرمرد
old woman	pirzan	پیرزن

30. Human anatomy

organism (body)	orgānism	ارگانیسم
heart	qalb	قلب
blood	xun	خون
artery	sorxrag	سرخرگ
vein	siyāhrag	سیاهرگ

brain	maqz	مغز
nerve	asab	عصب
nerves	a'sāb	اعصاب
vertebra	mohre	مهره
spine (backbone)	sotun-e faqarāt	ستون فقرات

stomach (organ)	me'de	معده
intestines, bowels	rude	روده
intestine (e.g. large ~)	rude	روده
liver	kabed	کبد
kidney	kolliye	کلیه

bone	ostexān	استخوان
skeleton	eskelet	اسکلت
rib	dande	دنده
skull	jomjome	جمجمه

muscle	azole	عضله
biceps	azole-ye dosar	عضلۀ دوسر
triceps	azole-ye se sar	عضلۀ سه سر
tendon	tāndon	تاندون
joint	mofassal	مفصل

lungs	rie	ریه
genitals	andām hā-ye tanāsol-i	اندام های تناسلی
skin	pust	پوست

31. Head

head	sar	سر
face	surat	صورت
nose	bini	بینی
mouth	dahān	دهان

eye	češm	چشم
eyes	češm-hā	چشم ها
pupil	mardomak	مردمک
eyebrow	abru	ابرو
eyelash	može	مژه
eyelid	pelek	پلک

tongue	zabān	زبان
tooth	dandān	دندان
lips	lab-hā	لب ها
cheekbones	ostexānhā-ye gune	استخوان های گونه
gum	lase	لثه
palate	saqf-e dahān	سقف دهان

nostrils	surāxhā-ye bini	سوراخ های بینی
chin	čāne	چانه
jaw	fak	فک
cheek	gune	گونه

forehead	pišāni	پیشانی
temple	gijgāh	گیجگاه
ear	guš	گوش
back of the head	pas gardan	پس گردن
neck	gardan	گردن
throat	galu	گلو

hair	mu-hā	مو ها
hairstyle	model-e mu	مدل مو
haircut	model-e mu	مدل مو
wig	kolāh-e gis	کلاه گیس

moustache	sebil	سبیل
beard	riš	ریش
to have (a beard, etc.)	gozāštan	گذاشتن
plait	muy-ye bāfte	موی بافته
sideboards	xatt-e riš	خط ریش

red-haired (adj)	muqermez	موقرمز
grey (hair)	sefid-e mu	سفید مو
bald (adj)	tās	طاس
bald patch	tāsi	طاسی
ponytail	dom-e asbi	دم اسبی
fringe	čatri	چتری

32. Human body

hand	dast	دست
arm	bāzu	بازو
finger	angošt	انگشت
toe	šast-e pā	شصت پا
thumb	šost	شست
little finger	angošt-e kučak	انگشت کوچک
nail	nāxon	ناخن
fist	mošt	مشت
palm	kaf-e dast	کف دست
wrist	moč-e dast	مچ دست
forearm	sā'ed	ساعد
elbow	āranj	آرنج
shoulder	ketf	کتف
leg	pā	پا
foot	pā	پا
knee	zānu	زانو
calf (part of leg)	sāq	ساق
hip	rān	ران
heel	pāšne-ye pā	پاشنهٔ پا
body	badan	بدن
stomach	šekam	شکم
chest	sine	سینه
breast	sine	سینه
flank	pahlu	پهلو
back	pošt	پشت
lower back	kamar	کمر
waist	dur-e kamar	دور کمر
navel (belly button)	nāf	ناف
buttocks	nešiman-e gāh	نشیمن گاه
bottom	bāsan	باسن
beauty spot	xāl	خال
birthmark (café au lait spot)	xāl-e mādarzād	خال مادرزاد
tattoo	xāl kubi	خال کوبی
scar	jā-ye zaxm	جای زخم

Clothing & Accessories

33. Outerwear. Coats

clothes	lebās	لباس
outerwear	lebās-e ru	لباس رو
winter clothing	lebās-e zemestāni	لباس زمستانی
coat (overcoat)	pāltow	پالتو
fur coat	pālto-ye pustin	پالتوی پوستین
fur jacket	kot-e pustin	کت پوستین
down coat	kāpšan	کاپشن
jacket (e.g. leather ~)	kot	کت
raincoat (trenchcoat, etc.)	bārāni	بارانی
waterproof (adj)	zed-e āb	ضد آب

34. Men's & women's clothing

shirt (button shirt)	pirāhan	پیراهن
trousers	šalvār	شلوار
jeans	jin	جین
suit jacket	kot	کت
suit	kat-o šalvār	کت و شلوار
dress (frock)	lebās	لباس
skirt	dāman	دامن
blouse	boluz	بلوز
knitted jacket (cardigan, etc.)	jeliqe-ye kešbāf	جلیقه کشباف
jacket (of woman's suit)	kot	کت
T-shirt	tey šarr-at	تی شرت
shorts (short trousers)	šalvarak	شلوارک
tracksuit	lebās-e varzeši	لباس ورزشی
bathrobe	howle-ye hamām	حوله حمام
pyjamas	pižāme	پیژامه
jumper (sweater)	poliver	پلیور
pullover	poliver	پلیور
waistcoat	jeliqe	جلیقه
tailcoat	kat-e dāman gerd	کت دامن گرد
dinner suit	esmoking	اسموکینگ
uniform	oniform	اونیفورم
workwear	lebās-e kār	لباس کار
boiler suit	rupuš	روپوش
coat (e.g. doctor's smock)	rupuš	روپوش

35. Clothing. Underwear

underwear	lebās-e zir	لباس زیر
pants	šort-e bākser	شورت باکسر
panties	šort-e zanāne	شورت زنانه
vest (singlet)	zir-e pirāhan-i	زیر پیراهنی
socks	jurāb	جوراب
nightgown	lebās-e xāb	لباس خواب
bra	sine-ye band	سینه بند
knee highs (knee-high socks)	sāq	ساق
tights	jurāb-e šalvāri	جوراب شلواری
stockings (hold ups)	jurāb-e sāqeboland	جوراب ساقه بلند
swimsuit, bikini	māyo	مایو

36. Headwear

hat	kolāh	کلاه
trilby hat	šāpo	شاپو
baseball cap	kolāh beysbāl	کلاه بیس بال
flatcap	kolāh-e taxt	کلاه تخت
beret	kolāh barre	کلاه بره
hood	kolāh-e bārāni	کلاه بارانی
panama hat	kolāh-e dowre-ye boland	کلاه دوره بلند
knit cap (knitted hat)	kolāh-e bāftani	کلاه بافتنی
headscarf	rusari	روسری
women's hat	kolāh-e zanāne	کلاه زنانه
hard hat	kolāh-e imeni	کلاه ایمنی
forage cap	kolāh-e pādegān	کلاه پادگان
helmet	kolāh-e imeni	کلاه ایمنی
bowler	kolāh-e namadi	کلاه نمدی
top hat	kolāh-e ostovānei	کلاه استوانه ای

37. Footwear

footwear	kafš	کفش
shoes (men's shoes)	putin	پوتین
shoes (women's shoes)	kafš	کفش
boots (e.g., cowboy ~)	čakme	چکمه
carpet slippers	dampāyi	دمپایی
trainers	kafš katān-i	کفش کتانی
trainers	kafš katān-i	کفش کتانی
sandals	sandal	صندل
cobbler (shoe repairer)	kaffāš	کفاش
heel	pāšne-ye kafš	پاشنهٔ کفش

pair (of shoes)	yek joft	یک جفت
lace (shoelace)	band-e kafš	بند کفش
to lace up (vt)	band-e kafš bastan	بند کفش بستن
shoehorn	pāšne keš	پاشنه کش
shoe polish	vāks	واکس

38. Textile. Fabrics

cotton (n)	panbe	پنبه
cotton (as adj)	panbe i	پنبه ای
flax (n)	katān	کتان
flax (as adj)	katāni	کتانی

silk (n)	abrišam	ابریشم
silk (as adj)	abrišami	ابریشمی
wool (n)	pašm	پشم
wool (as adj)	pašmi	پشمی

velvet	maxmal	مخمل
suede	jir	جیر
corduroy	maxmal-e kebriti	مخمل کبریتی

nylon (n)	nāylon	نایلون
nylon (as adj)	nāyloni	نایلونی
polyester (n)	poliester	پلی استر
polyester (as adj)	poliester	پلیاستر

leather (n)	čarm	چرم
leather (as adj)	čarmi	چرمی
fur (n)	xaz	خز
fur (e.g. ~ coat)	xaz	خز

39. Personal accessories

gloves	dastkeš	دستکش
mittens	dastkeš-e yek angošti	دستکش یک انگشتی
scarf (muffler)	šāl-e gardan	شال گردن

glasses	eynak	عینک
frame (eyeglass ~)	qāb	قاب
umbrella	čatr	چتر
walking stick	asā	عصا
hairbrush	bores-e mu	برس مو
fan	bādbezan	بادبزن

tie (necktie)	kerāvāt	کراوات
bow tie	pāpiyon	پاپیون
braces	band šalvār	بند شلوار
handkerchief	dastmāl	دستمال

| comb | šāne | شانه |
| hair slide | sanjāq-e mu | سنجاق مو |

| hairpin | sanjāq-e mu | سنجاق مو |
| buckle | sagak | سگک |

| belt | kamarband | کمربند |
| shoulder strap | tasme | تسمه |

bag (handbag)	keyf	کیف
handbag	keyf-e zanāne	کیف زنانه
rucksack	kule pošti	کولهٔ پشتی

40. Clothing. Miscellaneous

fashion	mod	مد
in vogue (adj)	mod	مد
fashion designer	tarrāh-e lebas	طراح لباس

collar	yaqe	یقه
pocket	jib	جیب
pocket (as adj)	jibi	جیبی
sleeve	āstin	آستین
hanging loop	band-e āviz	بند آویز
flies (on trousers)	zip	زیپ

zip (fastener)	zip	زیپ
fastener	sagak	سگک
button	dokme	دکمه
buttonhole	surāx-e dokme	سوراخ دکمه
to come off (ab. button)	kande šodan	کنده شدن

to sew (vi, vt)	duxtan	دوختن
to embroider (vi, vt)	golduzi kardan	گلدوزی کردن
embroidery	golduzi	گلدوزی
sewing needle	suzan	سوزن
thread	nax	نخ
seam	darz	درز

to get dirty (vi)	kasif šodan	کثیف شدن
stain (mark, spot)	lakke	لکه
to crease, crumple (vi)	čoruk šodan	چروک شدن
to tear, to rip (vt)	pāre kardan	پاره کردن
clothes moth	šab parre	شب پره

41. Personal care. Cosmetics

toothpaste	xamir-e dandān	خمیر دندان
toothbrush	mesvāk	مسواک
to clean one's teeth	mesvāk zadan	مسواک زدن

razor	tiq	تیغ
shaving cream	kerem-e riš tarāši	کرم ریش تراشی
to shave (vi)	riš tarāšidan	ریش تراشیدن
soap	sābun	صابون

shampoo	šāmpu	شامپو
scissors	qeyči	قیچی
nail file	sohan-e nāxon	سوهان ناخن
nail clippers	nāxon gir	ناخن گیر
tweezers	mučin	موچین

cosmetics	lavāzem-e ārāyeši	لوازم آرایشی
face mask	māsk	ماسک
manicure	mānikur	مانیکور
to have a manicure	mānikur kardan	مانیکور کردن
pedicure	pedikur	پدیکور

make-up bag	kife lavāzem-e ārāyeši	کیف لوازم آرایشی
face powder	pudr	پودر
powder compact	ja'be-ye pudr	جعبة پودر
blusher	sorxāb	سرخاب

perfume (bottled)	atr	عطر
toilet water (lotion)	atr	عطر
lotion	losiyon	لوسیون
cologne	odkolon	اودکلن

eyeshadow	sāye-ye češm	سایه چشم
eyeliner	medād čašm	مداد چشم
mascara	rimel	ریمل

lipstick	mātik	ماتیک
nail polish	lāk-e nāxon	لاک ناخن
hair spray	esperey-ye mu	اسپری مو
deodorant	deodyrant	دئودورانت

cream	kerem	کرم
face cream	kerem-e surat	کرم صورت
hand cream	kerem-e dast	کرم دست
anti-wrinkle cream	kerem-e zedd-e čoruk	کرم ضد چروک
day cream	kerem-e ruz	کرم روز
night cream	kerem-e šab	کرم شب
day (as adj)	ruzāne	روزانه
night (as adj)	šab	شب

tampon	tāmpon	تامپون
toilet paper (toilet roll)	kāqaz-e tuālet	کاغذ توالت
hair dryer	sešovār	سشوار

42. Jewellery

jewellery	javāherāt	جواهرات
precious (e.g. ~ stone)	qeymati	قیمتی
hallmark stamp	ayār	عیار

ring	angoštar	انگشتر
wedding ring	halqe	حلقه
bracelet	alangu	النگو
earrings	gušvāre	گوشواره

necklace (~ of pearls)	gardan band	گردن بند
crown	tāj	تاج
bead necklace	gardan band	گردن بند

diamond	almās	الماس
emerald	zomorrod	زمرد
ruby	yāqut	یاقوت
sapphire	yāqut-e kabud	یاقوت کبود
pearl	morvārid	مروارید
amber	kahrobā	کهربا

43. Watches. Clocks

watch (wristwatch)	sā'at-e moči	ساعت مچی
dial	safhe-ye sā'at	صفحهٔ ساعت
hand (of clock, watch)	aqrabe	عقربه
metal bracelet	band-e sāat	بند ساعت
watch strap	band-e čarmi	بند چرمی

battery	bātri	باطری
to be flat (battery)	tamām šodan bātri	تمام شدن باتری
to change a battery	bātri avaz kardan	باطری عوض کردن
to run fast	jelo oftādan	جلو افتادن
to run slow	aqab māndan	عقب ماندن

wall clock	sā'at-e divāri	ساعت دیواری
hourglass	sā'at-e šeni	ساعت شنی
sundial	sā'at-e āftābi	ساعت آفتابی
alarm clock	sā'at-e zang dār	ساعت زنگ دار
watchmaker	sā'at sāz	ساعت ساز
to repair (vt)	ta'mir kardan	تعمیر کردن

Food. Nutricion

44. Food

meat	gušt	گوشت
chicken	morq	مرغ
poussin	juje	جوجه
duck	ordak	اردک
goose	qāz	غاز
game	gušt-e šekār	گوشت شکار
turkey	gušt-e buqalamun	گوشت بوقلمون

pork	gušt-e xuk	گوشت خوک
veal	gušt-e gusāle	گوشت گوساله
lamb	gušt-e gusfand	گوشت گوسفند
beef	gušt-e gāv	گوشت گاو
rabbit	xarguš	خرگوش

sausage (bologna, pepperoni, etc.)	kālbās	کالباس
vienna sausage (frankfurter)	sosis	سوسیس
bacon	beykon	بیکن
ham	žāmbon	ژامبون
gammon	rān xuk	ران خوک

pâté	pāte	پاته
liver	jegar	جگر
mince (minced meat)	hamberger	همبرگر
tongue	zabān	زبان

egg	toxm-e morq	تخم مرغ
eggs	toxm-e morq-ha	تخم مرغ ها
egg white	sefide-ye toxm-e morq	سفیده تخم مرغ
egg yolk	zarde-ye toxm-e morq	زرده تخم مرغ

fish	māhi	ماهی
seafood	qazā-ye daryāyi	غذای دریایی
crustaceans	saxtpustān	سختپوستان
caviar	xāviār	خاویار

crab	xarčang	خرچنگ
prawn	meygu	میگو
oyster	sadaf-e xorāki	صدف خوراکی
spiny lobster	xarčang-e xārdār	خرچنگ خاردار
octopus	hašt pā	هشت پا
squid	māhi-ye morakkab	ماهی مرکب

sturgeon	māhi-ye xāviar	ماهی خاویار
salmon	māhi-ye salemon	ماهی سالمون
halibut	halibut	هالیبوت

cod	māhi-ye rowqan	ماهی روغن
mackerel	māhi-ye esqumeri	ماهی اسقومری
tuna	tan māhi	تن ماهی
eel	mārmāhi	مارماهی

trout	māhi-ye qezelālā	ماهی قزل آلا
sardine	sārdin	ساردین
pike	ordak māhi	اردک ماهی
herring	māhi-ye šur	ماهی شور

bread	nān	نان
cheese	panir	پنیر
sugar	qand	قند
salt	namak	نمک

rice	berenj	برنج
pasta (macaroni)	mākāroni	ماکارونی
noodles	rešte-ye farangi	رشته فرنگی

butter	kare	کره
vegetable oil	rowqan-e nabāti	روغن نباتی
sunflower oil	rowqan āftābgardān	روغن آفتاب گردان
margarine	mārgārin	مارگارین

| olives | zeytun | زیتون |
| olive oil | rowqan-e zeytun | روغن زیتون |

milk	šir	شیر
condensed milk	šir-e čegāl	شیر چگال
yogurt	mās-at	ماست
soured cream	xāme-ye torš	خامهٔ ترش
cream (of milk)	saršir	سرشیر

| mayonnaise | māyonez | مایونز |
| buttercream | xāme | خامه |

cereal grains (wheat, etc.)	hobubāt	حبوبات
flour	ārd	آرد
tinned food	konserv-hā	کنسرو ها

cornflakes	bereštuk	برشتوک
honey	asal	عسل
jam	morabbā	مربا
chewing gum	ādāms	آدامس

45. Drinks

water	āb	آب
drinking water	āb-e āšāmidani	آب آشامیدنی
mineral water	āb-e ma'dani	آب معدنی

still (adj)	bedun-e gāz	بدون گاز
carbonated (adj)	gāzdār	گازدار
sparkling (adj)	gāzdār	گازدار

| ice | yax | يخ |
| with ice | yax dār | يخ دار |

non-alcoholic (adj)	bi alkol	بى الكل
soft drink	nušābe-ye bi alkol	نوشابۀ بى الكل
refreshing drink	nušābe-ye xonak	نوشابۀ خنک
lemonade	limunād	ليموناد

spirits	mašrubāt-e alkoli	مشروبات الكلى
wine	šarāb	شراب
white wine	šarāb-e sefid	شراب سفيد
red wine	šarāb-e sorx	شراب سرخ

liqueur	likor	ليكور
champagne	šāmpāyn	شامپاين
vermouth	vermut	ورموت

whisky	viski	ويسكى
vodka	vodkā	ودكا
gin	jin	جين
cognac	konyāk	كنياک
rum	araq-e neyšekar	عرق نيشكر

coffee	qahve	قهوه
black coffee	qahve-ye talx	قهوۀ تلخ
white coffee	šir-qahve	شيرقهوه
cappuccino	kāpočino	كاپوچينو
instant coffee	qahve-ye fowri	قهوه فورى

milk	šir	شير
cocktail	kuktel	كوكتل
milkshake	kuktele šir	كوكتل شير

juice	āb-e mive	آب ميوه
tomato juice	āb-e gowjefarangi	آب گوجه فرنگى
orange juice	āb-e porteqāl	آب پرتقال
freshly squeezed juice	āb-e mive-ye taze	آب ميوۀ تازه

beer	ābejow	آبجو
lager	ābejow-ye sabok	آبجوى سبک
bitter	ābejow-ye tire	آبجوى تيره

tea	čāy	چاى
black tea	čāy-e siyāh	چاى سياه
green tea	čāy-e sabz	چاى سبز

46. Vegetables

| vegetables | sabzijāt | سبزيجات |
| greens | sabzi | سبزى |

tomato	gowje farangi	گوجه فرنگى
cucumber	xiyār	خيار
carrot	havij	هويج

potato	sib zamini	سیب زمینی
onion	piyāz	پیاز
garlic	sir	سیر

cabbage	kalam	کلم
cauliflower	gol kalam	گل کلم
Brussels sprouts	koll-am boruksel	کلم بروکسل
broccoli	kalam borokli	کلم بروکلی

beetroot	čoqondar	چغندر
aubergine	bādenjān	بادنجان
courgette	kadu sabz	کدو سبز
pumpkin	kadu tanbal	کدو تنبل
turnip	šalqam	شلغم

parsley	ja'fari	جعفری
dill	šavid	شوید
lettuce	kāhu	کاهو
celery	karafs	کرفس
asparagus	mārčube	مارچوبه
spinach	esfenāj	اسفناج

pea	noxod	نخود
beans	lubiyā	لوبیا
maize	zorrat	ذرت
kidney bean	lubiyā qermez	لوبیا قرمز

sweet paper	felfel	فلفل
radish	torobče	تربچه
artichoke	kangar farangi	کنگرفرنگی

47. Fruits. Nuts

fruit	mive	میوه
apple	sib	سیب
pear	golābi	گلابی
lemon	limu	لیمو
orange	porteqāl	پرتقال
strawberry (garden ~)	tut-e farangi	توت فرنگی

tangerine	nārengi	نارنگی
plum	ālu	آلو
peach	holu	هلو
apricot	zardālu	زردآلو
raspberry	tamešk	تمشک
pineapple	ānānās	آناناس

banana	mowz	موز
watermelon	hendevāne	هندوانه
grape	angur	انگور
sour cherry	ālbālu	آلبالو
sweet cherry	gilās	گیلاس
melon	xarboze	خربزه
grapefruit	gerip forut	گریپ فوروت

avocado	āvokādo	اووكادو
papaya	pāpāyā	پاپایا
mango	anbe	انبه
pomegranate	anār	انار

redcurrant	angur-e farangi-ye sorx	انگور فرنگی سرخ
blackcurrant	angur-e farangi-ye siyāh	انگور فرنگی سیاه
gooseberry	angur-e farangi	انگور فرنگی
bilberry	zoqāl axte	زغال اخته
blackberry	šāh tut	شاه توت

raisin	kešmeš	کشمش
fig	anjir	انجیر
date	xormā	خرما

peanut	bādām zamin-i	بادام زمینی
almond	bādām	بادام
walnut	gerdu	گردو
hazelnut	fandoq	فندق
coconut	nārgil	نارگیل
pistachios	peste	پسته

48. Bread. Sweets

bakers' confectionery (pastry)	širini jāt	شیرینی جات
bread	nān	نان
biscuits	biskuit	بیسکوییت

chocolate (n)	šokolāt	شکلات
chocolate (as adj)	šokolāti	شکلاتی
candy (wrapped)	āb nabāt	آب نبات
cake (e.g. cupcake)	nān-e širini	نان شیرینی
cake (e.g. birthday ~)	širini	شیرینی

| pie (e.g. apple ~) | keyk | کیک |
| filling (for cake, pie) | čāšni | چاشنی |

jam (whole fruit jam)	morabbā	مربا
marmalade	mārmālād	مارمالاد
waffles	vāfel	وافل
ice-cream	bastani	بستنی
pudding (Christmas ~)	puding	پودینگ

49. Cooked dishes

course, dish	qazā	غذا
cuisine	qazā	غذا
recipe	dastur-e poxt	دستور پخت
portion	pors	پرس

| salad | sālād | سالاد |
| soup | sup | سوپ |

clear soup (broth)	pāye-ye sup	پایه سوپ
sandwich (bread)	sāndevič	ساندویچ
fried eggs	nimru	نیمرو

| hamburger (beefburger) | hamberger | همبرگر |
| beefsteak | esteyk | استیک |

side dish	moxallafāt	مخلفات
spaghetti	espāgeti	اسپاگتی
mash	pure-ye sibi zamini	پورهٔ سیب زمینی
pizza	pitzā	پیتزا
porridge (oatmeal, etc.)	šurbā	شوربا
omelette	ommol-at	املت

boiled (e.g. ~ beef)	āb paz	آب پز
smoked (adj)	dudi	دودی
fried (adj)	sorx šode	سرخ شده
dried (adj)	xošk	خشک
frozen (adj)	yax zade	یخ زده
pickled (adj)	torši	ترشی

sweet (sugary)	širin	شیرین
salty (adj)	šur	شور
cold (adj)	sard	سرد
hot (adj)	dāq	داغ
bitter (adj)	talx	تلخ
tasty (adj)	xoš mazze	خوش مزه

to cook in boiling water	poxtan	پختن
to cook (dinner)	poxtan	پختن
to fry (vt)	sorx kardan	سرخ کردن
to heat up (food)	garm kardan	گرم کردن

to salt (vt)	namak zadan	نمک زدن
to pepper (vt)	felfel pāšidan	فلفل پاشیدن
to grate (vt)	rande kardan	رنده کردن
peel (n)	pust	پوست
to peel (vt)	pust kandan	پوست کندن

50. Spices

salt	namak	نمک
salty (adj)	šur	شور
to salt (vt)	namak zadan	نمک زدن

black pepper	felfel-e siyāh	فلفل سیاه
red pepper (milled ~)	felfel-e sorx	فلفل سرخ
mustard	xardal	خردل
horseradish	torob-e kuhi	ترب کوهی

condiment	adviye	ادویه
spice	adviye	ادویه
sauce	ses	سس
vinegar	serke	سرکه

anise	rāziyāne	رازیانه
basil	reyhān	ریحان
cloves	mixak	میخک
ginger	zanjefil	زنجفیل
coriander	gešniz	گشنیز
cinnamon	dārčin	دارچین

sesame	konjed	کنجد
bay leaf	barg-e bu	برگ بو
paprika	paprika	پاپریکا
caraway	zire	زیره
saffron	za'ferān	زعفران

51. Meals

| food | qazā | غذا |
| to eat (vi, vt) | xordan | خوردن |

breakfast	sobhāne	صبحانه
to have breakfast	sobhāne xordan	صبحانه خوردن
lunch	nāhār	ناهار
to have lunch	nāhār xordan	ناهار خوردن
dinner	šām	شام
to have dinner	šām xordan	شام خوردن

| appetite | eštehā | اشتها |
| Enjoy your meal! | nuš-e jān | نوش جان |

to open (~ a bottle)	bāz kardan	باز کردن
to spill (liquid)	rixtan	ریختن
to spill out (vi)	rixtan	ریختن
to boil (vi)	jušidan	جوشیدن
to boil (vt)	jušāndan	جوشاندن
boiled (~ water)	jušide	جوشیده
to chill, cool down (vt)	sard kardan	سرد کردن
to chill (vi)	sard šodan	سرد شدن

| taste, flavour | maze | مزه |
| aftertaste | maze | مزه |

to slim down (lose weight)	lāqar kardan	لاغر کردن
diet	režim	رژیم
vitamin	vitāmin	ویتامین
calorie	kālori	کالری
vegetarian (n)	giyāh xār	گیاه خوار
vegetarian (adj)	giyāh xāri	گیاه خواری

fats (nutrient)	čarbi-hā	چربی ها
proteins	porotein	پروتئین
carbohydrates	karbohidrāt-hā	کربو هیدرات ها

slice (of lemon, ham)	qet'e	قطعه
piece (of cake, pie)	tekke	تکه
crumb (of bread, cake, etc.)	zarre	ذره

52. Table setting

spoon	qāšoq	قاشق
knife	kārd	کارد
fork	čangāl	چنگال
cup (e.g., coffee ~)	fenjān	فنجان
plate (dinner ~)	bošqāb	بشقاب
saucer	na'lbeki	نعلبکی
serviette	dastmāl	دستمال
toothpick	xelāl-e dandān	خلال دندان

53. Restaurant

restaurant	resturān	رستوران
coffee bar	kāfe	کافه
pub, bar	bār	بار
tearoom	qahve xāne	قهوه خانه
waiter	pišxedmat	پیشخدمت
waitress	pišxedmat	پیشخدمت
barman	motesaddi-ye bār	متصدی بار
menu	meno	منو
wine list	kārt-e šarāb	کارت شراب
to book a table	miz rezerv kardan	میز رزرو کردن
course, dish	qazā	غذا
to order (meal)	sefāreš dādan	سفارش دادن
to make an order	sefāreš dādan	سفارش دادن
aperitif	mašrub-e piš qazā	مشروب پیش غذا
starter	piš qazā	پیش غذا
dessert, pudding	deser	دسر
bill	surat hesāb	صورت حساب
to pay the bill	surat-e hesāb rā pardāxtan	صورت حساب را پرداختن
to give change	baqiye rā dādan	بقیه را دادن
tip	an'ām	انعام

Family, relatives and friends

54. Personal information. Forms

name (first name)	esm	اسم
surname (last name)	nām-e xānevādegi	نام خانوادگی
date of birth	tārix-e tavallod	تاریخ تولد
place of birth	mahall-e tavallod	محل تولد
nationality	melliyat	ملیت
place of residence	mahall-e sokunat	محل سکونت
country	kešvar	کشور
profession (occupation)	šoql	شغل
gender, sex	jens	جنس
height	qad	قد
weight	vazn	وزن

55. Family members. Relatives

mother	mādar	مادر
father	pedar	پدر
son	pesar	پسر
daughter	doxtar	دختر
younger daughter	doxtar-e kučak	دختر کوچک
younger son	pesar-e kučak	پسر کوچک
eldest daughter	doxtar-e bozorg	دختر بزرگ
eldest son	pesar-e bozorg	پسر بزرگ
brother	barādar	برادر
elder brother	barādar-e bozorg	برادر بزرگ
younger brother	barādar-e kučak	برادر کوچک
sister	xāhar	خواهر
elder sister	xāhar-e bozorg	خواهر بزرگ
younger sister	xāhar-e kučak	خواهر کوچک
cousin (masc.)	pesar 'amu	پسر عمو
cousin (fem.)	doxtar amu	دخترعمو
mummy	māmān	مامان
dad, daddy	bābā	بابا
parents	vāledeyn	والدین
child	kudak	کودک
children	bače-hā	بچه ها
grandmother	mādarbozorg	مادربزرگ
grandfather	pedar-bozorg	پدربزرگ

grandson	nave	نوه
granddaughter	nave	نوه
grandchildren	nave-hā	نوه ها

uncle	amu	عمو
aunt	xāle yā amme	خاله یا عمه
nephew	barādar-zāde	برادرزاده
niece	xāhar-zāde	خواهرزاده

mother-in-law (wife's mother)	mādarzan	مادرزن
father-in-law (husband's father)	pedar-šowhar	پدرشوهر
son-in-law (daughter's husband)	dāmād	داماد
stepmother	nāmādari	نامادری
stepfather	nāpedari	ناپدری

infant	nowzād	نوزاد
baby (infant)	širxār	شیرخوار
little boy, kid	pesar-e kučulu	پسر کوچولو

wife	zan	زن
husband	šowhar	شوهر
spouse (husband)	hamsar	همسر
spouse (wife)	hamsar	همسر

married (masc.)	mote'ahhel	متاهل
married (fem.)	mote'ahhel	متاهل
single (unmarried)	mojarrad	مجرد
bachelor	mojarrad	مجرد
divorced (masc.)	talāq gerefte	طلاق گرفته
widow	bive zan	بیوه زن
widower	bive	بیوه

relative	xišāvand	خویشاوند
close relative	aqvām-e nazdik	اقوام نزدیک
distant relative	aqvām-e dur	اقوام دور
relatives	aqvām	اقوام

orphan (boy or girl)	yatim	یتیم
guardian (of a minor)	qayyem	قیم
to adopt (a boy)	be pesari gereftan	به پسری گرفتن
to adopt (a girl)	be doxtari gereftan	به دختری گرفتن

56. Friends. Colleagues

friend (masc.)	dust	دوست
friend (fem.)	dust	دوست
friendship	dusti	دوستی
to be friends	dust budan	دوست بودن

| pal (masc.) | rafiq | رفیق |
| pal (fem.) | rafiq | رفیق |

partner	šarik	شریک
chief (boss)	ra'is	رئیس
superior (n)	ra'is	رئیس
owner, proprietor	sāheb	صاحب
subordinate (n)	zirdast	زیردست
colleague	hamkār	همکار

acquaintance (person)	āšnā	آشنا
fellow traveller	hamsafar	همسفر
classmate	ham kelās	هم کلاس

neighbour (masc.)	hamsāye	همسایه
neighbour (fem.)	hamsāye	همسایه
neighbours	hamsāye-hā	همسایه ها

57. Man. Woman

woman	zan	زن
girl (young woman)	doxtar	دختر
bride	arus	عروس

beautiful (adj)	zibā	زیبا
tall (adj)	qad boland	قد بلند
slender (adj)	xoš andām	خوش اندام
short (adj)	qad kutāh	قد کوتاه

blonde (n)	mu bur	مو بور
brunette (n)	mu siyāh	مو سیاه
ladies' (adj)	zanāne	زنانه
virgin (girl)	bākere	باکره
pregnant (adj)	bārdār	باردار

man (adult male)	mard	مرد
blonde haired man	mu bur	مو بور
dark haired man	mu siyāh	مو سیاه
tall (adj)	qad boland	قد بلند
short (adj)	qad kutāh	قد کوتاه
rude (rough)	xašen	خشن
stocky (adj)	tanumand	تنومند
robust (adj)	tanumand	تنومند
strong (adj)	nirumand	نیرومند
strength	niru	نیرو

stout, fat (adj)	čāq	چاق
swarthy (adj)	sabze ru	سبزه رو
slender (well-built)	xoš andām	خوش اندام
elegant (adj)	barāzande	برازنده

58. Age

| age | sen | سن |
| youth (young age) | javāni | جوانی |

young (adj)	javān	جوان
younger (adj)	kučaktar	کوچکتر
older (adj)	bozorgtar	بزرگتر

young man	mard-e javān	مرد جوان
teenager	nowjavān	نوجوان
guy, fellow	mard	مرد

| old man | pirmard | پیرمرد |
| old woman | pirzan | پیرزن |

adult (adj)	bāleq	بالغ
middle-aged (adj)	miyānsāl	میانسال
elderly (adj)	sālmand	سالمند
old (adj)	mosen	مسن

retirement	mostamerri	مستمری
to retire (from job)	bāznešaste šodan	بازنشسته شدن
pensioner	bāznešaste	بازنشسته

59. Children

child	kudak	کودک
children	bače-hā	بچه ها
twins	doqolu	دوقلو

cradle	gahvāre	گهواره
rattle	jeqjeqe	جغجغه
nappy	pušak	پوشک

dummy, comforter	pestānak	پستانک
pram	kāleske	کالسکه
nursery	kudakestān	کودکستان
babysitter	parastār bače	پرستار بچه

childhood	kudaki	کودکی
doll	arusak	عروسک
toy	asbāb bāzi	اسباب بازی
construction set (toy)	xāne sāzi	خانه سازی
well-bred (adj)	bā tarbiyat	با تربیت
ill-bred (adj)	bi tarbiyat	بی تربیت
spoilt (adj)	lus	لوس

to be naughty	šeytanat kardan	شیطنت کردن
mischievous (adj)	bāziguš	بازیگوش
mischievousness	šeytāni	شیطانی
mischievous child	šeytān	شیطان

| obedient (adj) | moti' | مطیع |
| disobedient (adj) | sarkeš | سرکش |

docile (adj)	āqel	عاقل
clever (intelligent)	bāhuš	باهوش
child prodigy	kudak nābeqe	کودک نابغه

60. Married couples. Family life

to kiss (vt)	busidan	بوسیدن
to kiss (vi)	hamdigar rā busidan	همدیگررا بوسیدن
family (n)	xānevāde	خانواده
family (as adj)	xānevādegi	خانوادگی
couple	zoj	زوج
marriage (state)	ezdevāj	ازدواج
hearth (home)	kāšāne	کاشانه
dynasty	selsele	سلسله
date	qarār	قرار
kiss	buse	بوسه
love (for sb)	ešq	عشق
to love (sb)	dust dāštan	دوست داشتن
beloved	mahbub	محبوب
tenderness	mehrbāni	مهربانی
tender (affectionate)	mehrbān	مهربان
faithfulness	vafā	وفا
faithful (adj)	vafādār	وفادار
care (attention)	tavajjoh	توجه
caring (~ father)	ba molāheze	با ملاحظه
newlyweds	tāze ezdevāj karde	تازه ازدواج کرده
honeymoon	māh-e asal	ماه عسل
to get married (ab. woman)	ezdevāj kardan	ازدواج کردن
to get married (ab. man)	ezdevāj kardan	ازدواج کردن
wedding	arusi	عروسی
golden wedding	panjāhomin sālgard-e arusi	پنجاهمین سالگرد عروسی
anniversary	sālgard	سالگرد
lover (masc.)	ma'šuq	معشوق
mistress (lover)	ma'šuqe	معشوقه
adultery	xiyānat	خیانت
to cheat on ... (commit adultery)	xiyānat kardan	خیانت کردن
jealous (adj)	hasud	حسود
to be jealous	hasud budan	حسود بودن
divorce	talāq	طلاق
to divorce (vi)	talāq gereftan	طلاق گرفتن
to quarrel (vi)	da'vā kardan	دعوا کردن
to be reconciled (after an argument)	āšti kardan	آشتی کردن
together (adv)	bāham	باهم
sex	seks	سکس
happiness	xošbaxti	خوشبختی
happy (adj)	xošbaxt	خوشبخت
misfortune (accident)	badbaxti	بدبختی
unhappy (adj)	badbaxt	بدبخت

Character. Feelings. Emotions

61. Feelings. Emotions

English	Persian (transliteration)	Persian
feeling (emotion)	ehsās	احساس
feelings	ehsāsat	احساسات
to feel (vt)	ehsās kardan	احساس کردن
hunger	gorosnegi	گرسنگی
to be hungry	gorosne budan	گرسنه بودن
thirst	tešnegi	تشنگی
to be thirsty	tešne budan	تشنه بودن
sleepiness	xāb āludegi	خواب آلودگی
to feel sleepy	xābālud budan	خواب آلود بودن
tiredness	xastegi	خستگی
tired (adj)	xaste	خسته
to get tired	xaste šodan	خسته شدن
mood (humour)	xolq	خلق
boredom	bi hoselegi	بی حوصلگی
to be bored	hosele sar raftan	حوصله سررفتن
seclusion	guše nešini	گوشه نشینی
to seclude oneself	guše nešini kardan	گوشه نشینی کردن
to worry (make anxious)	negarān kardan	نگران کردن
to be worried	negarān šodan	نگران شدن
worrying (n)	negarāni	نگرانی
anxiety	negarāni	نگرانی
preoccupied (adj)	moztareb	مضطرب
to be nervous	asabi šodan	عصبی شدن
to panic (vi)	vahšat kardan	وحشت کردن
hope	omid	امید
to hope (vi, vt)	omid dāštan	امید داشتن
certainty	etminān	اطمینان
certain, sure (adj)	motmaen	مطمئن
uncertainty	adam-e etminān	عدم اطمینان
uncertain (adj)	nā motmaen	نا مطمئن
drunk (adj)	mast	مست
sober (adj)	hošyār	هوشیار
weak (adj)	za'if	ضعیف
happy (adj)	xošbaxt	خوشبخت
to scare (vt)	tarsāndan	ترساندن
fury (madness)	qeyz	غیظ
rage (fury)	xašm	خشم
depression	afsordegi	افسردگی
discomfort (unease)	nārāhati	ناراحتی

comfort	āsāyeš	آسایش
to regret (be sorry)	afsus xordan	افسوس خوردن
regret	afsus	افسوس
bad luck	bad šāns-i	بد شانسی
sadness	delxori	دلخوری

shame (remorse)	šarm	شرم
gladness	šādi	شادی
enthusiasm, zeal	eštiyāq	اشتیاق
enthusiast	moštāq	مشتاق
to show enthusiasm	eštiyāq dāštan	اشتیاق داشتن

62. Character. Personality

character	šaxsiyat	شخصیت
character flaw	naqs	نقص
mind, reason	aql	عقل

conscience	vejdān	وجدان
habit (custom)	ādat	عادت
ability (talent)	este'dād	استعداد
can (e.g. ~ swim)	tavānestan	توانستن

patient (adj)	bā howsele	با حوصله
impatient (adj)	bi hosele	بی حوصله
curious (inquisitive)	konjkāv	کنجکاو
curiosity	konjkāvi	کنجکاوی

modesty	forutani	فروتنی
modest (adj)	forutan	فروتن
immodest (adj)	gostāx	گستاخ

laziness	tanbali	تنبلی
lazy (adj)	tanbal	تنبل
lazy person (masc.)	tanbal	تنبل

cunning (n)	mokāri	مکاری
cunning (as adj)	makkār	مکار
distrust	bad gomāni	بد گمانی
distrustful (adj)	bad gomān	بد گمان

generosity	sexāvat	سخاوت
generous (adj)	ba sexāvat	با سخاوت
talented (adj)	bā este'dād	با استعداد
talent	este'dād	استعداد

courageous (adj)	šojā'	شجاع
courage	šojā'at	شجاعت
honest (adj)	sādeq	صادق
honesty	sedāqat	صداقت

careful (cautious)	bā ehtiyāt	با احتیاط
brave (courageous)	bi bāk	بی باک
serious (adj)	jeddi	جدی

strict (severe, stern)	saxt gir	سخت گیر
decisive (adj)	mosammam	مصمم
indecisive (adj)	do del	دو دل
shy, timid (adj)	xejālati	خجالتی
shyness, timidity	xejālat	خجالت

confidence (trust)	e'temād	اعتماد
to believe (trust)	bāvar kardan	باور کردن
trusting (credulous)	zud bāvar	زود باور

sincerely (adv)	sādeqāne	صادقانه
sincere (adj)	sādeq	صادق
sincerity	sedāqat	صداقت
open (person)	sarih	صریح

calm (adj)	ārām	آرام
frank (sincere)	rok	رک
naïve (adj)	sāde lowh	ساده لوح
absent-minded (adj)	sar be havā	سر به هوا
funny (odd)	xande dār	خنده دار

greed	hers	حرص
greedy (adj)	haris	حریص
stingy (adj)	xasis	خسیس
evil (adj)	badjens	بدجنس
stubborn (adj)	lajuj	لجوج
unpleasant (adj)	nāxošāyand	ناخوشایند

selfish person (masc.)	xodxāh	خودخواه
selfish (adj)	xodxāhi	خودخواهی
coward	tarsu	ترسو
cowardly (adj)	tarsu	ترسو

63. Sleep. Dreams

to sleep (vi)	xābidan	خوابیدن
sleep, sleeping	xāb	خواب
dream	royā	رویا
to dream (in sleep)	xāb didan	خواب دیدن
sleepy (adj)	xāb ālud	خواب آلود

bed	taxt-e xāb	تخت خواب
mattress	tošak	تشک
blanket (eiderdown)	patu	پتو
pillow	bālešt	بالشت
sheet	malāfe	ملافه

insomnia	bi-xābi	بیخوابی
sleepless (adj)	bi xāb	بی خواب
sleeping pill	xāb āvar	خواب آور
to take a sleeping pill	xābāvar xordan	خواب آور خوردن

to feel sleepy	xābālud budan	خواب آلود بودن
to yawn (vi)	xamyāze kešidan	خمیازه کشیدن

to go to bed	be raxtexāb raftan	به رختخواب رفتن
to make up the bed	raxtexāb-e pahn kardan	رختخواب پهن کردن
to fall asleep	xābidan	خوابیدن
nightmare	kābus	کابوس
snore, snoring	xoropof	خروپف
to snore (vi)	xoropof kardan	خروپف کردن
alarm clock	sā'at-e zang dār	ساعت زنگ دار
to wake (vt)	bidār kardan	بیدار کردن
to wake up	bidār šodan	بیدار شدن
to get up (vi)	boland šodan	بلند شدن
to have a wash	dast-o ru šostan	دست و روشستن

64. Humour. Laughter. Gladness

humour (wit, fun)	šuxi	شوخی
sense of humour	šux ta'bi	شوخ طبعی
to enjoy oneself	šādi kardan	شادی کردن
cheerful (merry)	šād	شاد
merriment (gaiety)	šādi	شادی
smile	labxand	لبخند
to smile (vi)	labxand zadan	لبخند زدن
to start laughing	xandidan	خندیدن
to laugh (vi)	xandidan	خندیدن
laugh, laughter	xande	خنده
anecdote	latife	لطیفه
funny (anecdote, etc.)	xande dār	خنده دار
funny (odd)	xande dār	خنده دار
to joke (vi)	šuxi kardan	شوخی کردن
joke (verbal)	šuxi	شوخی
joy (emotion)	šādi	شادی
to rejoice (vi)	xošhāl šodan	خوشحال شدن
joyful (adj)	xošhāl	خوشحال

65. Discussion, conversation. Part 1

communication	ertebāt	ارتباط
to communicate	ertebāt dāštan	ارتباط داشتن
conversation	mokāleme	مکالمه
dialogue	goftogu	گفتگو
discussion (discourse)	mobāhese	مباحثه
dispute (debate)	mošājere	مشاجره
to dispute	mošājere kardan	مشاجره کردن
interlocutor	ham soxan	هم سخن
topic (theme)	mowzu'	موضوع
point of view	noqte nazar	نقطه نظر

| opinion (point of view) | nazar | نظر |
| speech (talk) | soxanrāni | سخنرانی |

discussion (of report, etc.)	mozākere	مذاکره
to discuss (vt)	bahs kardan	بحث کردن
talk (conversation)	goftogu	گفتگو
to talk (to chat)	goftogu kardan	گفتگو کردن
meeting	didār	دیدار
to meet (vi, vt)	molāqāt kardan	ملاقات کردن

proverb	zarb-ol-masal	ضرب المثل
saying	zarb-ol-masal	ضرب المثل
riddle (poser)	mo'ammā	معما
to pose a riddle	mo'ammā matrah kardan	معما مطرح کردن
password	ramz	رمز
secret	rāz	راز

oath (vow)	sowgand	سوگند
to swear (an oath)	sowgand xordan	سوگند خوردن
promise	va'de	وعده
to promise (vt)	qowl dādan	قول دادن

advice (counsel)	nasihat	نصیحت
to advise (vt)	nasihat kardan	نصیحت کردن
to follow one's advice	nasihat-e kasi rā donbāl kardan	نصیحت کسی را دنبال کردن
to listen to ... (obey)	guš kardan	گوش کردن

news	xabar	خبر
sensation (news)	hayajān	هیجان
information (data)	ettelā'āt	اطلاعات
conclusion (decision)	natije	نتیجه
voice	sedā	صدا
compliment	ta'rif	تعریف
kind (nice)	bā mohabbat	با محبت

word	kalame	کلمه
phrase	ebārat	عبارت
answer	javāb	جواب

| truth | haqiqat | حقیقت |
| lie | doruq | دروغ |

thought	fekr	فکر
idea (inspiration)	fekr	فکر
fantasy	fāntezi	فانتزی

66. Discussion, conversation. Part 2

respected (adj)	mohtaram	محترم
to respect (vt)	ehterām gozāštan	احترام گذاشتن
respect	ehterām	احترام
Dear ... (letter)	gerāmi	گرامی
to introduce (sb to sb)	mo'arrefi kardan	معرفی کردن

to make acquaintance	āšnā šodan	آشنا شدن
intention	qasd	قصد
to intend (have in mind)	qasd dāštan	قصد داشتن
wish	ārezu	آرزو
to wish (~ good luck)	ārezu kardan	آرزو کردن
surprise (astonishment)	ta'ajjob	تعجب
to surprise (amaze)	mote'ajjeb kardan	متعجب کردن
to be surprised	mote'ajjeb šodan	متعجب شدن
to give (vt)	dādan	دادن
to take (get hold of)	bardāštan	برداشتن
to give back	bargardāndan	برگرداندن
to return (give back)	pas dādan	پس دادن
to apologize (vi)	ozr xāstan	عذر خواستن
apology	ozr xāhi	عذر خواهی
to forgive (vt)	baxšidan	بخشیدن
to talk (speak)	harf zadan	حرف زدن
to listen (vi)	guš dādan	گوش دادن
to hear out	xub guš dādan	خوب گوش دادن
to understand (vt)	fahmidan	فهمیدن
to show (to display)	nešān dādan	نشان دادن
to look at …	negāh kardan	نگاه کردن
to call (yell for sb)	sedā kardan	صدا کردن
to distract (disturb)	mozāhem šodan	مزاحم شدن
to disturb (vt)	mozāhem šodan	مزاحم شدن
to pass (to hand sth)	dādan	دادن
demand (request)	xāheš	خواهش
to request (ask)	xāheš kardan	خواهش کردن
demand (firm request)	taqāzā	تقاضا
to demand (request firmly)	darxāst kardan	درخواست کردن
to tease (call names)	dast endâxtan	دست انداختن
to mock (make fun of)	masxare kardan	مسخره کردن
mockery, derision	masxare	مسخره
nickname	laqab	لقب
insinuation	kenāye	کنایه
to insinuate (imply)	kenāye zadan	کنایه زدن
to mean (vt)	ma'ni dāštan	معنی داشتن
description	towsif	توصیف
to describe (vt)	towsif kardan	توصیف کردن
praise (compliments)	tahsin	تحسین
to praise (vt)	tahsin kardan	تحسین کردن
disappointment	nāomidi	ناامیدی
to disappoint (vt)	nāomid kardan	ناامید کردن
to be disappointed	nāomid šodan	ناامید شدن
supposition	farz	فرض
to suppose (assume)	farz kardan	فرض کردن

| warning (caution) | extār | اخطار |
| to warn (vt) | extār dādan | اخطار دادن |

67. Discussion, conversation. Part 3

| to talk into (convince) | rāzi kardan | راضی کردن |
| to calm down (vt) | ārām kardan | آرام کردن |

silence (~ is golden)	sokut	سکوت
to be silent (not speaking)	sāket māndan	ساکت ماندن
to whisper (vi, vt)	najvā kardan	نجوا کردن
whisper	najvā	نجوا

| frankly, sincerely (adv) | sādeqāne | صادقانه |
| in my opinion ... | be nazar-e man | به نظرمن |

detail (of the story)	joz'iyāt	جزئیات
detailed (adj)	mofassal	مفصل
in detail (adv)	be tafsil	به تفصیل

| hint, clue | sarnax | سرنخ |
| to give a hint | sarnax dādan | سرنخ دادن |

look (glance)	nazar	نظر
to have a look	nazar andāxtan	نظر انداختن
fixed (look)	bi harekat	بی حرکت
to blink (vi)	pelk zadan	پلک زدن
to wink (vi)	češmak zadan	چشمک زدن
to nod (in assent)	sar-e tekān dādan	سر تکان دادن

sigh	āh	آه
to sigh (vi)	āh kešidan	آه کشیدن
to shudder (vi)	larzidan	لرزیدن
gesture	žest	ژست
to touch (one's arm, etc.)	lams kardan	لمس کردن
to seize (e.g., ~ by the arm)	gereftan	گرفتن
to tap (on the shoulder)	zadan	زدن

Look out!	movāzeb bāš!	مواظب باش!
Really?	vāqe'an?	واقعاً؟
Are you sure?	motmaenn-i?	مطمئنی؟
Good luck!	movaffaq bāšid!	موفق باشید!
I see!	albate!	البته!
What a pity!	heyf!	حیف!

68. Agreement. Refusal

consent	movāfeqat	موافقت
to consent (vi)	movāfeqat kardan	موافقت کردن
approval	ta'id	تایید
to approve (vt)	ta'id kardan	تایید کردن
refusal	emtenā'	امتناع

to refuse (vi, vt)	rad kardan	رد کردن
Great!	āli	عالی
All right!	xub	خوب
Okay! (I agree)	besyār xob!	بسیارخوب!

forbidden (adj)	mamnu'	ممنوع
it's forbidden	mamnu' ast	ممنوع است
it's impossible	qeyr-e momken ast	غیر ممکن است
incorrect (adj)	nādorost	نادرست

to reject (~ a demand)	rad kardan	رد کردن
to support (cause, idea)	poštibāni kardan	پشتیبانی کردن
to accept (~ an apology)	qabul kardan	قبول کردن

to confirm (vt)	ta'yid kardan	تآیید کردن
confirmation	ta'yid	تآیید
permission	ejāze	اجازه
to permit (vt)	ejāze dādan	اجازه دادن
decision	tasmim	تصمیم
to say nothing (hold one's tongue)	sokut kardan	سکوت کردن

condition (term)	šart	شرط
excuse (pretext)	bahāne	بهانه
praise (compliments)	tahsin	تحسین
to praise (vt)	tahsin kardan	تحسین کردن

69. Success. Good luck. Failure

success	movaffaqiyat	موفقیت
successfully (adv)	bā movaffaqiyat	با موفقیت
successful (adj)	movaffaqiyat āmiz	موفقیت آمیز

luck (good luck)	šāns	شانس
Good luck!	movaffaq bāšid!	موفق باشید!
lucky (e.g. ~ day)	šāns	شانس
lucky (fortunate)	xoš šāns	خوش شانس

failure	nākāmi	ناکامی
misfortune	bad šāns-i	بد شانسی
bad luck	bad šāns-i	بد شانسی
unsuccessful (adj)	nā movaffaq	نا موفق
catastrophe	fāje'e	فاجعه

pride	eftexār	افتخار
proud (adj)	maqrur	مغرور
to be proud	eftexār kardan	افتخارکردن

winner	barande	برنده
to win (vi)	piruz šodan	پیروز شدن
to lose (not win)	bāxtan	باختن
try	talāš	تلاش
to try (vi)	talāš kardan	تلاش کردن
chance (opportunity)	šāns	شانس

70. Quarrels. Negative emotions

shout (scream)	faryād	فریاد
to shout (vi)	faryād zadan	فریاد زدن
to start to cry out	faryād zadan	فریاد زدن
quarrel	da'vā	دعوا
to quarrel (vi)	da'vā kardan	دعوا کردن
fight (squabble)	mošājere	مشاجره
to make a scene	janjāl kardan	جنجال کردن
conflict	dargiri	درگیری
misunderstanding	su'-e tafāhom	سوء تفاهم
insult	towhin	توهین
to insult (vt)	towhin kardan	توهین کردن
insulted (adj)	towhin šode	توهین شده
resentment	ranješ	رنجش
to offend (vt)	ranjāndan	رنجاندن
to take offence	ranjidan	رنجیدن
indignation	xašm	خشم
to be indignant	xašmgin šodan	خشمگین شدن
complaint	šekāyat	شکایت
to complain (vi, vt)	šekāyat kardan	شکایت کردن
apology	ozr xāhi	عذر خواهی
to apologize (vi)	ozr xāstan	عذر خواستن
to beg pardon	ozr xāstan	عذر خواستن
criticism	enteqād	انتقاد
to criticize (vt)	enteqād kardan	انتقاد کردن
accusation	ettehām	اتهام
to accuse (vt)	mottaham kardan	متهم کردن
revenge	enteqām	انتقام
to avenge (get revenge)	enteqām gereftan	انتقام گرفتن
to pay back	talāfi darāvardan	تلافی درآوردن
disdain	tahqir	تحقیر
to despise (vt)	tahqir kardan	تحقیر کردن
hatred, hate	nefrat	نفرت
to hate (vt)	motenaffer budan	متنفر بودن
nervous (adj)	asabi	عصبی
to be nervous	asabi šodan	عصبی شدن
angry (mad)	xašmgin	خشمگین
to make angry	xašmgin kardan	خشمگین کردن
humiliation	tahqir	تحقیر
to humiliate (vt)	tahqir kardan	تحقیر کردن
to humiliate oneself	tahqir šodan	تحقیر شدن
shock	šok	شوک
to shock (vt)	šokke kardan	شوک کردن
trouble (e.g. serious ~)	moškel	مشکل

unpleasant (adj)	nāxošāyand	ناخوشایند
fear (dread)	tars	ترس
terrible (storm, heat)	eftezāh	افتضاح
scary (e.g. ~ story)	vahšatnāk	وحشتناک
horror	vahšat	وحشت
awful (crime, news)	vahšat āvar	وحشت آور

to begin to tremble	larzidan	لرزیدن
to cry (weep)	gerye kardan	گریه کردن
to start crying	gerye sar dādan	گریه سر دادن
tear	ašk	اشک

fault	taqsir	تقصیر
guilt (feeling)	gonāh	گناه
dishonor (disgrace)	ār	عار
protest	e'terāz	اعتراض
stress	fešār	فشار

to disturb (vt)	mozāhem šodan	مزاحم شدن
to be furious	xašmgin budan	خشمگین بودن
angry (adj)	xašmgin	خشمگین
to end (~ a relationship)	qat' kardan	قطع کردن
to swear (at sb)	fohš dādan	فحش دادن

to scare (become afraid)	tarsidan	ترسیدن
to hit (strike with hand)	zadan	زدن
to fight (street fight, etc.)	zad-o-xord kardan	زد و خورد کردن

to settle (a conflict)	hal-o-fasl kardan	حل و فصل کردن
discontented (adj)	nārāzi	ناراضی
furious (adj)	qazabnāk	غضبناک

| It's not good! | xub nist! | خوب نیست! |
| It's bad! | bad ast! | بد است! |

Medicine

71. Diseases

illness	bimāri	بیماری
to be ill	bimār budan	بیمار بودن
health	salāmati	سلامتی

runny nose (coryza)	āb-e rizeš-e bini	آب ریزش بینی
tonsillitis	varam-e lowze	ورم لوزه
cold (illness)	sarmā xordegi	سرما خوردگی
to catch a cold	sarmā xordan	سرما خوردن

bronchitis	boronšit	برنشیت
pneumonia	zātorrie	ذات الریه
flu, influenza	ānfolānzā	آنفولانزا

shortsighted (adj)	nazdik bin	نزدیک بین
longsighted (adj)	durbin	دوربین
strabismus (crossed eyes)	enherāf-e čašm	انحراف چشم
squint-eyed (adj)	luč	لوچ
cataract	āb morvārid	آب مروارید
glaucoma	ab-e siyāh	آب سیاه

stroke	sekte-ye maqzi	سکته مغزی
heart attack	sekte-ye qalbi	سکته قلبی
myocardial infarction	ānfārktus	آنفارکتوس
paralysis	falaji	فلجی
to paralyse (vt)	falj kardan	فلج کردن

allergy	ālerži	آلرژی
asthma	āsm	آسم
diabetes	diyābet	دیابت

| toothache | dandān-e dard | دندان درد |
| caries | pusidegi | پوسیدگی |

diarrhoea	eshāl	اسهال
constipation	yobusat	یبوست
stomach upset	nārāhati-ye me'de	ناراحتی معده
food poisoning	masmumiyat	مسمومیت
to get food poisoning	masmum šodan	مسموم شدن

arthritis	varam-e mafāsel	ورم مفاصل
rickets	rāšitism	راشیتیسم
rheumatism	romātism	روماتیسم
atherosclerosis	tasallob-e šarāin	تصلب شرائین

| gastritis | varam-e me'de | ورم معده |
| appendicitis | āpāndisit | آپاندیسیت |

cholecystitis	eltehāb-e kise-ye safrā	التهاب کیسه صفرا
ulcer	zaxm	زخم
measles	sorxak	سرخک
rubella (German measles)	sorxje	سرخجه
jaundice	yaraqān	یرقان
hepatitis	hepātit	هپاتیت
schizophrenia	šizoferni	شیزوفرنی
rabies (hydrophobia)	hāri	هاری
neurosis	extelāl-e a'sāb	اختلال اعصاب
concussion	zarbe-ye maqzi	ضربه مغزی
cancer	saratān	سرطان
sclerosis	eskeleroz	اسکلروز
multiple sclerosis	eskeleroz čandgāne	اسکلروز چندگانه
alcoholism	alkolism	الکلیسم
alcoholic (n)	alkoli	الکلی
syphilis	siflis	سیفلیس
AIDS	eydz	ایدز
tumour	tumor	تومور
malignant (adj)	bad xim	بد خیم
benign (adj)	xoš xim	خوش خیم
fever	tab	تب
malaria	mālāriyā	مالاریا
gangrene	qānqāriyā	قانقاریا
seasickness	daryā-zadegi	دریازدگی
epilepsy	sar'	صرع
epidemic	epidemi	اپیدمی
typhus	hasbe	حصبه
tuberculosis	sel	سل
cholera	vabā	وبا
plague (bubonic ~)	tā'un	طاعون

72. Symptoms. Treatments. Part 1

symptom	alāem-e bimāri	علائم بیماری
temperature	damā	دما
high temperature (fever)	tab	تب
pulse	nabz	نبض
dizziness (vertigo)	sargije	سرگیجه
hot (adj)	dāq	داغ
shivering	ra'še	رعشه
pale (e.g. ~ face)	rang paride	رنگ پریده
cough	sorfe	سرفه
to cough (vi)	sorfe kardan	سرفه کردن
to sneeze (vi)	atse kardan	عطسه کردن
faint	qaš	غش

to faint (vi)	qaš kardan	غش کردن
bruise (hématome)	kabudi	کبودی
bump (lump)	barāmadegi	برآمدگی
to bang (bump)	barxord kardan	برخورد کردن
contusion (bruise)	kuftegi	کوفتگی
to get a bruise	zarb didan	ضرب دیدن

to limp (vi)	langidan	لنگیدن
dislocation	dar raftegi	دررفتگی
to dislocate (vt)	dar raftan	دررفتن
fracture	šekastegi	شکستگی
to have a fracture	dočār-e šekastegi šodan	دچار شکستگی شدن

cut (e.g. paper ~)	boridegi	بریدگی
to cut oneself	boridan	بریدن
bleeding	xunrizi	خونریزی

| burn (injury) | suxtegi | سوختگی |
| to get burned | dočār-e suxtegi šodan | دچار سوختگی شدن |

to prick (vt)	surāx kardan	سوراخ کردن
to prick oneself	surāx kardan	سوراخ کردن
to injure (vt)	āsib resāndan	آسیب رساندن
injury	zaxm	زخم
wound	zaxm	زخم
trauma	zarbe	ضربه

to be delirious	hazyān goftan	هذیان گفتن
to stutter (vi)	loknat dāštan	لکنت داشتن
sunstroke	āftāb-zadegi	آفتابزدگی

73. Symptoms. Treatments. Part 2

| pain, ache | dard | درد |
| splinter (in foot, etc.) | xār | خار |

sweat (perspiration)	araq	عرق
to sweat (perspire)	araq kardan	عرق کردن
vomiting	estefrāq	استفراغ
convulsions	tašannoj	تشنج

pregnant (adj)	bārdār	باردار
to be born	motevalled šodan	متولد شدن
delivery, labour	vaz'-e haml	وضع حمل
to deliver (~ a baby)	be donyā āvardan	به دنیا آوردن
abortion	seqt-e janin	سقط جنین

breathing, respiration	tanaffos	تنفس
in-breath (inhalation)	estenšāq	استنشاق
out-breath (exhalation)	bāzdam	بازدم
to exhale (breathe out)	bāzdamidan	بازدمیدن
to inhale (vi)	nafas kešidan	نفس کشیدن
disabled person	ma'lul	معلول
cripple	falaj	فلج

drug addict	mo'tād	معتاد
deaf (adj)	kar	کر
mute (adj)	lāl	لال
deaf mute (adj)	kar-o lāl	کر و لال

| mad, insane (adj) | divāne | دیوانه |
| madman (demented person) | divāne | دیوانه |

| madwoman | divāne | دیوانه |
| to go insane | divāne šodan | دیوانه شدن |

gene	žen	ژن
immunity	masuniyat	مصونیت
hereditary (adj)	mowrusi	موروثی
congenital (adj)	mādarzād	مادرزاد

virus	virus	ویروس
microbe	mikrob	میکروب
bacterium	bākteri	باکتری
infection	ofunat	عفونت

74. Symptoms. Treatments. Part 3

| hospital | bimārestān | بیمارستان |
| patient | bimār | بیمار |

diagnosis	tašxis	تشخیص
cure	mo'āleje	معالجه
medical treatment	darmān	درمان
to get treatment	darmān šodan	درمان شدن
to treat (~ a patient)	mo'āleje kardan	معالجه کردن
to nurse (look after)	parastāri kardan	پرستاری کردن
care (nursing ~)	parastāri	پرستاری

operation, surgery	amal-e jarrāhi	عمل جراحی
to bandage (head, limb)	pānsemān kardan	پانسمان کردن
bandaging	pānsemān	پانسمان

vaccination	vāksināsyon	واکسیناسیون
to vaccinate (vt)	vāksine kardan	واکسینه کردن
injection	tazriq	تزریق
to give an injection	tazriq kardan	تزریق کردن

attack	hamle	حمله
amputation	qat'-e ozv	قطع عضو
to amputate (vt)	qat' kardan	قطع کردن
coma	komā	کما
to be in a coma	dar komā budan	در کما بودن
intensive care	morāqebat-e viže	مراقبت ویژه

to recover (~ from flu)	behbud yāftan	بهبود یافتن
condition (patient's ~)	hālat	حالت
consciousness	huš	هوش
memory (faculty)	hāfeze	حافظه

to pull out (tooth)	dandān kešidan	دندان کشیدن
filling	por kardan	پر کردن
to fill (a tooth)	por kardan	پر کردن
hypnosis	hipnotizm	هیپنوتیزم
to hypnotize (vt)	hipnotizm kardan	هیپنوتیزم کردن

75. Doctors

doctor	pezešk	پزشک
nurse	parastār	پرستار
personal doctor	pezešk-e šaxsi	پزشک شخصی
dentist	dandān pezešk	دندان پزشک
optician	češm-pezešk	چشم پزشک
general practitioner	pezešk omumi	پزشک عمومی
surgeon	jarrāh	جراح
psychiatrist	ravānpezešk	روانپزشک
paediatrician	pezešk-e kudakān	پزشک کودکان
psychologist	ravānšenās	روانشناس
gynaecologist	motexasses-e zanān	متخصص زنان
cardiologist	motexasses-e qalb	متخصص قلب

76. Medicine. Drugs. Accessories

medicine, drug	dāru	دارو
remedy	darmān	درمان
to prescribe (vt)	tajviz kardan	تجویز کردن
prescription	nosxe	نسخه
tablet, pill	qors	قرص
ointment	pomād	پماد
ampoule	āmpul	آمپول
mixture	šarbat	شربت
syrup	šarbat	شربت
pill	kapsul	کپسول
powder	pudr	پودر
gauze bandage	bānd	باند
cotton wool	panbe	پنبه
iodine	yod	ید
plaster	časb-e zaxm	چسب زخم
eyedropper	qatre čekān	قطره چکان
thermometer	damāsanj	دماسنج
syringe	sorang	سرنگ
wheelchair	vilčer	ویلچر
crutches	čub zir baqal	چوب زیر بغل
painkiller	mosaken	مسکن
laxative	moshel	مسهل

spirits (ethanol)	alkol	الکل
medicinal herbs	giyāhān-e dāruyi	گیاهان دارویی
herbal (~ tea)	giyāhi	گیاهی

77. Smoking. Tobacco products

tobacco	tutun	توتون
cigarette	sigār	سیگار
cigar	sigār	سیگار
pipe	pip	پیپ
packet (of cigarettes)	baste	بسته

matches	kebrit	کبریت
matchbox	quti-ye kebrit	قوطی کبریت
lighter	fandak	فندک
ashtray	zir-sigāri	زیرسیگاری
cigarette case	quti-ye sigār	قوطی سیگار

| cigarette holder | čub-e sigār | چوب سیگار |
| filter (cigarette tip) | filter | فیلتر |

to smoke (vi, vt)	sigār kešidan	سیگار کشیدن
to light a cigarette	sigār rowšan kardan	سیگار روشن کردن
smoking	sigār kešidan	سیگار کشیدن
smoker	sigāri	سیگاری

cigarette end	tah-e sigār	ته سیگار
smoke, fumes	dud	دود
ash	xākestar	خاکستر

HUMAN HABITAT

City

78. City. Life in the city

city, town	šahr	شهر
capital city	pāytaxt	پایتخت
village	rustā	روستا

city map	naqše-ye šahr	نقشهٔ شهر
city centre	markaz-e šahr	مرکز شهر
suburb	hume-ye šahr	حومهٔ شهر
suburban (adj)	hume-ye šahr	حومهٔ شهر

outskirts	hume	حومه
environs (suburbs)	hume	حومه
city block	mahalle	محله
residential block (area)	mahalle-ye maskuni	محلهٔ مسکونی

traffic	obur-o morur	عبور و مرور
traffic lights	čerāq-e rāhnamā	چراغ راهنما
public transport	haml-o naql-e šahri	حمل و نقل شهری
crossroads	čahārrāh	چهارراه

zebra crossing	xatt-e āber-e piyāde	خط عابرپیاده
pedestrian subway	zir-e gozar	زیر گذر
to cross (~ the street)	obur kardan	عبور کردن
pedestrian	piyāde	پیاده
pavement	piyāde row	پیاده رو

bridge	pol	پل
embankment (river walk)	xiyābān-e sāheli	خیابان ساحلی
fountain	češme	چشمه

allée (garden walkway)	bāq rāh	باغ راه
park	pārk	پارک
boulevard	bolvār	بولوار
square	meydān	میدان
avenue (wide street)	xiyābān	خیابان
street	xiyābān	خیابان
side street	kuče	کوچه
dead end	bon bast	بن بست

house	xāne	خانه
building	sāxtemān	ساختمان
skyscraper	āsemānxarāš	آسمانخراش
facade	namā	نما
roof	bām	بام

window	panjere	پنجره
arch	tāq-e qowsi	طاق قوسی
column	sotun	ستون
corner	nabš	نبش

shop window	vitrin	ویترین
signboard (store sign, etc.)	tāblo	تابلو
poster	poster	پوستر
advertising poster	poster-e tabliqāti	پوستر تبلیغاتی
hoarding	bilbord	بیلبورد

rubbish	āšqāl	آشغال
rubbish bin	satl-e āšqāl	سطل آشغال
to litter (vi)	kasif kardan	کثیف کردن
rubbish dump	jā-ye dafn-e āšqāl	جای دفن آشغال

telephone box	kābin-e telefon	کابین تلفن
lamppost	tir-e barq	تیر برق
bench (park ~)	nimkat	نیمکت

police officer	polis	پلیس
police	polis	پلیس
beggar	gedā	گدا
homeless (n)	bi xānomān	بی خانمان

79. Urban institutions

shop	maqāze	مغازه
chemist, pharmacy	dāruxāne	داروخانه
optician (spectacles shop)	eynak foruši	عینک فروشی
shopping centre	markaz-e tejāri	مرکز تجاری
supermarket	supermārket	سوپرمارکت

bakery	nānvāyi	نانوایی
baker	nānvā	نانوا
cake shop	qannādi	قنادی
grocery shop	baqqāli	بقالی
butcher shop	gušt foruši	گوشت فروشی

| greengrocer | sabzi foruši | سبزی فروشی |
| market | bāzār | بازار |

coffee bar	kāfe	کافه
restaurant	resturān	رستوران
pub, bar	bār	بار
pizzeria	pitzā-foruši	پیتزا فروشی

hairdresser	ārāyešgāh	آرایشگاه
post office	post	پست
dry cleaners	xošk-šuyi	خشکشویی
photo studio	ātolye-ye akkāsi	آتلیة عکاسی

| shoe shop | kafš foruši | کفش فروشی |
| bookshop | ketāb-foruši | کتاب فروشی |

sports shop	maqāze-ye varzeši	مغازهٔ ورزشی
clothes repair shop	ta'mir-e lebās	تعمیر لباس
formal wear hire	kerāye-ye lebās	کرایهٔ لباس
video rental shop	kerāye-ye film	کرایهٔ فیلم

circus	sirak	سیرک
zoo	bāq-e vahš	باغ وحش
cinema	sinamā	سینما
museum	muze	موزه
library	ketābxāne	کتابخانه

theatre	teātr	تئاتر
opera (opera house)	operā	اپرا
nightclub	kābāre	کاباره
casino	kāzino	کازینو

mosque	masjed	مسجد
synagogue	kenešt	کنشت
cathedral	kelisā-ye jāme'	کلیسای جامع
temple	ma'bad	معبد
church	kelisā	کلیسا

college	anistito	انستیتو
university	dānešgāh	دانشگاه
school	madrese	مدرسه

prefecture	ostāndāri	استانداری
town hall	šahrdāri	شهرداری
hotel	hotel	هتل
bank	bānk	بانک

embassy	sefārat	سفارت
travel agency	āžāns-e jahāngardi	آژانس جهانگردی
information office	daftar-e ettelāāt	دفتر اطلاعات
currency exchange	sarrāfi	صرافی

| underground, tube | metro | مترو |
| hospital | bimārestān | بیمارستان |

| petrol station | pomp-e benzin | پمپ بنزین |
| car park | pārking | پارکینگ |

80. Signs

signboard (store sign, etc.)	tāblo	تابلو
notice (door sign, etc.)	nevešte	نوشته
poster	poster	پوستر
direction sign	rāhnamā	راهنما
arrow (sign)	alāmat	علامت

caution	ehtiyāt	احتیاط
warning sign	alāmat-e hošdār	علامت هشدار
to warn (vt)	hošdār dādan	هشدار دادن
rest day (weekly ~)	ruz-e ta'til	روز تعطیل

| timetable (schedule) | jadval | جدول |
| opening hours | sā'athā-ye kāri | ساعت های کاری |

WELCOME!	xoš āmadid	خوش آمدید
ENTRANCE	vorud	ورود
WAY OUT	xoruj	خروج

PUSH	hel dādan	هل دادن
PULL	bekešid	بکشید
OPEN	bāz	باز
CLOSED	baste	بسته

| WOMEN | zanāne | زنانه |
| MEN | mardāne | مردانه |

DISCOUNTS	taxfif	تخفیف
SALE	harāj	حراج
NEW!	jadid	جدید
FREE	majjāni	مجانی

ATTENTION!	tavajjoh	توجه
NO VACANCIES	otāq-e xāli nadārim	اتاق خالی نداریم
RESERVED	rezerv šode	رزرو شده

| ADMINISTRATION | edāre | اداره |
| STAFF ONLY | xāse personel | خاص پرسنل |

BEWARE OF THE DOG!	movāzeb-e sag bāšid	مواظب سگ باشید
NO SMOKING	sigār kešidan mamnu'	سیگار کشیدن ممنوع
DO NOT TOUCH!	dast nazanid	دست نزنید

DANGEROUS	xatarnāk	خطرناک
DANGER	xatar	خطر
HIGH VOLTAGE	voltāj bālā	ولتاژ بالا
NO SWIMMING!	šenā mamnu'	شنا ممنوع
OUT OF ORDER	xārāb	خراب

FLAMMABLE	qābel-e ehterāq	قابل احتراق
FORBIDDEN	mamnu'	ممنوع
NO TRESPASSING!	obur mamnu'	عبور ممنوع
WET PAINT	rang-e xis	رنگ خیس

81. Urban transport

bus, coach	otobus	اتوبوس
tram	terāmvā	تراموا
trolleybus	otobus-e barqi	اتوبوس برقی
route (of bus, etc.)	xat	خط
number (e.g. bus ~)	šomāre	شماره

to go by ...	raftan bā	رفتن با
to get on (~ the bus)	savār šodan	سوار شدن
to get off ...	piyāde šodan	پیاده شدن
stop (e.g. bus ~)	istgāh-e otobus	ایستگاه اتوبوس

next stop	istgāh-e ba'di	ایستگاه بعدی
terminus	istgāh-e āxar	ایستگاه آخر
timetable	barnāme	برنامه
to wait (vi)	montazer budan	منتظر بودن

| ticket | belit | بلیط |
| fare | qeymat-e belit | قیمت بلیت |

cashier (ticket seller)	sanduqdār	صندوقدار
ticket inspection	kontorol-e belit	کنترل بلیط
ticket inspector	kontorol či	کنترل چی

to be late (for ...)	ta'xir dāštan	تأخیرداشتن
to miss (~ the train, etc.)	az dast dādan	از دست دادن
to be in a hurry	ajale kardan	عجله کردن

taxi, cab	tāksi	تاکسی
taxi driver	rānande-ye tāksi	راننده تاکسی
by taxi	bā tāksi	با تاکسی
taxi rank	istgāh-e tāksi	ایستگاه تاکسی
to call a taxi	tāksi gereftan	تاکسی گرفتن
to take a taxi	tāksi gereftan	تاکسی گرفتن

traffic	obur-o morur	عبور و مرور
traffic jam	terāfik	ترافیک
rush hour	sā'at-e šoluqi	ساعت شلوغی
to park (vi)	pārk kardan	پارک کردن
to park (vt)	pārk kardan	پارک کردن
car park	pārking	پارکینگ

underground, tube	metro	مترو
station	istgāh	ایستگاه
to take the tube	bā metro raftan	با مترو رفتن
train	qatār	قطار
train station	istgāh-e rāh-e āhan	ایستگاه راه آهن

82. Sightseeing

monument	mojassame	مجسمه
fortress	qal'e	قلعه
palace	kāx	کاخ
castle	qal'e	قلعه
tower	borj	برج
mausoleum	ārāmgāh	آرامگاه

architecture	me'māri	معماری
medieval (adj)	qorun-e vasati	قرون وسطی
ancient (adj)	qadimi	قدیمی
national (adj)	melli	ملی
famous (monument, etc.)	mašhur	مشهور

tourist	turist	توریست
guide (person)	rāhnamā-ye tur	راهنمای تور
excursion, sightseeing tour	gardeš	گردش

| to show (vt) | nešān dādan | نشان دادن |
| to tell (vt) | hekāyat kardan | حکایت کردن |

to find (vt)	peydā kardan	پیدا کردن
to get lost (lose one's way)	gom šodan	گم شدن
map (e.g. underground ~)	naqše	نقشه
map (e.g. city ~)	naqše	نقشه

souvenir, gift	sowqāti	سوغاتی
gift shop	forušgāh-e sowqāti	فروشگاه سوغاتی
to take pictures	aks gereftan	عکس گرفتن
to have one's picture taken	aks gereftan	عکس گرفتن

83. Shopping

to buy (purchase)	xarid kardan	خرید کردن
shopping	xarid	خرید
to go shopping	xarid kardan	خرید کردن
shopping	xarid	خرید

| to be open (ab. shop) | bāz budan | باز بودن |
| to be closed | baste budan | بسته بودن |

footwear, shoes	kafš	کفش
clothes, clothing	lebās	لباس
cosmetics	lavāzem-e ārāyeši	لوازم آرایشی
food products	mavādd-e qazāyi	مواد غذایی
gift, present	hedye	هدیه

| shop assistant (masc.) | forušande | فروشنده |
| shop assistant (fem.) | forušande-ye zan | فروشنده زن |

cash desk	sanduq	صندوق
mirror	āyene	آینه
counter (shop ~)	pišxān	پیشخوان
fitting room	otāq porov	اتاق پرو

to try on	emtehān kardan	امتحان کردن
to fit (ab. dress, etc.)	monāseb budan	مناسب بودن
to fancy (vt)	dust dāštan	دوست داشتن

price	qeymat	قیمت
price tag	barčasb-e qeymat	برچسب قیمت
to cost (vt)	qeymat dāštan	قیمت داشتن
How much?	čeqadr?	چقدر؟
discount	taxfif	تخفیف

inexpensive (adj)	arzān	ارزان
cheap (adj)	arzān	ارزان
expensive (adj)	gerān	گران
It's expensive	gerān ast	گران است

| hire (n) | kerāye | کرایه |
| to hire (~ a dinner jacket) | kerāye kardan | کرایه کردن |

| credit (trade credit) | vām | وام |
| on credit (adv) | xarid-e e'tebāri | خرید اعتباری |

84. Money

money	pul	پول
currency exchange	tabdil-e arz	تبدیل ارز
exchange rate	nerx-e arz	نرخ ارز
cashpoint	xodpardāz	خودپرداز
coin	sekke	سکه

| dollar | dolār | دلار |
| euro | yuro | یورو |

lira	lire	لیره
Deutschmark	mārk	مارک
franc	farānak	فرانک
pound sterling	pond-e esterling	پوند استرلینگ
yen	yen	ین

debt	qarz	قرض
debtor	bedehkār	بدهکار
to lend (money)	qarz dādan	قرض دادن
to borrow (vi, vt)	qarz gereftan	قرض گرفتن

bank	bānk	بانک
account	hesāb-e bānki	حساب بانکی
to deposit (vt)	rixtan	ریختن
to deposit into the account	be hesāb rixtan	به حساب ریختن
to withdraw (vt)	az hesāb bardāštan	از حساب برداشتن

credit card	kārt-e e'tebāri	کارت اعتباری
cash	pul-e naqd	پول نقد
cheque	ček	چک
to write a cheque	ček neveštan	چک نوشتن
chequebook	daste-ye ček	دسته چک

wallet	kif-e pul	کیف پول
purse	kif-e pul	کیف پول
safe	gāvsanduq	گاوصندوق

heir	vāres	وارث
inheritance	mirās	میراث
fortune (wealth)	dārāyi	دارایی

lease	ejāre	اجاره
rent (money)	kerāye-ye xāne	کرایه خانه
to rent (sth from sb)	ejāre kardan	اجاره کردن

price	qeymat	قیمت
cost	arzeš	ارزش
sum	jam'-e kol	جمع کل
to spend (vt)	xarj kardan	خرج کردن
expenses	maxārej	مخارج

| to economize (vi, vt) | sarfeju-yi kardan | صرفه جویی کردن |
| economical | maqrun besarfe | مقرون به صرفه |

to pay (vi, vt)	pardāxtan	پرداختن
payment	pardāxt	پرداخت
change (give the ~)	pul-e xerad	پول خرد

tax	māliyāt	مالیات
fine	jarime	جریمه
to fine (vt)	jarime kardan	جریمه کردن

85. Post. Postal service

post office	post	پست
post (letters, etc.)	post	پست
postman	nāme resān	نامه رسان
opening hours	sā'athā-ye kāri	ساعت های کاری

letter	nāme	نامه
registered letter	nāme-ye sefāreši	نامه سفارشی
postcard	kārt-e postāl	کارت پستال
telegram	telegrām	تلگرام
parcel	baste posti	بسته پستی
money transfer	havāle	حواله

to receive (vt)	gereftan	گرفتن
to send (vt)	ferestādan	فرستادن
sending	ersāl	ارسال

address	nešāni	نشانی
postcode	kod-e posti	کد پستی
sender	ferestande	فرستنده
receiver	girande	گیرنده

| name (first name) | esm | اسم |
| surname (last name) | nām-e xānevādegi | نام خانوادگی |

postage rate	ta'refe	تعرفه
standard (adj)	ādi	عادی
economical (adj)	ādi	عادی

weight	vazn	وزن
to weigh (~ letters)	vazn kardan	وزن کردن
envelope	pākat	پاکت
postage stamp	tambr	تمبر
to stamp an envelope	tamr zadan	تمبر زدن

Dwelling. House. Home

86. House. Dwelling

house	xāne	خانه
at home (adv)	dar xāne	در خانه
yard	hayāt	حیاط
fence (iron ~)	hesār	حصار
brick (n)	ājor	آجر
brick (as adj)	ājori	آجری
stone (n)	sang	سنگ
stone (as adj)	sangi	سنگی
concrete (n)	boton	بتن
concrete (as adj)	botoni	بتنی
new (new-built)	jadid	جدید
old (adj)	qadimi	قدیمی
decrepit (house)	maxrube	مخروبه
modern (adj)	modern	مدرن
multistorey (adj)	čandtabaqe	چندطبقه
tall (~ building)	boland	بلند
floor, storey	tabaqe	طبقه
single-storey (adj)	yek tabaqe	یک طبقه
ground floor	tabaqe-ye pāin	طبقهٔ پائین
top floor	tabaqe-ye bālā	طبقهٔ بالا
roof	bām	بام
chimney	dudkeš	دودکش
roof tiles	saqf-e kazeb	سقف کاذب
tiled (adj)	sofāli	سفالی
loft (attic)	zir-širvāni	زیرشیروانی
window	panjere	پنجره
glass	šiše	شیشه
window ledge	tāqče-ye panjare	طاقچهٔ پنجره
shutters	kerkere	کرکره
wall	divār	دیوار
balcony	bālkon	بالکن
downpipe	nāvdān	ناودان
upstairs (to be ~)	bālā	بالا
to go upstairs	bālā raftan	بالا رفتن
to come down (the stairs)	pāyin āmadan	پایین آمدن
to move (to new premises)	asbābkeši kardan	اسباب کشی کردن

87. House. Entrance. Lift

entrance	darb-e vorudi	درب ورودی
stairs (stairway)	pellekān	پلکان
steps	pelle-hā	پله ها
banisters	narde	نرده
lobby (hotel ~)	lābi	لابی
postbox	sanduq-e post	صندوق پست
waste bin	zobāle dān	زباله دان
refuse chute	šuting zobale	شوتینگ زباله
lift	āsānsor	آسانسور
goods lift	bālābar	بالابر
lift cage	kābin-e āsānsor	کابین آسانسور
to take the lift	āsānsor gereftan	آسانسور گرفتن
flat	āpārtemān	آپارتمان
residents (~ of a building)	sākenān	ساکنان
neighbour (masc.)	hamsāye	همسایه
neighbour (fem.)	hamsāye	همسایه
neighbours	hamsāye-hā	همسایه ها

88. House. Electricity

electricity	barq	برق
light bulb	lāmp	لامپ
switch	kelid	کلید
fuse (plug fuse)	fiyuz	فیوز
cable, wire (electric ~)	sim	سیم
wiring	sim keši	سیم کشی
electricity meter	kontor	کنتور
readings	dastgāh-e xaneš	دستگاه خوانش

89. House. Doors. Locks

door	darb	درب
gate (vehicle ~)	darvāze	دروازه
handle, doorknob	dastgire-ye dar	دستگیرهٔ در
to unlock (unbolt)	bāz kardan	باز کردن
to open (vt)	bāz kardan	باز کردن
to close (vt)	bastan	بستن
key	kelid	کلید
bunch (of keys)	daste	دسته
to creak (door, etc.)	qežqež kardan	غژغژ کردن
creak	qež qež	غژ غژ
hinge (door ~)	lowlā	لولا
doormat	pādari	پادری
door lock	qofl	قفل

keyhole	surāx kelid	سوراخ کلید
crossbar (sliding bar)	kolun-e dar	کلون در
door latch	čeft	چفت
padlock	qofl	قفل

to ring (~ the door bell)	zang zadan	زنگ زدن
ringing (sound)	zang	زنگ
doorbell	zang-e dar	زنگ در
doorbell button	zang	زنگ
knock (at the door)	dar zadan	درزدن
to knock (vi)	dar zadan	درزدن

code	kod	کد
combination lock	qofl-e ramz dār	قفل رمز دار
intercom	āyfon	آیفون
number (on the door)	pelāk-e manzel	پلاک منزل
doorplate	pelāk	پلاک
peephole	češmi	چشمی

90. Country house

village	rustā	روستا
vegetable garden	jāliz	جالیز
fence	parčin	پرچین
picket fence	hesār	حصار
wicket gate	darvāze	دروازه

granary	anbār	انبار
cellar	zirzamin	زیرزمین
shed (garden ~)	ālonak	آلونک
well (water)	čāh	چاه

stove (wood-fired ~)	boxāri	بخاری
to stoke the stove	rowšan kardan-e boxāri	روشن کردن بخاری
firewood	hizom	هیزم
log (firewood)	kande-ye čub	کندۀ چوب

veranda	eyvān-e sarpušide	ایوان سرپوشیده
deck (terrace)	terās	تراس
stoop (front steps)	vorudi-e xāne	ورودی خانه
swing (hanging seat)	tāb	تاب

91. Villa. Mansion

country house	xāne-ye xārej-e šahr	خانۀ خارج شهر
country-villa	vilā	ویلا
wing (~ of a building)	bāl	بال

garden	bāq	باغ
park	pārk	پارک
tropical glasshouse	golxāne	گلخانه
to look after (garden, etc.)	negahdāri kardan	نگهداری کردن

swimming pool	estaxr	استخر
gym (home gym)	sālon-e varzeš	سالن ورزش
tennis court	zamin-e tenis	زمین تنیس
home theater (room)	sinamā	سینما
garage	gārāž	گاراژ

| private property | melk-e xosusi | ملک خصوصی |
| private land | melk-e xosusi | ملک خصوصی |

| warning (caution) | hošdār | هشدار |
| warning sign | alāmat-e hošdār | علامت هشدار |

security	hefāzat	حفاظت
security guard	negahbān	نگهبان
burglar alarm	dozdgir	دزدگیر

92. Castle. Palace

castle	qal'e	قلعه
palace	kāx	کاخ
fortress	qal'e	قلعه
wall (round castle)	divār	دیوار
tower	borj	برج
keep, donjon	borj-e asli	برج اصلی

portcullis	darb-e kešowyi	درب کشویی
subterranean passage	rāh-e zirzamini	راه زیرزمینی
moat	xandaq	خندق
chain	zanjir	زنجیر
arrow loop	mazqal	مزغل

magnificent (adj)	mojallal	مجلل
majestic (adj)	bāšokuh	باشکوه
impregnable (adj)	nofoz nāpazir	نفوذ ناپذیر
medieval (adj)	qorun-e vasati	قرون وسطی

93. Flat

flat	āpārtemān	آپارتمان
room	otāq	اتاق
bedroom	otāq-e xāb	اتاق خواب
dining room	otāq-e qazāxori	اتاق غذاخوری
living room	mehmānxāne	مهمانخانه
study (home office)	daftar	دفتر

entry room	tālār-e vorudi	تالار ورودی
bathroom	hammām	حمام
water closet	tuālet	توالت

ceiling	saqf	سقف
floor	kaf	کف
corner	guše	گوشه

94. Flat. Cleaning

to clean (vi, vt)	tamiz kardan	تمیز کردن
to put away (to stow)	morattab kardan	مرتب کردن
dust	gard	گرد
dusty (adj)	gard ālud	گرد آلود
to dust (vt)	gardgiri kardan	گردگیری کردن
vacuum cleaner	jāru barqi	جارو برقی
to vacuum (vt)	jāru barq-i kešidan	جارو برقی کشیدن
to sweep (vi, vt)	jāru kardan	جارو کردن
sweepings	āšqāl	آشغال
order	nazm	نظم
disorder, mess	bi nazmi	بی نظمی
mop	jāru-ye dastedār	جاروی دسته دار
duster	kohne	کهنه
short broom	jārub	جاروب
dustpan	xāk andāz	خاک انداز

95. Furniture. Interior

furniture	mobl	مبل
table	miz	میز
chair	sandali	صندلی
bed	taxt-e xāb	تخت خواب
sofa, settee	kānāpe	کاناپه
armchair	mobl-e rāhati	مبل راحتی
bookcase	qafase-ye ketāb	قفسه کتاب
shelf	qafase	قفسه
wardrobe	komod	کمد
coat rack (wall-mounted ~)	raxt āviz	رخت آویز
coat stand	čub lebāsi	چوب لباسی
chest of drawers	komod	کمد
coffee table	miz-e pišdasti	میز پیشدستی
mirror	āyene	آینه
carpet	farš	فرش
small carpet	qāliče	قالیچه
fireplace	šumine	شومینه
candle	šam'	شمع
candlestick	šam'dān	شمعدان
drapes	parde	پرده
wallpaper	kāqaz-e divāri	کاغذ دیواری
blinds (jalousie)	kerkere	کرکره
table lamp	čerāq-e rumizi	چراغ رومیزی
wall lamp (sconce)	čerāq-e divāri	چراغ دیواری

| standard lamp | ābāžur | آباژور |
| chandelier | luster | لوستر |

leg (of chair, table)	pāye	پایه
armrest	daste-ye sandali	دستۀ صندلی
back (backrest)	pošti	پشتی
drawer	kešow	کشو

96. Bedding

bedclothes	raxt-e xāb	رخت خواب
pillow	bālešt	بالشت
pillowslip	rubalešt	روبالشت
duvet	patu	پتو
sheet	malāfe	ملافه
bedspread	rutaxti	روتختی

97. Kitchen

kitchen	āšpazxāne	آشپزخانه
gas	gāz	گاز
gas cooker	ojāgh-e gāz	اجاق گاز
electric cooker	ojāgh-e barghi	اجاق برقی
oven	fer	فر
microwave oven	māykrofer	مایکروفر

refrigerator	yaxčāl	یخچال
freezer	fereyzer	فریزر
dishwasher	māšin-e zarfšuyi	ماشین ظرفشویی

mincer	čarx-e gušt	چرخ گوشت
juicer	ābmive giri	آبمیوه گیری
toaster	towster	توستر
mixer	maxlut kon	مخلوط کن

coffee machine	qahve sāz	قهوه ساز
coffee pot	qahve juš	قهوه جوش
coffee grinder	āsiyāb-e qahve	آسیاب قهوه

kettle	ketri	کتری
teapot	quri	قوری
lid	sarpuš	سرپوش
tea strainer	čāy sāf kon	چای صاف کن

spoon	qāšoq	قاشق
teaspoon	qāšoq čāy xori	قاشق چای خوری
soup spoon	qāšoq sup xori	قاشق سوپ خوری
fork	čangāl	چنگال
knife	kārd	کارد

| tableware (dishes) | zoruf | ظروف |
| plate (dinner ~) | bošqāb | بشقاب |

saucer	na'lbeki	نعلبکی
shot glass	gilās-e vodkā	گیلاس ودکا
glass (tumbler)	estekān	استکان
cup	fenjān	فنجان

sugar bowl	qandān	قندان
salt cellar	namakdān	نمکدان
pepper pot	felfeldān	فلفلدان
butter dish	zarf-e kare	ظرف کره

stock pot (soup pot)	qāblame	قابلمه
frying pan (skillet)	tābe	تابه
ladle	malāqe	ملاقه
colander	ābkeš	آبکش
tray (serving ~)	sini	سینی

bottle	botri	بطری
jar (glass)	šiše	شیشه
tin (can)	quti	قوطی

bottle opener	dar bāz kon	در بازکن
tin opener	dar bāz kon	در بازکن
corkscrew	dar bāz kon	در بازکن
filter	filter	فیلتر
to filter (vt)	filter kardan	فیلتر کردن

| waste (food ~, etc.) | āšqāl | آشغال |
| waste bin (kitchen ~) | satl-e zobāle | سطل زباله |

98. Bathroom

bathroom	hammām	حمام
water	āb	آب
tap	šir	شیر
hot water	āb-e dāq	آب داغ
cold water	āb-e sard	آب سرد

toothpaste	xamir-e dandān	خمیر دندان
to clean one's teeth	mesvāk zadan	مسواک زدن
toothbrush	mesvāk	مسواک

to shave (vi)	riš tarāšidan	ریش تراشیدن
shaving foam	xamir-e eslāh	خمیر اصلاح
razor	tiq	تیغ

to wash (one's hands, etc.)	šostan	شستن
to have a bath	hamām kardan	حمام کردن
shower	duš	دوش
to have a shower	duš gereftan	دوش گرفتن

bath	vān hammām	وان حمام
toilet (toilet bowl)	tuālet-e farangi	توالت فرنگی
sink (washbasin)	sink	سینک
soap	sābun	صابون

soap dish	jā sābun	جا صابون
sponge	abr	ابر
shampoo	šāmpu	شامپو
towel	howle	حوله
bathrobe	howle-ye hamām	حوله حمام

laundry (process)	raxčuyi	لباسشویی
washing machine	māšin-e lebas-šui	ماشین لباسشویی
to do the laundry	šostan-e lebās	شستن لباس
washing powder	pudr-e lebas-šui	پودر لباسشویی

99. Household appliances

TV, telly	televiziyon	تلویزیون
tape recorder	zabt-e sowt	ضبط صوت
video	video	ویدئو
radio	rādiyo	رادیو
player (CD, MP3, etc.)	paxš konande	پخش کننده

video projector	video porožektor	ویدئو پروژکتور
home cinema	sinamā-ye xānegi	سینمای خانگی
DVD player	paxš konande-ye di vi di	پخش کننده دی وی دی
amplifier	āmpli-fāyer	آمپلی فایر
video game console	konsul-e bāzi	کنسول بازی

video camera	durbin-e filmbardāri	دوربین فیلمبرداری
camera (photo)	durbin-e akkāsi	دوربین عکاسی
digital camera	durbin-e dijitāl	دوربین دیجیتال

vacuum cleaner	jāru barqi	جارو برقی
iron (e.g. steam ~)	oto	اتو
ironing board	miz-e otu	میز اتو

telephone	telefon	تلفن
mobile phone	telefon-e hamrāh	تلفن همراه
typewriter	māšin-e tahrir	ماشین تحریر
sewing machine	čarx-e xayyāti	چرخ خیاطی

microphone	mikrofon	میکروفون
headphones	guši	گوشی
remote control (TV)	kontorol az rāh-e dur	کنترل از راه دور

CD, compact disc	si-di	سیدی
cassette, tape	kāst	کاست
vinyl record	safhe-ye gerāmāfon	صفحه گرامافون

100. Repairs. Renovation

renovations	ta'mir	تعمیر
to renovate (vt)	ta'mir kardan	تعمیر کردن
to repair, to fix (vt)	ta'mir kardan	تعمیر کردن
to put in order	morattab kardan	مرتب کردن

to redo (do again)	dobāre anjām dādan	دوباره انجام دادن
paint	rang	رنگ
to paint (~ a wall)	rang kardan	رنگ کردن
house painter	naqqāš	نقاش
paintbrush	qalam mu	قلم مو

whitewash	sefid kāri	سفید کاری
to whitewash (vt)	sefid kāri kardan	سفید کاری کردن

wallpaper	kāqaz-e divāri	کاغذ دیواری
to wallpaper (vt)	kāqaz-e divāri kardan	کاغذ دیواری کردن
varnish	lāk	لاک
to varnish (vt)	lāk zadan	لاک زدن

101. Plumbing

water	āb	آب
hot water	āb-e dāq	آب داغ
cold water	āb-e sard	آب سرد
tap	šir	شیر

drop (of water)	qatre	قطره
to drip (vi)	čakidan	چکیدن
to leak (ab. pipe)	našt kardan	نشت کردن
leak (pipe ~)	našt	نشت
puddle	čāle	چاله

pipe	lule	لوله
valve (e.g., ball ~)	šir-e falake	شیر فلکه
to be clogged up	masdud šodan	مسدود شدن

tools	abzār	ابزار
adjustable spanner	āčār-e farānse	آچار فرانسه
to unscrew (lid, filter, etc.)	bāz kardan	باز کردن
to screw (tighten)	pič kardan	پیچ کردن

to unclog (vt)	lule bāz kardan	لوله باز کردن
plumber	lule keš	لوله کش
basement	zirzamin	زیرزمین
sewerage (system)	fāzelāb	فاضلاب

102. Fire. Conflagration

fire (accident)	ātaš suzi	آتش سوزی
flame	šo'le	شعله
spark	jaraqqe	جرقه
smoke (from fire)	dud	دود
torch (flaming stick)	maš'al	مشعل
campfire	ātaš	آتش

petrol	benzin	بنزین
paraffin	naft-e sefid	نفت سفید

flammable (adj)	sutani	سوختنی
explosive (adj)	mavādd-e monfajere	مواد منفجره
NO SMOKING	sigār kešidan mamnu'	سیگار کشیدن ممنوع
safety	amniyat	امنیت
danger	xatar	خطر
dangerous (adj)	xatarnāk	خطرناک
to catch fire	ātaš gereftan	آتش گرفتن
explosion	enfejār	انفجار
to set fire	ātaš zadan	آتش زدن
arsonist	ātaš afruz	آتش افروز
arson	ātaš zadan-e amdi	آتش زدن عمدی
to blaze (vi)	šo'levar budan	شعله ور بودن
to burn (be on fire)	suxtan	سوختن
to burn down	suxtan	سوختن
to call the fire brigade	ātaš-e nešāni rā xabar kardan	آتش نشانی را خبر کردن
firefighter, fireman	ātaš nešān	آتش نشان
fire engine	māšin-e ātašnešāni	ماشین آتش نشانی
fire brigade	tim-e ātašnešāni	تیم آتش نشانی
fire engine ladder	nardebān-e ātašnešāni	نردبان آتش نشانی
fire hose	šelang-e ātaš-nešāni	شلنگ آتش نشانی
fire extinguisher	kapsul-e ātašnešāni	کپسول آتش نشانی
helmet	kolāh-e imeni	کلاه ایمنی
siren	āžir-e xatar	آژیر خطر
to cry (for help)	faryād zadan	فریاد زدن
to call for help	be komak talabidan	به کمک طلبیدن
rescuer	nejāt-e dahande	نجات دهنده
to rescue (vt)	najāt dādan	نجات دادن
to arrive (vi)	residan	رسیدن
to extinguish (vt)	xāmuš kardan	خاموش کردن
water	āb	آب
sand	šen	شن
ruins (destruction)	xarābe	خرابه
to collapse (building, etc.)	foru rixtan	فرو ریختن
to fall down (vi)	rizeš kardan	ریزش کردن
to cave in (ceiling, floor)	foru rixtan	فرو ریختن
piece of debris	qet'e	قطعه
ash	xākestar	خاکستر
to suffocate (die)	xafe šodan	خفه شدن
to be killed (perish)	košte šodan	کشته شدن

HUMAN ACTIVITIES

Job. Business. Part 1

103. Office. Working in the office

office (company ~)	daftar	دفتر
office (of director, etc.)	daftar	دفتر
reception desk	pazir-aš	پذیرش
secretary	monši	منشی
secretary (fem.)	monši	منشی
director	modir	مدیر
manager	modir	مدیر
accountant	hesābdār	حسابدار
employee	kārmand	کارمند
furniture	mobl	مبل
desk	miz	میز
desk chair	sandali dastedār	صندلی دسته دار
drawer unit	kešow	کشو
coat stand	čub lebāsi	چوب لباسی
computer	kāmpiyuter	کامپیوتر
printer	pirinter	پرینتر
fax machine	faks	فکس
photocopier	dastgāh-e kopi	دستگاه کپی
paper	kāqaz	کاغذ
office supplies	lavāzem-e tahrir	لوازم تحریر
mouse mat	māows pad	ماوس پد
sheet of paper	varaq	ورق
binder	puše	پوشه
catalogue	kātālog	کاتالوگ
phone directory	rāhnamā	راهنما
documentation	asnād	اسناد
brochure (e.g. 12 pages ~)	borušur	بروشور
leaflet (promotional ~)	borušur	بروشور
sample	nemune	نمونه
training meeting	āmuzeš	آموزش
meeting (of managers)	jalase	جلسه
lunch time	vaqt-e nāhār	وقت ناهار
to make a copy	kopi gereftan	کپی گرفتن
to make multiple copies	kopi gereftan	کپی گرفتن
to receive a fax	faks gereftan	فکس گرفتن
to send a fax	faks ferestādan	فکس فرستادن

to call (by phone)	telefon zadan	تلفن زدن
to answer (vt)	javāb dādan	جواب دادن
to put through	vasl šodan	وصل شدن

to arrange, to set up	sāzmān dādan	سازمان دادن
to demonstrate (vt)	nemāyeš dādan	نمایش دادن
to be absent	qāyeb budan	غایب بودن
absence	qeybat	غیبت

104. Business processes. Part 1

occupation	šoql	شغل
firm	šerkat	شرکت
company	kompāni	کمپانی
corporation	šerkat-e sahami	شرکت سهامی
enterprise	šerkat	شرکت
agency	namāyandegi	نمایندگی

agreement (contract)	qarārdād	قرارداد
contract	qarārdād	قرارداد
deal	mo'āmele	معامله
order (to place an ~)	sefāreš	سفارش
terms (of the contract)	šart	شرط

wholesale (adv)	omde furuši	عمده فروشی
wholesale (adj)	omde	عمده
wholesale (n)	omde furuši	عمده فروشی
retail (adj)	xorde-foruši	خرده فروشی
retail (n)	xorde-foruši	خرده فروشی

competitor	raqib	رقیب
competition	reqābat	رقابت
to compete (vi)	reqābat kardan	رقابت کردن

| partner (associate) | šarik | شریک |
| partnership | mošārek-at | مشارکت |

crisis	bohrān	بحران
bankruptcy	varšekastegi	ورشکستگی
to go bankrupt	varšekast šodan	ورشکست شدن
difficulty	saxti	سختی
problem	moškel	مشکل
catastrophe	fāje'e	فاجعه

economy	eqtesād	اقتصاد
economic (~ growth)	eqtesādi	اقتصادی
economic recession	rokud-e eqtesādi	رکود اقتصادی

| goal (aim) | hadaf | هدف |
| task | hadaf | هدف |

to trade (vi)	tejārat kardan	تجارت کردن
network (distribution ~)	šabake-ye towzi'	شبکۀ توزیع
inventory (stock)	fehrest anbār	فهرست انبار

range (assortment)	majmu'e	مجموعه
leader (leading company)	rahbar	رهبر
large (~ company)	bozorg	بزرگ
monopoly	enhesār	انحصار

theory	nazariye	نظریه
practice	amal	عمل
experience (in my ~)	tajrobe	تجربه
trend (tendency)	gerāyeš	گرایش
development	pišraft	پیشرفت

105. Business processes. Part 2

| profit (foregone ~) | sud | سود |
| profitable (~ deal) | sudāvar | سودآور |

delegation (group)	hey'at-e namāyandegān	هیئت نمایندگان
salary	hoquq	حقوق
to correct (an error)	eslāh kardan	اصلاح کردن
business trip	ma'muriyat	مأموریت
commission	komisiyon	کمیسیون

to control (vt)	kontorol kardan	کنترل کردن
conference	konferāns	کنفرانس
licence	parvāne	پروانه
reliable (~ partner)	motmaen	مطمئن

initiative (undertaking)	ebtekār	ابتکار
norm (standard)	me'yār	معیار
circumstance	vaz'iyat	وضعیت
duty (of employee)	vazife	وظیفه

organization (company)	šerkat	شرکت
organization (process)	sāzmāndehi	سازماندهی
organized (adj)	sāzmān yāfte	سازمان یافته
cancellation	laqv	لغو
to cancel (call off)	laqv kardan	لغو کردن
report (official ~)	gozāreš	گزارش

patent	govāhi-ye sabt-e exterā'	گواهی ثبت اختراع
to patent (obtain patent)	govāhi exterā' gereftan	گواهی اختراع گرفتن
to plan (vt)	barnāmerizi kardan	برنامه ریزی کردن

bonus (money)	pādāš	پاداش
professional (adj)	herfe i	حرفه ای
procedure	tašrifāt	تشریفات

to examine (contract, etc.)	barresi kardan	بررسی کردن
calculation	mohāsebe	محاسبه
reputation	e'tebār	اعتبار
risk	risk	ریسک

| to manage, to run | edāre kardan | اداره کردن |
| information | ettelā'āt | اطلاعات |

| property | dārāyi | دارایی |
| union | ettehādiye | اتحادیه |

life insurance	bime-ye omr	بیمهٔ عمر
to insure (vt)	bime kardan	بیمه کردن
insurance	bime	بیمه

auction (~ sale)	harāj	حراج
to notify (inform)	xabar dādan	خبر دادن
management (process)	edāre	اداره
service (~ industry)	xedmat	خدمت

forum	ham andiši	هم اندیشی
to function (vi)	amal kardan	عمل کردن
stage (phase)	marhale	مرحله
legal (~ services)	hoquqi	حقوقی
lawyer (legal advisor)	hoquq dān	حقوق دان

106. Production. Works

plant	kārxāne	کارخانه
factory	kārxāne	کارخانه
workshop	kārgāh	کارگاه
works, production site	towlidi	تولیدی

industry (manufacturing)	san'at	صنعت
industrial (adj)	san'ati	صنعتی
heavy industry	sanāye-'e sangin	صنایع سنگین
light industry	sanāye-'e sabok	صنایع سبک

products	towlidāt	تولیدات
to produce (vt)	towlid kardan	تولید کردن
raw materials	mavādd-e xām	مواد خام

foreman (construction ~)	sarkāregar	سرکارگر
workers team (crew)	daste-ye kāregaran	دسته کارگران
worker	kārgar	کارگر

working day	ruz-e kāri	روز کاری
pause (rest break)	esterāhat	استراحت
meeting	jalase	جلسه
to discuss (vt)	bahs kardan	بحث کردن

plan	barnāme	برنامه
to fulfil the plan	barnāme rā ejrā kardan	برنامه را اجرا کردن
rate of output	nerx-e tolid	نرخ تولید
quality	keyfiyat	کیفیت
control (checking)	kontorol	کنترل
quality control	kontorol-e keyfi	کنترل کیفی

workplace safety	amniyat-e kār	امنیت کار
discipline	enzebāt	انضباط
violation (of safety rules, etc.)	naqz	نقض
to violate (rules)	naqz kardan	نقض کردن

strike	e'tesāb	اعتصاب
striker	e'tesāb konande	اعتصاب کننده
to be on strike	e'tesāb kardan	اعتصاب کردن
trade union	ettehādiye-ye kārgari	اتحادیۀ کارگری

to invent (machine, etc.)	exterā' kardan	اختراع کردن
invention	exterā'	اختراع
research	tahqiq	تحقیق
to improve (make better)	behtar kardan	بهتر کردن
technology	fanāvari	فناوری
technical drawing	rasm-e fani	رسم فنی

load, cargo	bār	بار
loader (person)	bārbar	باربر
to load (vehicle, etc.)	bār kardan	بار کردن
loading (process)	bārgiri	بارگیری
to unload (vi, vt)	bārgiri	بارگیری
unloading	bārandāz-i	باراندازی

transport	haml-o naql	حمل و نقل
transport company	šerkat-e haml-o naql	شرکت حمل و نقل
to transport (vt)	haml kardan	حمل کردن

wagon	vāgon-e bari	واگن باری
tank (e.g., oil ~)	maxzan	مخزن
lorry	kāmiyon	کامیون

| machine tool | dastgāh | دستگاه |
| mechanism | mekānism | مکانیسم |

industrial waste	zāye'āt-e san'ati	ضایعات صنعتی
packing (process)	baste band-i	بسته بندی
to pack (vt)	baste bandi kardan	بسته بندی کردن

107. Contract. Agreement

contract	qarārdād	قرارداد
agreement	tavāfoq-e nāme	توافق نامه
addendum	zamime	ضمیمه

to sign a contract	qarārdād bastan	قرارداد بستن
signature	emzā'	امضاء
to sign (vt)	emzā kardan	امضا کردن
seal (stamp)	mehr	مهر

subject of contract	mowzu-'e qarārdād	موضوع قرارداد
clause	mādde	ماده
parties (in contract)	tarafeyn	طرفین
legal address	ādres-e hoquqi	آدرس حقوقی

to violate the contract	naqz kardan-e qarārdād	نقض کردن قرارداد
commitment (obligation)	ta'ahhod	تعهد
responsibility	mas'uliyat	مسئولیت
force majeure	šarāyet-e ezterāri	شرایط اضطراری

| dispute | xalāf | خلاف |
| penalties | eqdāmāt-e tanbihi | اقدامات تنبیهی |

108. Import & Export

import	vāredāt	واردات
importer	vāred konande	وارد کننده
to import (vt)	vāred kardan	وارد کردن
import (as adj.)	vāredāti	وارداتی

export (exportation)	sāderāt	صادرات
exporter	sāder konande	صادر کننده
to export (vi, vt)	sāder kardan	صادر کردن
export (as adj.)	sāderāti	صادراتی

| goods (merchandise) | kālā | کالا |
| consignment, lot | mahmule | محموله |

weight	vazn	وزن
volume	hajm	حجم
cubic metre	metr moka'ab	متر مکعب

manufacturer	towlid konande	تولید کننده
transport company	šerkat-e haml-o naql	شرکت حمل و نقل
container	kāntiner	کانتینر

border	marz	مرز
customs	gomrok	گمرک
customs duty	avārez-e gomroki	عوارض گمرکی
customs officer	ma'mur-e gomrok	مأمور گمرک
smuggling	qāčāq	قاچاق
contraband (smuggled goods)	ajnās-e qāčāq	اجناس قاچاق

109. Finances

share, stock	sahām	سهام
bond (certificate)	owrāq-e bahādār	اوراق بهادار
promissory note	safte	سفته

| stock exchange | burs | بورس |
| stock price | nerx-e sahām | نرخ سهام |

| to go down (become cheaper) | arzān šodan | ارزان شدن |
| to go up (become more expensive) | gerān šodan | گران شدن |

controlling interest	manāfe-'e kontoroli	منافع کنترلی
investment	sarmāye gozāri	سرمایه گذاری
to invest (vt)	sarmāye gozāri kardan	سرمایه گذاری کردن
percent	darsad	درصد

interest (on investment)	sud	سود
profit	sud	سود
profitable (adj)	sudāvar	سودآور
tax	māliyāt	مالیات
currency (foreign ~)	arz	ارز
national (adj)	melli	ملی
exchange (currency ~)	tabādol	تبادل
accountant	hesābdār	حسابدار
accounting	hesābdāri	حسابداری
bankruptcy	varšekastegi	ورشکستگی
collapse, ruin	šekast	شکست
ruin	varšekastegi	ورشکستگی
to be ruined (financially)	varšekast šodan	ورشکست شدن
inflation	tavarrom	تورم
devaluation	taqlil-e arzeš-e pul	تقلیل ارزش پول
capital	sarmāye	سرمایه
income	darāmad	درآمد
turnover	gardeš mo'āmelāt	گردش معاملات
resources	manābe'	منابع
monetary resources	manābe-'e puli	منابع پولی
overheads	maxārej-e kolli	مخارج کلی
to reduce (expenses)	kam kardan	کم کردن

110. Marketing

marketing	bāzāryābi	بازاریابی
market	bāzār	بازار
market segment	baxše bāzār	بخش بازار
product	mahsul	محصول
goods (merchandise)	kālā	کالا
brand	barand	برند
trademark	nešān tejāri	نشان تجاری
logotype	logo	لوگو
logo	logo	لوگو
demand	taqāzā	تقاضا
supply	arze	عرضه
need	ehtiyāj	احتیاج
consumer	masraf-e konande	مصرف کننده
analysis	tahlil	تحلیل
to analyse (vt)	tahlil kardan	تحلیل کردن
positioning	mowze' giri	موضع گیری
to position (vt)	mowze' giri kardan	موضع گیری کردن
price	qeymat	قیمت
pricing policy	siyāsat-e qeymat-e gozār-i	سیاست قیمت گذاری
price formation	qeymat gozāri	قیمت گذاری

111. Advertising

advertising	āgahi	آگهی
to advertise (vt)	tabliq kardan	تبلیغ کردن
budget	budje	بودجه

ad, advertisement	āgahi	آگهی
TV advertising	tabliqāt-e televiziyoni	تبلیغات تلویزیونی
radio advertising	tabliqāt-e rādiyoyi	تبلیغات رادیویی
outdoor advertising	āgahi-ye biruni	آگهی بیرونی

mass medias	resāne-hay-e jam'i	رسانه های جمعی
periodical (n)	našriye-ye dowrei	نشریۀ دوره ای
image (public appearance)	temsāl	تمثال

| slogan | šo'ār | شعار |
| motto (maxim) | šo'ār | شعار |

campaign	kampeyn	کمپین
advertising campaign	kampeyn-e tabliqāti	کمپین تبلیغاتی
target group	goruh-e hadaf	گروه هدف

business card	kārt-e vizit	کارت ویزیت
leaflet (promotional ~)	borušur	بروشور
brochure (e.g. 12 pages ~)	borušur	بروشور
pamphlet	ketābče	کتابچه
newsletter	xabarnāme	خبرنامه

signboard (store sign, etc.)	tāblo	تابلو
poster	poster	پوستر
hoarding	bilbord	بیلبورد

112. Banking

| bank | bānk | بانک |
| branch (of bank, etc.) | šo'be | شعبه |

| consultant | mošāver | مشاور |
| manager (director) | modir | مدیر |

bank account	hesāb-e bānki	حساب بانکی
account number	šomāre-ye hesāb	شمارۀ حساب
current account	hesāb-e jāri	حساب جاری
deposit account	hesāb-e pasandāz	حساب پس انداز

to open an account	hesāb-e bāz kardan	حساب باز کردن
to close the account	hesāb rā bastan	حساب را بستن
to deposit into the account	be hesāb rixtan	به حساب ریختن
to withdraw (vt)	az hesāb bardāštan	از حساب برداشتن

deposit	seporde	سپرده
to make a deposit	seporde gozāštan	سپرده گذاشتن
wire transfer	enteqāl	انتقال

to wire, to transfer	enteqāl dādan	انتقال دادن
sum	jam'-e kol	جمع کل
How much?	čeqadr?	چقدر؟

| signature | emzā' | امضاء |
| to sign (vt) | emzā kardan | امضا کردن |

credit card	kārt-e e'tebāri	کارت اعتباری
code (PIN code)	kod	کد
credit card number	šomāre-ye kārt-e e'tebāri	شماره کارت اعتباری
cashpoint	xodpardāz	خودپرداز

cheque	ček	چک
to write a cheque	ček neveštan	چک نوشتن
chequebook	daste-ye ček	دسته چک

loan (bank ~)	e'tebār	اعتبار
to apply for a loan	darxāst-e vam kardan	درخواست وام کردن
to get a loan	vām gereftan	وام گرفتن
to give a loan	vām dādan	وام دادن
guarantee	zemānat	ضمانت

113. Telephone. Phone conversation

telephone	telefon	تلفن
mobile phone	telefon-e hamrāh	تلفن همراه
answerphone	monši-ye telefoni	منشی تلفنی

| to call (by phone) | telefon zadan | تلفن زدن |
| call, ring | tamās-e telefoni | تماس تلفنی |

to dial a number	šomāre gereftan	شماره گرفتن
Hello!	alo!	الو!
to ask (vt)	porsidan	پرسیدن
to answer (vi, vt)	javāb dādan	جواب دادن
to hear (vt)	šenidan	شنیدن
well (adv)	xub	خوب
not well (adv)	bad	بد
noises (interference)	sedā	صدا

receiver	guši	گوشی
to pick up (~ the phone)	guši rā bar dāštan	گوشی را برداشتن
to hang up (~ the phone)	guši rā gozāštan	گوشی را گذاشتن

busy (engaged)	mašqul	مشغول
to ring (ab. phone)	zang zadan	زنگ زدن
telephone book	daftar-e telefon	دفتر تلفن

local (adj)	mahalli	محلی
local call	telefon-e dāxeli	تلفن داخلی
trunk (e.g. ~ call)	beyn-e šahri	بین شهری
trunk call	telefon-e beyn-e šahri	تلفن بین شهری
international (adj)	beynolmelali	بین المللی
international call	telefon-e beynolmelali	تلفن بین المللی

114. Mobile telephone

mobile phone	telefon-e hamrāh	تلفن همراه
display	namāyešgar	نمایشگر
button	dokme	دکمه
SIM card	sim-e kārt	سیم کارت
battery	bātri	باطری
to be flat (battery)	tamām šodan bātri	تمام شدن باتری
charger	šāržer	شارژ
menu	meno	منو
settings	tanzimāt	تنظیمات
tune (melody)	āhang	آهنگ
to select (vt)	entexāb kardan	انتخاب کردن
calculator	māšin-e hesāb	ماشین حساب
voice mail	monši-ye telefoni	منشی تلفنی
alarm clock	sā'at-e zang dār	ساعت زنگ دار
contacts	daftar-e telefon	دفتر تلفن
SMS (text message)	payāmak	پیامک
subscriber	moštarek	مشترک

115. Stationery

ballpoint pen	xodkār	خودکار
fountain pen	xodnevis	خودنویس
pencil	medād	مداد
highlighter	māžik	ماژیک
felt-tip pen	māžik	ماژیک
notepad	daftar-e yāddāšt	دفتر یادداشت
diary	daftar-e yāddāšt	دفتر یادداشت
ruler	xat keš	خط کش
calculator	māšin-e hesāb	ماشین حساب
rubber	pāk kon	پاک کن
drawing pin	punez	پونز
paper clip	gire	گیره
glue	časb	چسب
stapler	mangane-ye zan	منگنه زن
hole punch	pānč	پانچ
pencil sharpener	madād-e tarāš	مداد تراش

116. Various kinds of documents

account (report)	gozāreš	گزارش
agreement	tavāfoq-e nāme	توافق نامه

application form	form-e darxāst	فرم درخواست
authentic (adj)	asli	اصلی
badge (identity tag)	kārt-e šenāsāyi	کارت شناسایی
business card	kārt-e vizit	کارت ویزیت
certificate (~ of quality)	govāhi	گواهی
cheque (e.g. draw a ~)	ček	چک
bill (in restaurant)	surat hesāb	صورت حساب
constitution	qānun-e asāsi	قانون اساسی
contract (agreement)	qarārdād	قرارداد
copy	nosxe	نسخه
copy (of contract, etc.)	nosxe	نسخه
customs declaration	ežhār-nāme	اظهارنامه
document	sanad	سند
driving licence	govāhi-nāme-ye rānandegi	گواهینامۀ رانندگی
addendum	zamime	ضمیمه
form	porsešnāme	پرسشنامه
ID card (e.g., warrant card)	kārt-e šenāsāyi	کارت شناسایی
inquiry (request)	este'lām	استعلام
invitation card	da'vatnāme	دعوتنامه
invoice	surat hesāb	صورت حساب
law	qānun	قانون
letter (mail)	nāme	نامه
letterhead	sarnāme	سرنامه
list (of names, etc.)	fehrest	فهرست
manuscript	dast nevis	دست نویس
newsletter	xabarnāme	خبرنامه
note (short letter)	yāddāšt	یادداشت
pass (for worker, visitor)	javāz	جواز
passport	gozarnāme	گذرنامه
permit	mojavvez	مجوز
curriculum vitae, CV	rezume	رزومه
debt note, IOU	resid	رسید
receipt (for purchase)	resid	رسید
till receipt	resid	رسید
report (mil.)	gozāreš	گزارش
to show (ID, etc.)	erā'e kardan	ارائه کردن
to sign (vt)	emzā kardan	امضا کردن
signature	emzā'	امضاء
seal (stamp)	mehr	مهر
text	matn	متن
ticket (for entry)	belit	بلیط
to cross out	xat zadan	خط زدن
to fill in (~ a form)	por kardan	پر کردن
waybill (shipping invoice)	bārnāme	بارنامه
will (testament)	vasiyat-nāme	وصیتنامه

117. Kinds of business

accounting services	xadamāt-e hesābdāri	خدمات حسابداری
advertising	āgahi	آگهی
advertising agency	āžāns-e tabliqāti	آژانس تبلیغاتی
air-conditioners	tahviye-ye matbu'	تهویه مطبوع
airline	šerkat-e havāpeymāyi	شرکت هواپیمایی
alcoholic beverages	mašrubāt-e alkoli	مشروبات الکلی
antiques (antique dealers)	atiqe	عتیقه
art gallery (contemporary ~)	gāleri-ye honari	گالری هنری
audit services	xadamāt-e momayyezi	خدمات ممیزی
banking industry	bānk-dāri	بانکداری
beauty salon	sālon-e zibāyi	سالن زیبایی
bookshop	ketāb-foruši	کتاب فروشی
brewery	ābe jow-sāzi	آب جوسازی
business centre	markaz-e tejāri	مرکز تجاری
business school	moassese-ye bāzargāni	موسسه بازرگانی
casino	kāzino	کازینو
chemist, pharmacy	dāruxāne	داروخانه
cinema	sinamā	سینما
construction	sāxtemān	ساختمان
consulting	mošavere	مشاوره
dental clinic	dandān-e pezeški	دندان پزشکی
design	tarrāhi	طراحی
dry cleaners	xošk-šuyi	خشکشویی
employment agency	āžāns-e kāryābi	آژانس کاریابی
financial services	xadamāt-e māli	خدمات مالی
food products	mavādd-e qazāyi	مواد غذایی
furniture (e.g. house ~)	mobl	مبل
clothing, garment	lebās	لباس
hotel	hotel	هتل
ice-cream	bastani	بستنی
industry (manufacturing)	san'at	صنعت
insurance	bime	بیمه
Internet	internet	اینترنت
investments (finance)	sarmāye gozāri	سرمایه گذاری
jeweller	javāheri	جواهری
jewellery	javāherāt	جواهرات
laundry (shop)	xošk-šuyi	خشکشویی
legal adviser	xadamāt-e hoquqi	خدمات حقوقی
light industry	sanāye-'e sabok	صنایع سبک
magazine	majalle	مجله
mail-order selling	foruš-e sefāreš-e posti	فروش سفارش پستی
medicine	pezeški	پزشکی
museum	muze	موزه
news agency	xabar-gozāri	خبرگزاری
newspaper	ruznāme	روزنامه

nightclub	kābāre	کاباره
oil (petroleum)	naft	نفت
courier services	xadamāt-e post	خدمات پست
pharmaceutics	dārusāzi	داروسازی
printing (industry)	sahhāfi	صحافی
pub	bār	بار
publishing house	entešārāt	انتشارات

radio (~ station)	rādiyo	رادیو
real estate	amvāl-e qeyr-e manqul	اموال غیر منقول
restaurant	resturān	رستوران

security company	āžāns-e amniyati	آژانس امنیتی
shop	maqāze	مغازه
sport	varzeš	ورزش
stock exchange	burs	بورس
supermarket	supermārket	سوپرمارکت
swimming pool (public ~)	estaxr	استخر

tailor shop	xayyāti	خیاطی
television	televiziyon	تلویزیون
theatre	teātr	تئاتر
trade (commerce)	tejārat	تجارت
transport companies	haml-o naql	حمل و نقل
travel	turism	توریسم

undertakers	xadamat-e kafno dafn	خدمات کفن ودفن
veterinary surgeon	dāmpezešk	دامپزشک
warehouse	anbār	انبار
waste collection	jam āvari-ye zobāle	جمع آوری زباله

Job. Business. Part 2

118. Show. Exhibition

exhibition, show	namāyešgāh	نمایشگاه
trade show	namāyešgāh-e tejāri	نمایشگاه تجاری
participation	šerkat	شرکت
to participate (vi)	šerekat kardan	شرکت کردن
participant (exhibitor)	šerekat konande	شرکت کننده
director	ra'is	رئیس
organizers' office	daftar-e modiriyat	دفتر مدیریت
organizer	sāzmān dahande	سازمان دهنده
to organize (vt)	sāzmān dādan	سازمان دادن
participation form	darxāst-e šerkat	درخواست شرکت
to fill in (vt)	por kardan	پر کردن
details	joz'iyāt	جزئیات
information	ettelā'āt	اطلاعات
price (cost, rate)	arzeš	ارزش
including	šāmel	شامل
to include (vt)	šāmel šodan	شامل شدن
to pay (vi, vt)	pardāxtan	پرداختن
registration fee	haqq-e sabt	حق ثبت
entrance	vorud	ورود
pavilion, hall	qorfe	غرفه
to register (vt)	sabt kardan	ثبت کردن
badge (identity tag)	kārt-e šenāsāyi	کارت شناسایی
stand	qorfe	غرفه
to reserve, to book	rezerv kardan	رزرو کردن
display case	vitrin	ویترین
spotlight	nurafkan	نورافکن
design	tarh	طرح
to place (put, set)	qarār dādan	قرار دادن
to be placed	qarār gereftan	قرار گرفتن
distributor	towzi' konande	توزیع کننده
supplier	arze konande	عرضه کننده
to supply (vt)	arze kardan	عرضه کردن
country	kešvar	کشور
foreign (adj)	xāreji	خارجی
product	mahsul	محصول
association	anjoman	انجمن
conference hall	tālār-e konferāns	تالار کنفرانس

| congress | kongere | کنگره |
| contest (competition) | mosābeqe | مسابقه |

visitor (attendee)	bāzdid konande	بازدید کننده
to visit (attend)	bāzdid kardan	بازدید کردن
customer	moštari	مشتری

119. Mass Media

newspaper	ruznāme	روزنامه
magazine	majalle	مجله
press (printed media)	matbuāt	مطبوعات
radio	rādiyo	رادیو
radio station	istgāh-e rādiyoyi	ایستگاه رادیویی
television	televiziyon	تلویزیون

presenter, host	mojri	مجری
newsreader	guyande-ye axbār	گوینده اخبار
commentator	mofasser	مفسر

journalist	ruznāme negār	روزنامه نگار
correspondent (reporter)	xabarnegār	خبرنگار
press photographer	akkās-e matbuāti	عکاس مطبوعاتی
reporter	gozārešgar	گزارشگر

| editor | virāstār | ویراستار |
| editor-in-chief | sardabir | سردبیر |

to subscribe (to …)	moštarak šodan	مشترک شدن
subscription	ešterāk	اشتراک
subscriber	moštarek	مشترک
to read (vi, vt)	xāndan	خواندن
reader	xānande	خواننده

circulation (of newspaper)	tirāž	تیراژ
monthly (adj)	māhāne	ماهانه
weekly (adj)	haftegi	هفتگی
issue (edition)	šomāre	شماره
new (~ issue)	tāze	تازه

headline	sar xat-e xabar	سرخط خبر
short article	maqāle-ye kutāh	مقاله کوتاه
column (regular article)	sotun	ستون
article	maqāle	مقاله
page	safhe	صفحه

reportage, report	gozāreš	گزارش
event (happening)	vāqe'e	واقعه
sensation (news)	hayajān	هیجان
scandal	janjāl	جنجال
scandalous (adj)	janjāl āvar	جنجال آور
great (~ scandal)	bozorg	بزرگ
programme (e.g. cooking ~)	barnāme	برنامه
interview	mosāhebe	مصاحبه

| live broadcast | paxš-e mostaqim | پخش مستقیم |
| channel | kānāl | کانال |

120. Agriculture

agriculture	kešāvarzi	کشاورزی
peasant (masc.)	dehqān	دهقان
peasant (fem.)	dehqān	دهقان
farmer	kešāvarz	کشاورز

| tractor | terāktor | تراکتور |
| combine, harvester | kombāyn | کمباین |

plough	gāvāhan	گاوآهن
to plough (vi, vt)	šoxm zadan	شخم زدن
ploughland	zamin āmāde kešt	زمین آماده کشت
furrow (in field)	šiyār	شیار

to sow (vi, vt)	kāštan	کاشتن
seeder	bazrpāš	بذرپاش
sowing (process)	košt	کشت

| scythe | dās | داس |
| to mow, to scythe | dero kardan | درو کردن |

| spade (tool) | bil | بیل |
| to till (vt) | kandan | کندن |

hoe	kaj bil	کج بیل
to hoe, to weed	vajin kardan	وجین کردن
weed (plant)	alaf-e harz	علف هرز

watering can	āb pāš	آب پاش
to water (plants)	āb dādan	آب دادن
watering (act)	ābyāri	آبیاری

| pitchfork | čangak | چنگک |
| rake | šen keš | شن کش |

fertiliser	kud	کود
to fertilise (vt)	kud dādan	کود دادن
manure (fertiliser)	kud-e heyvāni	کود حیوانی

field	sahrā	صحرا
meadow	čaman	چمن
vegetable garden	jāliz	جالیز
orchard (e.g. apple ~)	bāq	باغ

to graze (vt)	čerāndan	چراندن
herdsman	čupān	چوپان
pasture	čerā-gāh	چراگاه

| cattle breeding | dāmparvari | دامپروری |
| sheep farming | gusfand dāri | گوسفند داری |

plantation	mazrae	مزرعه
row (garden bed ~s)	radif	ردیف
hothouse	golxāne	گلخانه
drought (lack of rain)	xošksāli	خشکسالی
dry (~ summer)	xošk	خشک
grain	dāne	دانه
cereal crops	qallāt	غلات
to harvest, to gather	mahsul-e jam' kardan	محصول جمع کردن
miller (person)	āsiyābān	آسیابان
mill (e.g. gristmill)	āsiyāb	آسیاب
to grind (grain)	qalle kubidan	غله کوبیدن
flour	ārd	آرد
straw	kāh	کاه

121. Building. Building process

building site	mahal-e sāxt-o sāz	محل ساخت و ساز
to build (vt)	sāxtan	ساختن
building worker	kārgar-e sāxtemāni	کارگر ساختمانی
project	porože	پروژه
architect	me'mār	معمار
worker	kārgar	کارگر
foundations (of a building)	šālude	شالوده
roof	bām	بام
foundation pile	pāye	پایه
wall	divār	دیوار
reinforcing bars	milgerd	میلگرد
scaffolding	dārbast	داربست
concrete	boton	بتن
granite	sang-e gerānit	سنگ گرانیت
stone	sang	سنگ
brick	ājor	آجر
sand	šen	شن
cement	simān	سیمان
plaster (for walls)	gač kāri	گچ کاری
to plaster (vt)	gačkār-i kardan	گچکاری کردن
paint	rang	رنگ
to paint (~ a wall)	rang kardan	رنگ کردن
barrel	boške	بشکه
crane	jarsaqil	جرثقیل
to lift, to hoist (vt)	boland kardan	بلند کردن
to lower (vt)	pāin āvardan	پائین آوردن
bulldozer	buldozer	بولدوزر
excavator	dastgāh-e haffāri	دستگاه حفاری

scoop, bucket	bil	بیل
to dig (excavate)	kandan	کندن
hard hat	kolāh-e imeni	کلاه ایمنی

122. Science. Research. Scientists

science	elm	علم
scientific (adj)	elmi	علمی
scientist	dānešmand	دانشمند
theory	nazariye	نظریه

axiom	qā'ede-ye kolli	قاعده کلی
analysis	tahlil	تحلیل
to analyse (vt)	tahlil kardan	تحلیل کردن
argument (strong ~)	dalil	دلیل
substance (matter)	mādde	ماده

hypothesis	farziye	فرضیه
dilemma	dorāhi	دوراهی
dissertation	pāyān nāme	پایان نامه
dogma	aqide	عقیده

doctrine	doktorin	دکترین
research	tahqiq	تحقیق
to research (vt)	tahghigh kardan	تحقیق کردن
tests (laboratory ~)	āzmāyeš	آزمایش
laboratory	āzmāyešgāh	آزمایشگاه

method	raveš	روش
molecule	molekul	مولکول
monitoring	nozzār-at	نظارت
discovery (act, event)	kašf	کشف

postulate	engāre	انگاره
principle	asl	اصل
forecast	piš bini	پیش بینی
to forecast (vt)	pišbini kardan	پیش بینی کردن

synthesis	santez	سنتز
trend (tendency)	gerāyeš	گرایش
theorem	qaziye	قضیه

| teachings | āmuzeš | آموزش |
| fact | haqiqat | حقیقت |

| expedition | safar | سفر |
| experiment | āzmāyeš | آزمایش |

academician	ozv-e ākādemi	عضو آکادمی
bachelor (e.g. ~ of Arts)	lisāns	لیسانس
doctor (PhD)	pezešk	پزشک
Associate Professor	dānešyār	دانشیار
Master (e.g. ~ of Arts)	foqe lisāns	فوق لیسانس
professor	porofosor	پروفسور

Professions and occupations

123. Job search. Dismissal

job	kār	کار
staff (work force)	kārmandān	کارمندان
personnel	kādr	کادر
career	šoql	شغل
prospects (chances)	durnamā	دورنما
skills (mastery)	mahārat	مهارت
selection (screening)	entexāb	انتخاب
employment agency	āžāns-e kāryābi	آژانس کاریابی
curriculum vitae, CV	rezume	رزومه
job interview	mosāhabe-ye kari	مصاحبه کاری
vacancy	post-e xāli	پست خالی
salary, pay	hoquq	حقوق
fixed salary	darāmad-e s ābet	درآمد ثابت
pay, compensation	pardāxt	پرداخت
position (job)	šoql	شغل
duty (of employee)	vazife	وظیفه
range of duties	šarh-e vazāyef	شرح وظایف
busy (I'm ~)	mašqul	مشغول
to fire (dismiss)	exrāj kardan	اخراج کردن
dismissal	exrāj	اخراج
unemployment	bikāri	بیکاری
unemployed (n)	bikār	بیکار
retirement	mostamerri	مستمری
to retire (from job)	bāznešaste šodan	بازنشسته شدن

124. Business people

director	modir	مدیر
manager (director)	modir	مدیر
boss	ra'is	رئیس
superior	māfowq	مافوق
superiors	roasā	رؤسا
president	ra'is jomhur	رئیس جمهور
chairman	ra'is	رئیس
deputy (substitute)	mo'āven	معاون
assistant	mo'āven	معاون

secretary	monši	منشی
personal assistant	dastyār-e šaxsi	دستیار شخصی
businessman	bāzargān	بازرگان
entrepreneur	kārāfarin	کارآفرین
founder	moasses	مؤسس
to found (vt)	ta'sis kardan	تأسیس کردن
founding member	hamkār	همکار
partner	šarik	شریک
shareholder	sahāmdār	سهامدار
millionaire	milyuner	میلیونر
billionaire	milyārder	میلیاردر
owner, proprietor	sāheb	صاحب
landowner	zamin-dār	زمین دار
client	xaridār	خریدار
regular client	xaridār-e dāemi	خریدار دائمی
buyer (customer)	xaridār	خریدار
visitor	bāzdid konande	بازدید کننده
professional (n)	herfe i	حرفه ای
expert	kāršenās	کارشناس
specialist	motexasses	متخصص
banker	kārmand-e bānk	کارمند بانک
broker	dallāl-e kārgozār	دلال کارگزار
cashier	sanduqdār	صندوقدار
accountant	hesābdār	حسابدار
security guard	negahbān	نگهبان
investor	sarmāye gozār	سرمایه گذار
debtor	bedehkār	بدهکار
creditor	talabkār	طلبکار
borrower	vām girande	وام گیرنده
importer	vāred konande	وارد کننده
exporter	sāder konande	صادر کننده
manufacturer	towlid konande	تولید کننده
distributor	towzi' konande	توزیع کننده
middleman	vāsete	واسطه
consultant	mošāver	مشاور
sales representative	namāyande	نماینده
agent	namāyande	نماینده
insurance agent	namāyande-ye bime	نمایندۀ بیمه

125. Service professions

cook	āšpaz	آشپز
chef (kitchen chef)	sarāšpaz	سرآشپز

baker	nānvā	نانوا
barman	motesaddi-ye bār	متصدی بار
waiter	pišxedmat	پیشخدمت
waitress	pišxedmat	پیشخدمت

lawyer, barrister	vakil	وکیل
lawyer (legal expert)	hoquq dān	حقوق دان
notary	daftardār	دفتردار

electrician	barq-e kār	برق کار
plumber	lule keš	لوله کش
carpenter	najjār	نجار

masseur	māsāž dahande	ماساژ دهنده
masseuse	māsāž dahande	ماساژ دهنده
doctor	pezešk	پزشک

taxi driver	rānande-ye tāksi	راننده تاکسی
driver	rānande	راننده
delivery man	peyk	پیک

chambermaid	mostaxdem	مستخدم
security guard	negahbān	نگهبان
flight attendant (fem.)	mehmāndār-e havāpeymā	مهماندار هواپیما

schoolteacher	mo'allem	معلم
librarian	ketābdār	کتابدار
translator	motarjem	مترجم
interpreter	motarjem-e šafāhi	مترجم شفاهی
guide	rāhnamā-ye tur	راهنمای تور

hairdresser	ārāyešgar	آرایشگر
postman	nāme resān	نامه رسان
salesman (store staff)	forušande	فروشنده

gardener	bāqbān	باغبان
domestic servant	nowkar	نوکر
maid (female servant)	xedmatkār	خدمتکار
cleaner (cleaning lady)	zan-e nezāfatči	زن نظافتچی

126. Military professions and ranks

private	sarbāz	سرباز
sergeant	goruhbān	گروهبان
lieutenant	sotvān	ستوان
captain	kāpitān	کاپیتان

major	sargord	سرگرد
colonel	sarhang	سرهنگ
general	ženerāl	ژنرال
marshal	māršāl	مارشال
admiral	daryāsālār	دریاسالار
military (n)	nezāmi	نظامی
soldier	sarbāz	سرباز

| officer | afsar | افسر |
| commander | farmändeh | فرمانده |

border guard	marzbän	مرزبان
radio operator	bisim či	بیسیم چی
scout (searcher)	etteläˈäti	اطلاعاتی
pioneer (sapper)	mohandes estehkämät	مهندس استحکامات
marksman	tirandäz	تیرانداز
navigator	nävbar	ناور

127. Officials. Priests

| king | šäh | شاه |
| queen | maleke | ملکه |

| prince | šähzäde | شاهزاده |
| princess | pranses | پرنسس |

| czar | tezär | تزار |
| czarina | maleke | ملکه |

president	raˈis jomhur	رئیس جمهور
Secretary (minister)	vazir	وزیر
prime minister	noxost vazir	نخست وزیر
senator	senätor	سناتور

diplomat	diplomät	دیپلمات
consul	konsul	کنسول
ambassador	safir	سفیر
counsillor (diplomatic officer)	mošäver	مشاور

official, functionary (civil servant)	kärmand	کارمند
prefect	baxšdär	بخشدار
mayor	šahrdär	شهردار

| judge | qäzi | قاضی |
| prosecutor | dädsetän | دادستان |

missionary	misiyoner	میسیونر
monk	räheb	راهب
abbot	räheb-e bozorg	راهب بزرگ
rabbi	xäxäm	خاخام

vizier	vazir	وزیر
shah	šäh	شاه
sheikh	šeyx	شیخ

128. Agricultural professions

| beekeeper | zanburdär | زنبوردار |
| shepherd | čupän | چوپان |

agronomist	motexasses-e kešāvarzi	متخصص کشاورزی
cattle breeder	dāmparvar	دامپرور
veterinary surgeon	dāmpezešk	دامپزشک

farmer	kešāvarz	کشاورز
winemaker	šarāb sāz	شراب ساز
zoologist	jānevar-šenās	جانور شناس
cowboy	gāvčerān	گاوچران

129. Art professions

actor	bāzigar	بازیگر
actress	bāzigar	بازیگر

singer (masc.)	xānande	خواننده
singer (fem.)	xānande	خواننده

dancer (masc.)	raqqās	رقاص
dancer (fem.)	raqqāse	رقاصه

performer (masc.)	honarpiše	هنرپیشه
performer (fem.)	honarpiše	هنرپیشه

musician	muzisiyan	موزیسین
pianist	piyānist	پیانیست
guitar player	gitārist	گیتاریست

conductor (orchestra ~)	rahbar-e orkestr	رهبر ارکستر
composer	āhangsāz	آهنگساز
impresario	modir-e operā	مدیر اپرا

film director	kārgardān	کارگردان
producer	tahiye konande	تهیه کننده
scriptwriter	senārist	سناریست
critic	montaqed	منتقد

writer	nevisande	نویسنده
poet	šā'er	شاعر
sculptor	mojassame sāz	مجسمه ساز
artist (painter)	naqqāš	نقاش

juggler	tardast	تردست
clown	dalqak	دلقک
acrobat	ākrobāt	آکروبات
magician	šo'bade bāz	شعبده باز

130. Various professions

doctor	pezešk	پزشک
nurse	parastār	پرستار
psychiatrist	ravānpezešk	روانپزشک
dentist	dandān pezešk	دندان پزشک

surgeon	jarrāh	جراح
astronaut	fazānavard	فضانورد
astronomer	setāre-šenās	ستاره شناس
pilot	xalabān	خلبان

driver (of taxi, etc.)	rānande	راننده
train driver	rānande	راننده
mechanic	mekānik	مکانیک

miner	ma'danči	معدنچی
worker	kārgar	کارگر
locksmith	qofl sāz	قفل ساز
joiner (carpenter)	najjār	نجار
turner (lathe machine operator)	tarrāš kār	تراش کار
building worker	kārgar-e sāxtemāni	کارگر ساختمانی
welder	juš kār	جوش کار

professor (title)	porofosor	پروفسور
architect	me'mār	معمار
historian	movarrex	مورخ
scientist	dānešmand	دانشمند
physicist	fizikdān	فیزیکدان
chemist (scientist)	šimi dān	شیمی دان

archaeologist	bāstān-šenās	باستان شناس
geologist	zamin-šenās	زمین شناس
researcher (scientist)	pažuhešgar	پژوهشگر

| babysitter | parastār bače | پرستار بچه |
| teacher, educator | āmuzgār | آموزگار |

editor	virāstār	ویراستار
editor-in-chief	sardabir	سردبیر
correspondent	xabarnegār	خبرنگار
typist (fem.)	māšin nevis	ماشین نویس

designer	tarāh	طراح
computer expert	kāršenās kāmpiyuter	کارشناس کامپیوتر
programmer	barnāme-ye nevis	برنامه نویس
engineer (designer)	mohandes	مهندس

sailor	malavān	ملوان
seaman	malavān	ملوان
rescuer	nejāt-e dahande	نجات دهنده

firefighter	ātaš nešān	آتش نشان
police officer	polis	پلیس
watchman	mohāfez	محافظ
detective	kārāgāh	کارآگاه

customs officer	ma'mur-e gomrok	مامور گمرک
bodyguard	mohāfez-e šaxsi	محافظ شخصی
prison officer	negahbān zendān	نگهبان زندان
inspector	bāzres	بازرس
sportsman	varzeškār	ورزشکار

trainer, coach	morabbi	مربی
butcher	qassāb	قصاب
cobbler (shoe repairer)	kaffāš	کفاش
merchant	bāzargān	بازرگان
loader (person)	bārbar	باربر

fashion designer	tarrāh-e lebas	طراح لباس
model (fem.)	model-e zan	مدل زن

131. Occupations. Social status

schoolboy	dāneš-āmuz	دانش آموز
student (college ~)	dānešju	دانشجو

philosopher	filsuf	فیلسوف
economist	eqtesāddān	اقتصاددان
inventor	moxtare'	مخترع

unemployed (n)	bikār	بیکار
pensioner	bāznešaste	بازنشسته
spy, secret agent	jāsus	جاسوس

prisoner	zendāni	زندانی
striker	e'tesāb konande	اعتصاب کننده
bureaucrat	ma'mur-e edāri	مأمور اداری
traveller (globetrotter)	mosāfer	مسافر

gay, homosexual (n)	hamjens-e bāz	همجنس باز
hacker	haker	هکر
hippie	hipi	هیپی

bandit	rāhzan	راهزن
hit man, killer	ādamkoš	آدمکش
drug addict	mo'tād	معتاد
drug dealer	forušande-ye mavādd-e moxadder	فروشندهٔ مواد مخدر
prostitute (fem.)	fāheše	فاحشه
pimp	jākeš	جاکش

sorcerer	jādugar	جادوگر
sorceress (evil ~)	jādugar	جادوگر
pirate	dozd-e daryāyi	دزد دریایی
slave	borde	برده
samurai	sāmurāyi	ساموراپی
savage (primitive)	vahši	وحشی

Sports

132. Kinds of sports. Sportspersons

sportsman	varzeškār	ورزشکار
kind of sport	anvā-e varzeš	انواع ورزش
basketball	basketbāl	بسکتبال
basketball player	basketbālist	بسکتبالیست
baseball	beysbāl	بیسبال
baseball player	beysbālist	بیسبالیست
football	futbāl	فوتبال
football player	futbālist	فوتبالیست
goalkeeper	darvāze bān	دروازه بان
ice hockey	hāki	هاکی
ice hockey player	hāki-ye bāz	هاکی باز
volleyball	vālibāl	والیبال
volleyball player	vālibālist	والیبالیست
boxing	boks	بوکس
boxer	boksor	بوکسور
wrestling	kešti	کشتی
wrestler	košti gir	کشتی گیر
karate	kārāte	کاراته
karate fighter	kārāte-e bāz	کاراته باز
judo	jodo	جودو
judo athlete	jodo bāz	جودو باز
tennis	tenis	تنیس
tennis player	tenis bāz	تنیس باز
swimming	šenā	شنا
swimmer	šenāgar	شناگر
fencing	šamširbāzi	شمشیربازی
fencer	šamširbāz	شمشیرباز
chess	šatranj	شطرنج
chess player	šatranj bāz	شطرنج باز
alpinism	kuhnavardi	کوهنوردی
alpinist	kuhnavard	کوهنورد
running	do	دو

runner	davande	دونده
athletics	varzeš	ورزش
athlete	varzeškār	ورزشکار

| horse riding | asb savāri | اسب سواری |
| horse rider | savārkār | سوارکار |

figure skating	raqs ruy yax	رقص روی یخ
figure skater (masc.)	eskeyt bāz	اسکیت باز
figure skater (fem.)	eskeyt bāz	اسکیت باز

| powerlifting | vazne bardār-i | وزنه برداری |
| powerlifter | vazne bardār | وزنه بردار |

| car racing | mosābeqe-ye otomobilrāni | مسابقۀ اتومبیلرانی |
| racing driver | otomobilrān | اتومبیلران |

| cycling | dočarxe savāri | دوچرخه سواری |
| cyclist | dočarxe savār | دوچرخه سوار |

long jump	pareš-e tul	پرش طول
pole vaulting	pareš bā neyze	پرش با نیزه
jumper	pareš konande	پرش کننده

133. Kinds of sports. Miscellaneous

American football	futbāl-e āmrikāyi	فوتبال آمریکایی
badminton	badminton	بدمینتون
biathlon	biatlon	بیاتلون
billiards	bilyārd	بیلیارد

bobsleigh	surtme	سورتمه
bodybuilding	badansāzi	بدنسازی
water polo	vāterpolo	واترپولو
handball	handbāl	هندبال
golf	golf	گلف

rowing	qāyeq rāni	قایق رانی
scuba diving	dāyving	دایوینگ
cross-country skiing	eski-ye sahrānavardi	اسکی صحرانوردی
table tennis (ping-pong)	ping pong	پینگ پونگ

sailing	qāyeq-rāni bādbani	قایق رانی بادبانی
rally	rāli	رالی
rugby	rāgbi	راگبی
snowboarding	snowbord	اسنوبرد
archery	tirandāzi bā kamān	تیراندازی با کمان

134. Gym

| barbell | hālter | هالتر |
| dumbbells | dambel | دمبل |

training machine	māšin-e tamrin	ماشین تمرین
exercise bicycle	dočarxe-ye tamrin	دوچرخه تمرین
treadmill	pist-e do	پیست دو

horizontal bar	bārfiks	بارفیکس
parallel bars	pārālel	پارالل
vault (vaulting horse)	xarak	خرک
mat (exercise ~)	tošak	تشک

skipping rope	tanāb	طناب
aerobics	āirobik	ایروبیک
yoga	yugā	یوگا

135. Ice hockey

ice hockey	hāki	هاکی
ice hockey player	hāki-ye bāz	هاکی باز
to play ice hockey	hākey bāzi kardan	هاکی بازی کردن
ice	yax	یخ

puck	mohre	مهره
ice hockey stick	čub-e hāki	چوب هاکی
ice skates	eskeyt ruy yax	اسکیت روی یخ

| board (ice hockey rink ~) | taxte | تخته |
| shot | šut | شوت |

goaltender	darvāze bān	دروازه بان
goal (score)	gol	گل
to score a goal	gol zadan	گل زدن

period	dowre	دوره
second period	dowre-ye dovvom	دورهٔ دوم
substitutes bench	nimkat-e zaxire	نیمکت ذخیره

136. Football

football	futbāl	فوتبال
football player	futbālist	فوتبالیست
to play football	futbāl bāzi kardan	فوتبال بازی کردن

major league	lig-e bartar	لیگ برتر
football club	bāšgāh-e futbāl	باشگاه فوتبال
coach	morabbi	مربی
owner, proprietor	sāheb	صاحب

team	tim	تیم
team captain	kāpitān-e tim	کاپیتان تیم
player	bāzikon	بازیکن
substitute	bāzikon-e zaxire	بازیکن ذخیره
forward	forvārd	فوروارد
centre forward	forvārd vasat	فوروارد وسط

scorer	golzan	گلزن
defender, back	defā'	دفاع
midfielder, halfback	hāfbak	هافبک

match	mosābeqe	مسابقه
to meet (vi, vt)	molāqāt kardan	ملاقات کردن
final	fināl	فینال
semi-final	nime nahāyi	نیمه نهایی
championship	mosābeqe-ye qahremāni	مسابقه قهرمانی

period, half	nime	نیمه
first period	nime-ye avval	نیمه اول
half-time	hāf tāym	هاف تایم

goal	darvāze	دروازه
goalkeeper	darvāze bān	دروازه بان
goalpost	tir-e darvāze	تیر دروازه
crossbar	tir-e ofoqi	تیر افقی
net	tur	تور
to concede a goal	gol xordan	گل خوردن

ball	tup	توپ
pass	pās	پاس
kick	zarbe	ضربه
to kick (~ the ball)	zarbe zadan	ضربه زدن
free kick (direct ~)	zarbe-ye xatā	ضربۀ خطا
corner kick	korner	کرنر

attack	hamle	حمله
counterattack	zedd-e hamle	ضد حمله
combination	mānovr	مانور

referee	dāvar	داور
to blow the whistle	sut zadan	سوت زدن
whistle (sound)	sut	سوت
foul, misconduct	xatā	خطا
to commit a foul	xatā kardan	خطا کردن
to send off	az zamin exrāj kardan	از زمین اخراج کردن

yellow card	kārt-e zard	کارت زرد
red card	kārt-e qermez	کارت قرمز
disqualification	rad-e salāhiyat	رد صلاحیت
to disqualify (vt)	rad-e salāhiyat kardan	رد صلاحیت کردن

penalty kick	penālti	پنالتی
wall	divār-e defā'i	دیوار دفاعی
to score (vi, vt)	gol zadan	گل زدن
goal (score)	gol	گل
to score a goal	gol zadan	گل زدن

substitution	ta'viz	تعویض
to replace (a player)	ta'viz kardan	تعویض کردن
rules	qavā'ed	قواعد
tactics	tāktik	تاکتیک
stadium	varzešgāh	ورزشگاه
terrace	teribun	تریبون

fan, supporter	tarafdār	طرفدار
to shout (vi)	faryād zadan	فریاد زدن
scoreboard	skorbord	اسکوربورد
score	emtiyāz	امتیاز
defeat	šekast	شکست
to lose (not win)	bāxtan	باختن
draw	mosāvi	مساوی
to draw (vi)	bāzi rā mosāvi kardan	بازی رامساوی کردن
victory	piruzi	پیروزی
to win (vi, vt)	piruz šodan	پیروز شدن
champion	qahremān	قهرمان
best (adj)	behtarin	بهترین
to congratulate (vt)	tabrik goftan	تبریک گفتن
commentator	mofasser	مفسر
to commentate (vt)	tafsir kardan	تفسیر کردن
broadcast	paxš	پخش

137. Alpine skiing

skis	eski	اسکی
to ski (vi)	eski kardan	اسکی کردن
mountain-ski resort	pist-e eski	پیست اسکی
ski lift	telesk-i	تلسکی
ski poles	čub-e eski	چوب اسکی
slope	šib	شیب
slalom	eslālom	اسلالوم

138. Tennis. Golf

golf	golf	گلف
golf club	bāšgāh-e golf	باشگاه گلف
golfer	bāzikon-e golf	بازیکن گلف
hole	gowdāl	گودال
club	čub-e golf	چوب گلف
golf trolley	čarx-e hāmele golf	چرخ حامل گلف
tennis	tenis	تنیس
tennis court	zamin-e tenis	زمین تنیس
serve	servis	سرویس
to serve (vt)	servis zadan	سرویس زدن
racket	rāket	راکت
net	tur	تور
ball	tup	توپ

139. Chess

chess	šatranj	شطرنج
chessmen	mohrehā-ye šatranj	مهره های شطرنج
chess player	šatranj bāz	شطرنج باز
chessboard	taxte-ye šatranj	تختهٔ شطرنج
chessman	mohre-ye šatranj	مهره شطرنج
White (white pieces)	sefid	سفید
Black (black pieces)	siyāh	سیاه
pawn	piyāde	پیاده
bishop	fil	فیل
knight	asb	اسب
rook	rox	رخ
queen	vazir	وزیر
king	šāh	شاه
move	harekat	حرکت
to move (vi, vt)	harekat kardan	حرکت کردن
to sacrifice (vt)	qorbāni kardan	قربانی کردن
castling	mohreye qal'e	مهرهٔ قلعه
check	kiš	کیش
checkmate	māt	مات
chess tournament	mosābeqe-ye šatranj	مسابقهٔ شطرنج
Grand Master	ostād-e bozorg	استاد بزرگ
combination	tarkib	ترکیب
game (in chess)	dor-e bazi	دوربازی
draughts	bāzi-ye čekerz	بازی چکرز

140. Boxing

boxing	boks	بوکس
fight (bout)	mobāreze	مبارزه
boxing match	mosābeqe-ye boks	مسابقه بوکس
round (in boxing)	rānd	راند
ring	ring	رینگ
gong	nāqus	ناقوس
punch	zarbe	ضربه
knockdown	nāk dān	ناک داون
knockout	nāk owt	ناک اوت
to knock out	nākowt kardan	ناک اوت کردن
boxing glove	dastkeš-e boks	دستکش بوکس
referee	dāvar	داور
lightweight	vazn-e sabok	وزن سبک
middleweight	vazn-e motevasset	وزن متوسط
heavyweight	vazn-e sangin	وزن سنگین

141. Sports. Miscellaneous

Olympic Games	bāzihā-ye olampik	بازی‌های المپیک
winner	barande	برنده
to be winning	piruz šodan	پیروز شدن
to win (vi)	piruz šodan	پیروز شدن
leader	rahbar	رهبر
to lead (vi)	lider budan	لیدر بودن
first place	rotbe-ye avval	رتبه اول
second place	rotbe-ye dovvom	رتبه دوم
third place	rotbe-ye sevvom	رتبه سوم
medal	medāl	مدال
trophy	kāp	کاپ
prize cup (trophy)	jām	جام
prize (in game)	jāyeze	جایزه
main prize	jāyeze-ye asli	جایزهٔ اصلی
record	rekord	رکورد
to set a record	rekord gozāštan	رکورد گذاشتن
final	fināl	فینال
final (adj)	pāyāni	پایانی
champion	qahremān	قهرمان
championship	mosābeqe-ye qahremāni	مسابقه قهرمانی
stadium	varzešgāh	ورزشگاه
terrace	teribun	تریبون
fan, supporter	tarafdār	طرفدار
opponent, rival	raqib	رقیب
start (start line)	šoru'	شروع
finish line	entehā	انتها
defeat	šekast	شکست
to lose (not win)	bāxtan	باختن
referee	dāvar	داور
jury (judges)	hey'at-e dāvarān	هیئت داوران
score	emtiyāz	امتیاز
draw	mosāvi	مساوی
to draw (vi)	bāzi rā mosāvi kardan	بازی رامساوی کردن
point	emtiyāz	امتیاز
result (final score)	natije	نتیجه
period	dowre	دوره
half-time	hāf tāym	هاف تایم
doping	doping	دوپینگ
to penalise (vt)	jarime kardan	جریمه کردن
to disqualify (vt)	rad-e salāhiyat kardan	رد صلاحیت کردن
apparatus	asbāb	اسباب

javelin	neyze	نیزه
shot (metal ball)	vazne	وزنه
ball (snooker, etc.)	tup	توپ
aim (target)	hadaf	هدف
target	nešangah	نشانگاه
to shoot (vi)	tirandāzi kardan	تیراندازی کردن
accurate (~ shot)	dorost	درست
trainer, coach	morabbi	مربی
to train (sb)	tamrin dādan	تمرین دادن
to train (vi)	tamrin kardan	تمرین کردن
training	tamrin	تمرین
gym	sālon-e varzeš	سالن ورزش
exercise (physical)	tamrin	تمرین
warm-up (athlete ~)	garm kardan	گرم کردن

Education

142. School

school	madrese	مدرسه
headmaster	modir-e madrese	مدیر مدرسه
pupil (boy)	dāneš-āmuz	دانش آموز
pupil (girl)	dāneš-āmuz	دانش آموز
schoolboy	dāneš-āmuz	دانش آموز
schoolgirl	dāneš-āmuz	دانش آموز
to teach (sb)	āmuxtan	آموختن
to learn (language, etc.)	yād gereftan	یاد گرفتن
to learn by heart	az hefz kardan	از حفظ کردن
to learn (~ to count, etc.)	yād gereftan	یاد گرفتن
to be at school	tahsil kardan	تحصیل کردن
to go to school	madrese raftan	مدرسه رفتن
alphabet	alefbā	الفبا
subject (at school)	mabhas	مبحث
classroom	kelās	کلاس
lesson	dars	درس
playtime, break	zang-e tafrih	زنگ تفریح
school bell	zang	زنگ
school desk	miz-e tahrir	میز تحریر
blackboard	taxte-ye siyāh	تخته سیاه
mark	nomre	نمره
good mark	nomre-ye xub	نمرهٔ خوب
bad mark	nomre-ye bad	نمرهٔ بد
to give a mark	nomre gozāštan	نمره گذاشتن
mistake, error	eštebāh	اشتباه
to make mistakes	eštebāh kardan	اشتباه کردن
to correct (an error)	eslāh kardan	اصلاح کردن
crib	taqallob	تقلب
homework	taklif manzel	تکلیف منزل
exercise (in education)	tamrin	تمرین
to be present	hozur dāštan	حضور داشتن
to be absent	qāyeb budan	غایب بودن
to miss school	az madrese qāyeb budan	ازمدرسه غایب بودن
to punish (vt)	tanbih kardan	تنبیه کردن
punishment	tanbih	تنبیه
conduct (behaviour)	raftār	رفتار

school report	gozāreš-e ruzāne	گزارش روزانه
pencil	medād	مداد
rubber	pāk kon	پاک کن
chalk	gač	گچ
pencil case	qalamdān	قلمدان

schoolbag	kif madrese	کیف مدرسه
pen	xodkār	خودکار
exercise book	daftar	دفتر
textbook	ketāb-e darsi	کتاب درسی
compasses	pargār	پرگار

to make technical drawings	rasm kardan	رسم کردن
technical drawing	rasm-e fani	رسم فنی

poem	še'r	شعر
by heart (adv)	az hefz	از حفظ
to learn by heart	az hefz kardan	از حفظ کردن

school holidays	ta'tilāt	تعطیلات
to be on holiday	dar ta'tilāt budan	در تعطیلات بودن
to spend holidays	ta'tilāt rā gozarāndan	تعطیلات را گذراندن

test (at school)	emtehān	امتحان
essay (composition)	enšā'	انشاء
dictation	dikte	دیکته
exam (examination)	emtehān	امتحان
to do an exam	emtehān dādan	امتحان دادن
experiment (e.g., chemistry ~)	āzmāyeš	آزمایش

143. College. University

academy	farhangestān	فرهنگستان
university	dānešgāh	دانشگاه
faculty (e.g., ~ of Medicine)	dāneškade	دانشکده

student (masc.)	dānešju	دانشجو
student (fem.)	dānešju	دانشجو
lecturer (teacher)	ostād	استاد

lecture hall, room	kelās	کلاس
graduate	fāreqottahsil	فارغ التحصیل

diploma	diplom	دیپلم
dissertation	pāyān nāme	پایان نامه

study (report)	tahqiqe elmi	تحقیق علمی
laboratory	āzmāyešgāh	آزمایشگاه

lecture	soxanrāni	سخنرانی
coursemate	ha mdowre i	هم دوره ای
scholarship, bursary	burse tahsili	بورس تحصیلی
academic degree	daraje-ye elmi	درجهٔ علمی

144. Sciences. Disciplines

mathematics	riyāziyāt	ریاضیات
algebra	jabr	جبر
geometry	hendese	هندسه

astronomy	setāre-šenāsi	ستاره شناسی
biology	zist-šenāsi	زیست شناسی
geography	joqrāfiyā	جغرافیا
geology	zamin-šenāsi	زمین شناسی
history	tārix	تاریخ

medicine	pezeški	پزشکی
pedagogy	olume tarbiyati	علوم تربیتی
law	hoquq	حقوق

physics	fizik	فیزیک
chemistry	šimi	شیمی
philosophy	falsafe	فلسفه
psychology	ravānšenāsi	روانشناسی

145. Writing system. Orthography

grammar	gerāmer	گرامر
vocabulary	vājegān	واژگان
phonetics	sadā-šenāsi	صداشناسی

noun	esm	اسم
adjective	sefat	صفت
verb	fe'l	فعل
adverb	qeyd	قید

pronoun	zamir	ضمیر
interjection	harf-e nedā	حرف ندا
preposition	harf-e ezāfe	حرف اضافه

root	riše-ye kalame	ریشه کلمه
ending	pasvand	پسوند
prefix	pišvand	پیشوند
syllable	hejā	هجا
suffix	pasvand	پسوند

stress mark	fešar-e hejā	فشار هجا
apostrophe	āpostrof	آپوستروف

full stop	noqte	نقطه
comma	virgul	ویرگول
semicolon	noqte virgul	نقطه ویرگول
colon	donoqte	دونقطه
ellipsis	čand noqte	چند نقطه

question mark	alāmat-e soāl	علامت سؤال
exclamation mark	alāmat-e taajjob	علامت تعجب

inverted commas	giyume	گیومه
in inverted commas	dar giyume	در گیومه
parenthesis	parāntez	پرانتز
in parenthesis	dar parāntez	در پرانتز

hyphen	xatt-e vāsel	خط واصل
dash	xatt-e tire	خط تیره
space (between words)	fāsele	فاصله

| letter | harf | حرف |
| capital letter | harf-e bozorg | حرف بزرگ |

| vowel (n) | sedādār | صدادار |
| consonant (n) | sāmet | صامت |

sentence	jomle	جمله
subject	nahād	نهاد
predicate	gozāre	گزاره

line	satr	سطر
on a new line	sar-e satr	سر سطر
paragraph	band	بند

word	kalame	کلمه
group of words	ebārat	عبارت
expression	bayān	بیان
synonym	moterādef	مترادف
antonym	motezād	متضاد

rule	qā'ede	قاعده
exception	estesnā	استثنا
correct (adj)	sahih	صحیح

conjugation	sarf	صرف
declension	sarf-e kalemāt	صرف کلمات
nominal case	hālat	حالت
question	soāl	سؤال
to underline (vt)	xatt kešidan	خط کشیدن
dotted line	noqte čin	نقطه چین

146. Foreign languages

language	zabān	زبان
foreign (adj)	xāreji	خارجی
foreign language	zabān-e xāreji	زبان خارجی
to study (vt)	dars xāndan	درس خواندن
to learn (language, etc.)	yād gereftan	یاد گرفتن

to read (vi, vt)	xāndan	خواندن
to speak (vi, vt)	harf zadan	حرف زدن
to understand (vt)	fahmidan	فهمیدن
to write (vt)	neveštan	نوشتن
fast (adv)	sari'	سریع
slowly (adv)	āheste	آهسته

fluently (adv)	ravān	روان
rules	qavā'ed	قواعد
grammar	gerāmer	گرامر
vocabulary	vājegān	واژگان
phonetics	āvā-šenāsi	آواشناسی
textbook	ketāb-e darsi	کتاب درسی
dictionary	farhang-e loqat	فرهنگ لغت
teach-yourself book	xod-āmuz	خودآموز
phrasebook	ketāb-e mokāleme	کتاب مکالمه
cassette, tape	kāst	کاست
videotape	kāst-e video	کاست ویدئو
CD, compact disc	si-di	سیدی
DVD	dey vey dey	دی وی دی
alphabet	alefbā	الفبا
to spell (vt)	heji kardan	هجی کردن
pronunciation	talaffoz	تلفظ
accent	lahje	لهجه
with an accent	bā lahje	با لهجه
without an accent	bi lahje	بی لهجه
word	kalame	کلمه
meaning	ma'ni	معنی
course (e.g. a French ~)	dowre	دوره
to sign up	nām-nevisi kardan	نام نویسی کردن
teacher	ostād	استاد
translation (process)	tarjome	ترجمه
translation (text, etc.)	tarjome	ترجمه
translator	motarjem	مترجم
interpreter	motarjem-e šafāhi	مترجم شفاهی
polyglot	čand zabāni	چند زبانی
memory	hāfeze	حافظه

147. Fairy tale characters

Santa Claus	bābā noel	بابا نوئل
Cinderella	sinderelā	سیندرلا
mermaid	pari-ye daryāyi	پری دریایی
Neptune	nepton	نپتون
magician, wizard	sāher	ساحر
fairy	sāher	ساحر
magic (adj)	jāduyi	جادویی
magic wand	asā-ye sehrāmiz	عصای سحرآمیز
fairy tale	afsāne	افسانه
miracle	mo'jeze	معجزه
dwarf	kutule	کوتوله

to turn into ...	tabdil šodan	تبدیل شدن
ghost	šabah	شبح
phantom	šabah	شبح
monster	qul	غول
dragon	eždehā	اژدها
giant	qul	غول

148. Zodiac Signs

Aries	borj-e haml	برج حمل
Taurus	borj-e sowr	برج ثور
Gemini	borj-e jowzā	برج جوزا
Cancer	saratān	سرطان
Leo	šir	شیر
Virgo	borj-e sonbole	برج سنبله
Libra	borj-e mizān	برج میزان
Scorpio	borj-e aqrab	برج عقرب
Sagittarius	borj-e qows	برج قوس
Capricorn	borj-e jeddi	برج جدی
Aquarius	borj-e dalow	برج دلو
Pisces	borj-e hut	برج حوت
character	šaxsiyat	شخصیت
character traits	xosusiyāt-e axlāqi	خصوصیات اخلاقی
behaviour	raftār	رفتار
to tell fortunes	fāl gereftan	فال گرفتن
fortune-teller	fālgir	فالگیر
horoscope	tāle' bini	طالع بینی

Arts

149. Theatre

theatre	teātr	تئاتر
opera	operā	اپرا
operetta	operā-ye kučak	اپرای کوچک
ballet	bāle	باله

theatre poster	e'lān-e namāyeš	اعلان نمایش
theatre company	hey'at honarpišegān	هیئت هنرپیشگان
tour	safar	سفر
to be on tour	dar tur budan	در تور بودن
to rehearse (vi, vt)	tamrin kardan	تمرین کردن
rehearsal	tamrin	تمرین
repertoire	roperator	رپراتور

performance	namāyeš	نمایش
theatrical show	namāyeš	نمایش
play	namāyeš nāme	نمایش نامه

ticket	belit	بلیط
booking office	belit-foruši	بلیت فروشی
lobby, foyer	lābi	لابی
coat check (cloakroom)	komod-e lebās	کمد لباس
cloakroom ticket	žeton	ژتون
binoculars	durbin	دوربین
usher	rāhnamā	راهنما

stalls (orchestra seats)	sandali-ye orkestr	صندلی ارکستر
balcony	bālkon	بالکن
dress circle	bālkon-e avval	بالکن اول
box	jāygāh-e vižhe	جایگاه ویژه
row	radif	ردیف
seat	jā	جا

audience	hozzār	حضار
spectator	tamāšāči	تماشاچی
to clap (vi, vt)	kaf zadan	کف زدن
applause	tašviq	تشویق
ovation	šādi-va soror	شادی و سرور

stage	sahne	صحنه
curtain	parde	پرده
scenery	sahne	صحنه
backstage	pošt-e sahne	پشت صحنه

scene (e.g. the last ~)	sahne	صحنه
act	parde	پرده
interval	ānterākt	آنتراکت

150. Cinema

actor	bāzigar	بازیگر
actress	bāzigar	بازیگر
cinema (industry)	sinamā	سینما
film	film	فیلم
episode	qesmat	قسمت
detective film	film-e polisi	فیلم پلیسی
action film	film-e akšen	فیلم اکشن
adventure film	film-e mājarāyi	فیلم ماجرایی
science fiction film	film-e elmi-ye taxayyoli	فیلم علمی تخیلی
horror film	film-e tarsnāk	فیلم ترسناک
comedy film	komedi	کمدی
melodrama	meloderām	ملودرام
drama	derām	درام
fictional film	film-e honari	فیلم هنری
documentary	film-e mostanad	فیلم مستند
cartoon	kārton	کارتون
silent films	film-e sāmet	فیلم صامت
role (part)	naqš	نقش
leading role	naqš-e asli	نقش اصلی
to play (vi, vt)	bāzi kardan	بازی کردن
film star	setāre-ye sinamā	ستارهٔ سینما
well-known (adj)	mašhur	مشهور
famous (adj)	mašhur	مشهور
popular (adj)	saršenās	سرشناس
script (screenplay)	senāriyo	سناریو
scriptwriter	senārist	سناریست
film director	kārgardān	کارگردان
producer	tahiye konande	تهیه کننده
assistant	dastyār	دستیار
cameraman	filmbardār	فیلمبردار
stuntman	badalkār	بدلکار
double (stuntman)	dublur	دوبلور
to shoot a film	film gereftan	فیلم گرفتن
audition, screen test	test	تست
shooting	film bardār-i	فیلم برداری
film crew	goruh film bar dār-i	گروه فیلم برداری
film set	mahal film bar dār-i	محل فیلم برداری
camera	durbin	دوربین
cinema	sinamā	سینما
screen (e.g. big ~)	parde	پرده
to show a film	film-e nešān dādan	فیلم نشان دادن
soundtrack	musiqi-ye matn	موسیقی متن
special effects	jelvehā-ye vižhe	جلوه های ویژه

subtitles	zirnevis	زیرنویس
credits	titrāj	تیتراژ
translation	tarjome	ترجمه

151. Painting

art	honar	هنر
fine arts	honarhā-ye zibā	هنرهای زیبا
art gallery	gāleri-ye honari	گالری هنری
art exhibition	namāyešgāh-e honari	نمایشگاه هنری
painting (art)	naqqāši	نقاشی
graphic art	honar-e gerāfik	هنر گرافیک
abstract art	honar-e ābestre	هنر آبستره
impressionism	ampersiyonism	امپرسیونیسم
picture (painting)	tasvir	تصویر
drawing	naqqāši	نقاشی
poster	poster	پوستر
illustration (picture)	tasvir	تصویر
miniature	minyātor	مینیاتور
copy (of painting, etc.)	nosxe	نسخه
reproduction	taksir	تکثیر
mosaic	muzāik	موزائیک
stained glass window	naqqāši ruy šiše	نقاشی روی شیشه
fresco	naqqāši ruy gač	نقاشی روی گچ
engraving	gerāvur	گراور
bust (sculpture)	mojassame-ye nimtane	مجسمهٔ نیم تنه
sculpture	mojassame sāz-i	مجسمه سازی
statue	mojassame	مجسمه
plaster of Paris	gač	گچ
plaster (as adj)	gači	گچی
portrait	temsāl	تمثال
self-portrait	tasvir-e naqqāš	تصویر نقاش
landscape painting	manzare	منظره
still life	tabi'at-e bijān	طبیعت بیجان
caricature	kārikātor	کاریکاتور
sketch	tarh-e moqaddamāti	طرح مقدماتی
paint	rang	رنگ
watercolor paint	āb-o rang	آب ورنگ
oil (paint)	rowqan	روغن
pencil	medād	مداد
Indian ink	morakkab	مرکب
charcoal	zoqāl	زغال
to draw (vi, vt)	naqqāši kardan	نقاشی کردن
to paint (vi, vt)	naqqāši kardan	نقاشی کردن
to pose (vi)	žest gereftan	ژست گرفتن
artist's model (masc.)	model-e naqqāši	مدل نقاشی

artist's model (fem.)	model-e naqqāši	مدل نقاشی
artist (painter)	naqqāš	نقاش
work of art	asar-e honari	اثر هنری
masterpiece	šāhkār	شاهکار
studio (artist's workroom)	kārgāh	کارگاه

canvas (cloth)	bum-e naqāši	بوم نقاشی
easel	sepāye-ye naqqāši	سه پایهٔ نقاشی
palette	taxte-ye rang	تختهٔ رنگ

frame (picture ~, etc.)	qāb	قاب
restoration	maremmat	مرمت
to restore (vt)	marammat kardan	مرمت کردن

152. Literature & Poetry

literature	adabiyāt	ادبیات
author (writer)	moallef	مؤلف
pseudonym	taxallos	تخلص

book	ketāb	کتاب
volume	jeld	جلد
table of contents	fehrest	فهرست
page	safhe	صفحه
main character	qahremān-e asli	قهرمان اصلی
autograph	dast-e xat	دست خط

short story	hekāyat	حکایت
story (novella)	dāstān	داستان
novel	ramān	رمان
work (writing)	ta'lif	تألیف
fable	afsāne	افسانه
detective novel	dastane jenai	داستان جنایی

poem (verse)	še'r	شعر
poetry	še'r	شعر
poem (epic, ballad)	še'r	شعر
poet	šā'er	شاعر

fiction	dāstān	داستان
science fiction	elmi-ye taxayyoli	علمی تخیلی
adventures	sargozašt	سرگذشت
educational literature	adabiyāt-e āmuzeši	ادبیات آموزشی
children's literature	adabiyāt-e kudak	ادبیات کودک

153. Circus

circus	sirak	سیرک
travelling circus	sirak-e sayār	سیرک سیار
programme	barnāme	برنامه
performance	namāyeš	نمایش
act (circus ~)	parde	پرده

circus ring	sahne-ye sirak	صحنه سیرک
pantomime (act)	pāntomim	پانتومیم
clown	dalqak	دلقک

acrobat	ākrobāt	آکروبات
acrobatics	band-e bāzi	بند بازی
gymnast	žimināstik kār	ژیمناستیک کار
gymnastics	žimināstik	ژیمناستیک
somersault	salto	سالتو

strongman	qavi heykal	قوی هیکل
tamer (e.g., lion ~)	rām konande	رام کننده
rider (circus horse ~)	savārkār	سوارکار
assistant	dastyār	دستیار

stunt	širin kāri	شیرین کاری
magic trick	šo'bade bāzi	شعبده بازی
conjurer, magician	šo'bade bāz	شعبده باز

juggler	tardast	تردست
to juggle (vi, vt)	tardasti kardan	تردستی کردن
animal trainer	morabbi-ye heyvānāt	مربی حیوانات
animal training	ta'lim heyvānāt	تعلیم حیوانات
to train (animals)	tarbiyat kardan	تربیت کردن

154. Music. Pop music

music	musiqi	موسیقی
musician	muzisiyan	موزیسین
musical instrument	abzār-e musiqi	ابزار موسیقی
to play ...	navāxtan	نواختن

guitar	gitār	گیتار
violin	viyolon	ویولون
cello	viyolonsel	ویولون سل
double bass	konterbās	کونترباس
harp	čang	چنگ

piano	piyāno	پیانو
grand piano	piyāno-e bozorg	پیانوی بزرگ
organ	arg	ارگ

wind instruments	sāzhā-ye bādi	سازهای بادی
oboe	abva	ابوا
saxophone	saksofon	ساکسوفون
clarinet	qare ney	قره نی
flute	folut	فلوت
trumpet	šeypur	شیپور

| accordion | ākordeon | آکوردئون |
| drum | tabl | طبل |

| duo | daste-ye do nafare | دسته دو نفره |
| trio | daste-ye se nafar-i | دستۀ سه نفری |

quartet	daste-ye čāhārnafari	دستهٔ چهارنفری
choir	kar	کر
orchestra	orkesr	ارکستر

pop music	musiqi-ye pāp	موسیقی پاپ
rock music	musiqi-ye rāk	موسیقی راک
rock group	goruh-e rāk	گروه راک
jazz	jāz	جاز

| idol | mahbub | محبوب |
| admirer, fan | havādār | هوادار |

concert	konsert	کنسرت
symphony	samfoni	سمفونی
composition	tasnif	تصنیف
to compose (write)	tasnif kardan	تصنیف کردن

singing (n)	āvāz	آواز
song	tarāne	ترانه
tune (melody)	āhang	آهنگ
rhythm	ritm	ریتم
blues	musiqi-ye boluz	موسیقی بلوز

sheet music	daftar-e not	دفتر نت
baton	čub-e rahbari	چوب رهبری
bow	ārše	آرشه
string	sim	سیم
case (e.g. guitar ~)	qalāf	غلاف

Rest. Entertainment. Travel

155. Trip. Travel

tourism, travel	gardešgari	گردشگری
tourist	turist	توریست
trip, voyage	mosāferat	مسافرت
adventure	mājarā	ماجرا
trip, journey	safar	سفر
holiday	moraxxasi	مرخصی
to be on holiday	dar moraxassi budan	در مرخصی بودن
rest	esterāhat	استراحت
train	qatār	قطار
by train	bā qatār	با قطار
aeroplane	havāpeymā	هواپیما
by aeroplane	bā havāpeymā	با هواپیما
by car	bā otomobil	با اتومبیل
by ship	dar kešti	با کشتی
luggage	bār	بار
suitcase	čamedān	چمدان
luggage trolley	čarx-e hamle bar	چرخ حمل بار
passport	gozarnāme	گذرنامه
visa	ravādid	روادید
ticket	belit	بلیط
air ticket	belit-e havāpeymā	بلیط هواپیما
guidebook	ketāb-e rāhnamā	کتاب راهنما
map (tourist ~)	naqše	نقشه
area (rural ~)	mahal	محل
place, site	jā	جا
exotica (n)	qarāyeb	غرایب
exotic (adj)	qarib	غریب
amazing (adj)	heyrat angiz	حیرت انگیز
group	goruh	گروه
excursion, sightseeing tour	gardeš	گردش
guide (person)	rāhnamā-ye tur	راهنمای تور

156. Hotel

hotel	hotel	هتل
motel	motel	متل
three-star (~ hotel)	se setāre	سه ستاره

five-star	panj setāre	پنج ستاره
to stay (in a hotel, etc.)	māndan	ماندن
room	otāq	اتاق
single room	otāq-e yeknafare	اتاق یک نفره
double room	otāq-e do nafare	اتاق دو نفره
to book a room	otāq rezerv kardan	اتاق رزرو کردن
half board	nim pānsiyon	نیم پانسیون
full board	pānsiyon	پانسیون
with bath	bā vān	با وان
with shower	bā duš	با دوش
satellite television	televiziyon-e māhvārei	تلویزیون ماهواره ای
air-conditioner	tahviye-ye matbu'	تهویه مطبوع
towel	howle	حوله
key	kelid	کلید
administrator	edāre-ye konande	اداره کننده
chambermaid	mostaxdem	مستخدم
porter	bārbar	باربر
doorman	darbān	دربان
restaurant	resturān	رستوران
pub, bar	bār	بار
breakfast	sobhāne	صبحانه
dinner	šām	شام
buffet	bufe	بوفه
lobby	lābi	لابی
lift	āsānsor	آسانسور
DO NOT DISTURB	mozāhem našavid	مزاحم نشوید
NO SMOKING	sigār kešidan mamnu'	سیگار کشیدن ممنوع

157. Books. Reading

book	ketāb	کتاب
author	moallef	مؤلف
writer	nevisande	نویسنده
to write (~ a book)	neveštan	نوشتن
reader	xānande	خواننده
to read (vi, vt)	xāndan	خواندن
reading (activity)	motāle'e	مطالعه
silently (to oneself)	be ārāmi	به آرامی
aloud (adv)	boland	بلند
to publish (vt)	montašer kardan	منتشر کردن
publishing (process)	entešār	انتشار
publisher	nāšer	ناشر
publishing house	entešārāt	انتشارات
to come out (be released)	montašer šodan	منتشر شدن

release (of a book)	našr	نشر
print run	tirāž	تیراژ
bookshop	ketāb-foruši	کتاب فروشی
library	ketābxāne	کتابخانه
story (novella)	dāstān	داستان
short story	hekāyat	حکایت
novel	ramān	رمان
detective novel	dastane jenai	داستان جنایی
memoirs	xāterāt	خاطرات
legend	afsāne	افسانه
myth	osture	اسطوره
poetry, poems	še'r	شعر
autobiography	zendegināme	زندگینامه
selected works	āsār-e montaxab	آثار منتخب
science fiction	elmi-ye taxayyoli	علمی تخیلی
title	onvān	عنوان
introduction	moqaddame	مقدمه
title page	safhe-ye onvān	صفحه عنوان
chapter	fasl	فصل
extract	gozide	گزیده
episode	qesmat	قسمت
plot (storyline)	suže	سوژه
contents	mazmun	مضمون
table of contents	fehrest	فهرست
main character	qahremān-e asli	قهرمان اصلی
volume	jeld	جلد
cover	jeld	جلد
binding	sahhāfi	صحافی
bookmark	čub-e alef	چوب الف
page	safhe	صفحه
to page through	varaq zadan	ورق زدن
margins	hāšiye	حاشیه
annotation	hāšiye nevisi	حاشیه نویسی
(marginal note, etc.)		
footnote	pāvaraqi	پاورقی
text	matn	متن
type, fount	font	فونت
misprint, typo	qalat čāpi	غلط چاپی
translation	tarjome	ترجمه
to translate (vt)	tarjome kardan	ترجمه کردن
original (n)	nosxe-ye asli	نسخهٔ اصلی
famous (adj)	mašhur	مشهور
unknown (not famous)	nāšenāxte	ناشناخته
interesting (adj)	jāleb	جالب

bestseller	por foruš	پر فروش
dictionary	farhang-e loqat	فرهنگ لغت
textbook	ketāb-e darsi	کتاب درسی
encyclopedia	dāyeratolma'āref	دایره المعارف

158. Hunting. Fishing

hunting	šekār	شکار
to hunt (vi, vt)	šekār kardan	شکار کردن
hunter	šekārči	شکارچی

to shoot (vi)	tirandāzi kardan	تیراندازی کردن
rifle	tofang	تفنگ
bullet (shell)	fešang	فشنگ
shot (lead balls)	sāčme	ساچمه

steel trap	tale	تله
snare (for birds, etc.)	dām	دام
to fall into the steel trap	dar tale oftādan	در تله افتادن
to lay a steel trap	tale gozāštan	تله گذاشتن

poacher	šekārči-ye qeyr-e qānuni	شکارچی غیر قانونی
game (in hunting)	šekār	شکار
hound dog	sag-e šekāri	سگ شکاری
safari	safar-e ektešāfi āfriqā	سفر اکتشافی آفریقا
mounted animal	heyvān-e model	حیوان مدل

fisherman	māhigir	ماهیگیر
fishing (angling)	māhigiri	ماهیگیری
to fish (vi)	māhi gereftan	ماهی گرفتن

fishing rod	čub māhi gir-i	چوب ماهی گیری
fishing line	nax-e māhigiri	نخ ماهیگیری
hook	qollāb	قلاب
float	šenāvar	شناور
bait	to'me	طعمه

| to cast a line | qollāb andāxtan | قلاب انداختن |
| to bite (ab. fish) | gāz gereftan | گاز گرفتن |

| catch (of fish) | seyd | صید |
| ice-hole | surāx dar yax | سوراخ دریخ |

| fishing net | tur | تور |
| boat | qāyeq | قایق |

to net (to fish with a net)	bā tur-e māhi gereftan	با تورماهی گرفتن
to cast[throw] the net	tur andāxtan	تور انداختن
to haul the net in	tur rā birun āvardan	تور را بیرون آوردن
to fall into the net	be tur oftādan	به تور افتادن

whaler (person)	seyād-e nahang	صیاد نهنگ
whaleboat	kešti-ye seyd-e nahang	کشتی صید نهنگ
harpoon	neyze	نیزه

159. Games. Billiards

billiards	bilyārd	بیلیارد
billiard room, hall	otāq-e bilyārd	اتاق بیلیارد
ball (snooker, etc.)	tup	توپ
to pocket a ball	tup vāred-e pākat kardan	توپ وارد پاکت کردن
cue	čub-e bilyārd	چوب بیلیارد
pocket	pākat	پاکت

160. Games. Playing cards

diamonds	xešt	خشت
spades	peyk	پیک
hearts	del	دل
clubs	xāj	خاج
ace	tak xāl	تک خال
king	šāh	شاه
queen	bi bi	بی بی
jack, knave	sarbāz	سرباز
playing card	varaq	ورق
cards	varaq	ورق
trump	xāl-e hokm	خال حکم
pack of cards	daste-ye varaq	دستۀ ورق
point	xāl	خال
to deal (vi, vt)	varaq dādan	ورق دادن
to shuffle (cards)	bar zadan	بر زدن
lead, turn (n)	harekat	حرکت
cardsharp	moteqalleb	متقلب

161. Casino. Roulette

casino	kāzino	کازینو
roulette (game)	rolet	رولت
bet	šart bandi	شرط بندی
to place bets	šart bandi kardan	شرط بندی کردن
red	sorx	سرخ
black	siyāh	سیاه
to bet on red	ru-ye sorx-e šart-bandi kardan	روی سرخ شرط بندی کردن
to bet on black	ru-ye siyāh-e šart-bandi kardan	روی سیاه شرط بندی کردن
croupier (dealer)	mas'ul-e bāzi	مسئول بازی
to spin the wheel	gardāndan-e čarx	گرداندن چرخ
rules (of game)	qavā'ede bāzi	قواعد بازی
chip	žeton	ژتون

to win (vi, vt)	piruz šodan	پیروز شدن
win (winnings)	bord	برد
to lose (~ 100 dollars)	bāxtan	باختن
loss (losses)	bāxt	باخت
player	bāzikon	بازیکن
blackjack (card game)	balak jak	بلک جک
craps (dice game)	tās bāzi	تاس بازی
dice (a pair of ~)	tās	تاس
fruit machine	māšin asal-at	ماشین اسلات

162. Rest. Games. Miscellaneous

to stroll (vi, vt)	gardeš kardan	گردش کردن
stroll (leisurely walk)	gardeš	گردش
car ride	siyāhat	سیاحت
adventure	mājarā	ماجرا
picnic	pik nik	پیک نیک
game (chess, etc.)	bāzi	بازی
player	bāzikon	بازیکن
game (one ~ of chess)	dor-e bazi	دوربازی
collector (e.g. philatelist)	kolleksiyoner	کلکسیونر
to collect (stamps, etc.)	jam'-e āvari kardan	جمع آوری کردن
collection	koleksiyon	کلکسیون
crossword puzzle	kalamāt-e moteqāte'	کلمات متقاطع
racecourse (hippodrome)	meydān-e asb-e davāni	میدان اسب دوانی
disco (discotheque)	disko	دیسکو
sauna	sonā	سونا
lottery	baxt-e āzmāyi	بخت آزمایی
camping trip	rāh peymāyi	راه پیمایی
camp	ordugāh	اردوگاه
tent (for camping)	čādor	چادر
compass	qotb namā	قطب نما
camper	kamp nešin	کمپ نشین
to watch (film, etc.)	tamāšā kardan	تماشا کردن
viewer	tamāšāči	تماشاچی
TV show (TV program)	barnāme-ye televiziyoni	برنامه تلویزیونی

163. Photography

camera (photo)	durbin-e akkāsi	دوربین عکاسی
photo, picture	aks	عکس
photographer	akkās	عکاس
photo studio	ātolye-ye akkāsi	آتلیهٔ عکاسی

photo album	ālbom-e aks	آلبوم عکس
camera lens	lenz-e durbin	لنز دوربین
telephoto lens	lenz-e tale-ye foto	لنز تله فوتو
filter	filter	فیلتر
lens	lenz	لنز

optics (high-quality ~)	optik	اپتیک
diaphragm (aperture)	diyāfrāgm	دیافراگم
exposure time (shutter speed)	sor'at-e bāz šodan-e lenz	سرعت بازشدن لنز
viewfinder	namā yāb	نما یاب

digital camera	durbin-e dijitāl	دوربین دیجیتال
tripod	se pāye	سه پایه
flash	feleš	فلش

to photograph (vt)	akkāsi kardan	عکاسی کردن
to take pictures	aks gereftan	عکس گرفتن
to have one's picture taken	aks gereftan	عکس گرفتن

focus	noqte-ye kānuni	نقطه کانونی
to focus	motemarkez kardan	متمرکز کردن
sharp, in focus (adj)	vāzeh	واضح
sharpness	vozuh	وضوح

| contrast | konterāst | کنتراست |
| contrast (as adj) | konterāst | کنتراست |

picture (photo)	aks	عکس
negative (n)	film-e negātiv	فیلم نگاتیو
film (a roll of ~)	film	فیلم
frame (still)	čārcub	چارچوب
to print (photos)	čāp kardan	چاپ کردن

164. Beach. Swimming

beach	pelāž	پلاژ
sand	šen	شن
deserted (beach)	xāli	خالی

suntan	hammām-e āftāb	حمام آفتاب
to get a tan	hammām-e āftāb gereftan	حمام آفتاب گرفتن
tanned (adj)	boronze	برنزه
sunscreen	kerem-e zedd-e āftāb	کرم ضد آفتاب

bikini	māyo-ye do tekke	مایوی دو تکه
swimsuit, bikini	māyo	مایو
swim trunks	māyo	مایو

swimming pool	estaxr	استخر
to swim (vi)	šenā kardan	شنا کردن
shower	duš	دوش
to change (one's clothes)	lebās avaz kardan	لباس عوض کردن
towel	howle	حوله

boat	qāyeq	قایق
motorboat	qāyeq-e motori	قایق موتوری
water ski	eski-ye ruy-ye āb	اسکی روی آب
pedalo	qāyeq-e pedāli	قایق پدالی
surfing	mowj savāri	موج سواری
surfer	mowj savār	موج سوار
scuba set	eskowba	اسکوبا
flippers (swim fins)	bālehā-ye qavvāsi	باله های غواصی
mask (diving ~)	māsk	ماسک
diver	qavvās	غواص
to dive (vi)	širje raftan	شیرجه رفتن
underwater (adv)	zir-e ābi	زیر آبی
beach umbrella	čatr	چتر
beach chair (sun lounger)	sandali-ye rāhati	صندلی راحتی
sunglasses	eynak āftābi	عینک آفتابی
air mattress	tošak-e ābi	تشک آبی
to play (amuse oneself)	bāzi kardan	بازی کردن
to go for a swim	ābtani kardan	آبتنی کردن
beach ball	tup	توپ
to inflate (vt)	bād kardan	باد کردن
inflatable, air (adj)	bādi	بادی
wave	mowj	موج
buoy (line of ~s)	šenāvar	شناور
to drown (ab. person)	qarq šodan	غرق شدن
to save, to rescue	najāt dādan	نجات دادن
life jacket	jeliqe-ye nejāt	جلیقۀ نجات
to observe, to watch	mošāhede kardan	مشاهده کردن
lifeguard	nejāt-e dahande	نجات دهنده

TECHNICAL EQUIPMENT. TRANSPORT

Technical equipment

165. Computer

computer	kāmpiyuter	کامپیوتر
notebook, laptop	lap tāp	لپ تاپ
to turn on	rowšan kardan	روشن کردن
to turn off	xāmuš kardan	خاموش کردن
keyboard	sahfe kelid	صحفه کلید
key	kelid	کلید
mouse	māows	ماوس
mouse mat	māows pad	ماوس پد
button	dokme	دکمه
cursor	makān namā	مکان نما
monitor	monitor	مونیتور
screen	safhe	صفحه
hard disk	hārd disk	هارد دیسک
hard disk capacity	hajm-e hard	حجم هارد
memory	hāfeze	حافظه
random access memory	hāfeze-ye ram	حافظه رم
file	parvande	پرونده
folder	puše	پوشه
to open (vt)	bāz kardan	باز کردن
to close (vt)	bastan	بستن
to save (vt)	zaxire kardan	ذخیره کردن
to delete (vt)	hazf kardan	حذف کردن
to copy (vt)	kopi kardan	کپی کردن
to sort (vt)	tabaqe bandi kardan	طبقه بندی کردن
to transfer (copy)	kopi kardan	کپی کردن
programme	barnāme	برنامه
software	narm afzār	نرم افزار
programmer	barnāme-ye nevis	برنامه نویس
to program (vt)	barnāme-nevisi kardan	برنامه نویسی کردن
hacker	haker	هکر
password	kalame-ye obur	کلمه عبور
virus	virus	ویروس
to find, to detect	peydā kardan	پیدا کردن
byte	bāyt	بایت

megabyte	megābāyt	مگابایت
data	dāde-hā	داده ها
database	pāygāh dāde-hā	پایگاه داده ها
cable (USB, etc.)	kābl	کابل
to disconnect (vt)	jodā kardan	جدا کردن
to connect (sth to sth)	vasl kardan	وصل کردن

166. Internet. E-mail

Internet	internet	اینترنت
browser	morurgar	مرورگر
search engine	motor-e jostoju	موتور جستجو
provider	erāe-ye dehande	ارائه دهنده
webmaster	tarrāh-e vebsāyt	طراح وب سایت
website	veb-sāyt	وب سایت
webpage	safhe-ye veb	صفحه وب
address (e-mail ~)	nešāni	نشانی
address book	daftarče-ye nešāni	دفترچه نشانی
postbox	sanduq-e post	صندوق پست
post	post	پست
full (adj)	por	پر
message	payām	پیام
incoming messages	payāmhā-ye vorudi	پیامهای ورودی
outgoing messages	payāmhā-ye xoruji	پیامهای خروجی
sender	ferestande	فرستنده
to send (vt)	ferestādan	فرستادن
sending (of mail)	ersāl	ارسال
receiver	girande	گیرنده
to receive (vt)	gereftan	گرفتن
correspondence	mokātebe	مکاتبه
to correspond (vi)	mokātebe kardan	مکاتبه کردن
file	parvande	پرونده
to download (vt)	dānlod kardan	دانلود کردن
to create (vt)	ijād kardan	ایجاد کردن
to delete (vt)	hazf kardan	حذف کردن
deleted (adj)	hazf šode	حذف شده
connection (ADSL, etc.)	ertebāt	ارتباط
speed	sor'at	سرعت
modem	modem	مودم
access	dastyābi	دستیابی
port (e.g. input ~)	dargāh	درگاه
connection (make a ~)	ertebāt	ارتباط
to connect to ... (vi)	vasl šodan	وصل شدن

| to select (vt) | entexāb kardan | انتخاب کردن |
| to search (for ...) | jostoju kardan | جستجو کردن |

167. Electricity

electricity	barq	برق
electric, electrical (adj)	barqi	برقی
electric power station	nirugāh	نیروگاه
energy	enerži	انرژی
electric power	niru-ye barq	نیروی برق

light bulb	lāmp	لامپ
torch	čerāq-e dasti	چراغ دستی
street light	čerāq-e barq	چراغ برق

light	nur	نور
to turn on	rowšan kardan	روشن کردن
to turn off	xāmuš kardan	خاموش کردن
to turn off the light	čerāq rā xāmuš kardan	چراغ را خاموش کردن

to burn out (vi)	suxtan	سوختن
short circuit	ettesāli	اتصالی
broken wire	sim qat' šode	سیم قطع شده
contact (electrical ~)	tamās	تماس

light switch	kelid	کلید
socket outlet	periz	پریز
plug	došāxe	دوشاخه
extension lead	sim-e sayār	سیم سیار

fuse	fiyuz	فیوز
cable, wire	sim	سیم
wiring	sim keši	سیم کشی

ampere	āmper	آمپر
amperage	šeddat-e jaryān	شدت جریان
volt	volt	ولت
voltage	voltāž	ولتاژ

| electrical device | vasile-ye barqi | وسیله برقی |
| indicator | šāxes | شاخص |

electrician	barq-e kār	برق کار
to solder (vt)	lahim kardan	لحیم کردن
soldering iron	hoviye	هویه
electric current	jaryān-e barq	جریان برق

168. Tools

tool, instrument	abzār	ابزار
tools	abzār	ابزار
equipment (factory ~)	tajhizāt	تجهیزات

hammer	čakoš	چکش
screwdriver	pič gušti	پیچ گوشتی
axe	tabar	تبر

saw	arre	اره
to saw (vt)	arre kardan	اره کردن
plane (tool)	rande	رنده
to plane (vt)	rande kardan	رنده کردن
soldering iron	hoviye	هویه
to solder (vt)	lahim kardan	لحیم کردن

file (tool)	sowhān	سوهان
carpenter pincers	gāzanbor	گازانبر
combination pliers	anbordast	انبردست
chisel	eskene	اسکنه

drill bit	sar-matte	سرمته
electric drill	matte barqi	مته برقی
to drill (vi, vt)	surāx kardan	سوراخ کردن

knife	kārd	کارد
pocket knife	čāqu-ye jibi	چاقوی جیبی
blade	tiqe	تیغه

sharp (blade, etc.)	tiz	تیز
dull, blunt (adj)	konad	کند
to get blunt (dull)	konad šodan	کند شدن
to sharpen (vt)	tiz kardan	تیز کردن

bolt	pič	پیچ
nut	mohre	مهره
thread (of a screw)	šiyār	شیار
wood screw	pič	پیچ

| nail | mix | میخ |
| nailhead | sar-e mix | سر میخ |

ruler (for measuring)	xat keš	خط کش
tape measure	metr	متر
spirit level	tarāz	تراز
magnifying glass	zarre bin	ذره بین

measuring instrument	abzār-e andāzegir-i	ابزاراندازه گیری
to measure (vt)	andāze gereftan	اندازه گرفتن
scale (of thermometer, etc.)	safhe-ye modarraj	صفحهٔ مدرج
readings	dastgāh-e xaneš	دستگاه خوانش

| compressor | komperesor | کمپرسور |
| microscope | mikroskop | میکروسکوپ |

pump (e.g. water ~)	pomp	پمپ
robot	robāt	روبات
laser	leyzer	لیزر

| spanner | āčār | آچار |
| adhesive tape | navār-e časb | نوار چسب |

glue	časb	چسب
sandpaper	kāqaz-e sonbāde	کاغذ سنباده
spring	fanar	فنر
magnet	āhan-e robā	آهن ربا
gloves	dastkeš	دستکش

rope	tanāb	طناب
cord	band	بند
wire (e.g. telephone ~)	sim	سیم
cable	kābl	کابل

sledgehammer	potk	پتک
prybar	deylam	دیلم
ladder	nardebān	نردبان
stepladder	nardebān-e sabok	نردبان سبک

to screw (tighten)	pič kardan	پیچ کردن
to unscrew (lid, filter, etc.)	bāz kardan	باز کردن
to tighten (e.g. with a clamp)	fešordan	فشردن
to glue, to stick	časbāndan	چسباندن
to cut (vt)	boridan	بریدن

malfunction (fault)	xarābi	خرابی
repair (mending)	ta'mir	تعمیر
to repair, to fix (vt)	ta'mir kardan	تعمیر کردن
to adjust (machine, etc.)	tanzim kardan	تنظیم کردن

to check (to examine)	barresi kardan	بررسی کردن
checking	barresi	بررسی
readings	dastgāh-e xaneš	دستگاه خوانش

| reliable, solid (machine) | motmaen | مطمئن |
| complex (adj) | pičide | پیچیده |

to rust (get rusted)	zang zadan	زنگ زدن
rusty (adj)	zang zade	زنگ زده
rust	zang	زنگ

Transport

169. Aeroplane

aeroplane	havāpeymā	هواپیما
air ticket	belit-e havāpeymā	بلیط هواپیما
airline	šerkat-e havāpeymāyi	شرکت هواپیمایی
airport	forudgāh	فرودگاه
supersonic (adj)	māvarā sowt	ماوراء صوت
captain	kāpitān	کاپیتان
crew	xadame	خدمه
pilot	xalabān	خلبان
stewardess	mehmāndār-e havāpeymā	مهماندار هواپیما
navigator	nāvbar	ناوبر
wings	bāl-hā	بال ها
tail	dam	دم
cockpit	kābin	کابین
engine	motor	موتور
undercarriage (landing gear)	šāssi	شاسی
turbine	turbin	توربین
propeller	parvāne	پروانه
black box	ja'be-ye siyāh	جعبه سیاه
yoke (control column)	farmān	فرمان
fuel	suxt	سوخت
safety card	dasturol'amal	دستورالعمل
oxygen mask	māsk-e oksižen	ماسک اکسیژن
uniform	oniform	اونیفورم
lifejacket	jeliqe-ye nejāt	جلیقة نجات
parachute	čatr-e nejāt	چترنجات
takeoff	parvāz	پرواز
to take off (vi)	parvāz kardan	پرواز کردن
runway	bānd-e forudgāh	باند فرودگاه
visibility	meydān did	میدان دید
flight (act of flying)	parvāz	پرواز
altitude	ertefā'	ارتفاع
air pocket	čāle-ye havāyi	چاله هوایی
seat	jā	جا
headphones	guši	گوشی
folding tray (tray table)	sini-ye tāšow	سینی تاشو
airplane window	panjere	پنجره
aisle	rāhrow	راهرو

170. Train

train	qatār	قطار
commuter train	qatār-e barqi	قطار برقی
express train	qatār-e sari'osseyr	قطارسریع السیر
diesel locomotive	lokomotiv-e dizel	لوکوموتیو دیزل
steam locomotive	lokomotiv-e boxar	لوکوموتیو بخار
coach, carriage	vāgon	واگن
buffet car	vāgon-e resturān	واگن رستوران
rails	reyl-hā	ریل ها
railway	rāh āhan	راه آهن
sleeper (track support)	reyl-e band	ریل بند
platform (railway ~)	sakku-ye rāh-āhan	سکوی راه آهن
platform (~ 1, 2, etc.)	masir	مسیر
semaphore	nešanar	نشانر
station	istgāh	ایستگاه
train driver	rānande	راننده
porter (of luggage)	bārbar	باربر
carriage attendant	rāhnamā-ye qatār	راهنمای قطار
passenger	mosāfer	مسافر
ticket inspector	kontorol či	کنترل چی
corridor (in train)	rāhrow	راهرو
emergency brake	tormoz-e ezterāri	ترمز اضطراری
compartment	kupe	کوپه
berth	taxt-e kupe	تخت کوپه
upper berth	taxt-e bālā	تخت بالا
lower berth	taxt-e pāyin	تخت پایین
bed linen, bedding	raxt-e xāb	رخت خواب
ticket	belit	بلیط
timetable	barnāme	برنامه
information display	barnāme-ye zamāni	برنامه زمانی
to leave, to depart	tark kardan	ترک کردن
departure (of train)	harekat	حرکت
to arrive (ab. train)	residan	رسیدن
arrival	vorud	ورود
to arrive by train	bā qatār āmadan	با قطار آمدن
to get on the train	savār-e qatār šodan	سوار قطار شدن
to get off the train	az qatār piyāde šodan	از قطار پیاده شدن
train crash	sānehe	سانحه
to derail (vi)	az xat xārej šodan	از خط خارج شدن
steam locomotive	lokomotiv-e boxar	لوکوموتیو بخار
stoker, fireman	ātaškār	آتشکار
firebox	ātašdān	آتشدان
coal	zoqāl sang	زغال سنگ

171. Ship

ship	kešti	کشتی
vessel	kešti	کشتی
steamship	kešti-ye boxāri	کشتی بخاری
riverboat	qāyeq-e rudxāne	قایق رودخانه
cruise ship	kešti-ye tafrihi	کشتی تفریحی
cruiser	razm nāv	رزم ناو
yacht	qāyeq-e tafrihi	قایق تفریحی
tugboat	yadak keš	یدک کش
barge	kešti-ye bārkeše yadaki	کشتی بارکش یدکی
ferry	kešti-ye farābar	کشتی فرابر
sailing ship	kešti-ye bādbāni	کشتی بادبانی
brigantine	košti dozdān daryā-yi	کشتی دزدان دریایی
ice breaker	kešti-ye yaxšekan	کشتی یخ شکن
submarine	zirdaryāyi	زیردریایی
boat (flat-bottomed ~)	qāyeq	قایق
dinghy	qāyeq-e tafrihi	قایق تفریحی
lifeboat	qāyeq-e nejāt	قایق نجات
motorboat	qāyeq-e motori	قایق موتوری
captain	kāpitān	کاپیتان
seaman	malavān	ملوان
sailor	malavān	ملوان
crew	xadame	خدمه
boatswain	sar malavān	سر ملوان
ship's boy	šāgerd-e malavān	شاگرد ملوان
cook	āšpaz-e kešti	آشپز کشتی
ship's doctor	pezešk-e kešti	پزشک کشتی
deck	arše-ye kešti	عرشهٔ کشتی
mast	dakal	دکل
sail	bādbān	بادبان
hold	anbār	انبار
bow (prow)	sine-ye kešti	سینه کشتی
stern	aqab kešti	عقب کشتی
oar	pāru	پارو
screw propeller	parvāne	پروانه
cabin	otāq-e kešti	اتاق کشتی
wardroom	otāq-e afsarān	اتاق افسران
engine room	motor xāne	موتور خانه
bridge	pol-e farmāndehi	پل فرماندهی
radio room	kābin-e bisim	کابین بی سیم
wave (radio)	mowj	موج
logbook	roxdād nāme	رخداد نامه
spyglass	teleskop	تلسکوپ
bell	nāqus	ناقوس

flag	parčam	پرچم
hawser (mooring ~)	tanāb	طناب
knot (bowline, etc.)	gereh	گره

| deckrails | narde | نرده |
| gangway | pol | پل |

anchor	langar	لنگر
to weigh anchor	langar kešidan	لنگر کشیدن
to drop anchor	langar andāxtan	لنگر انداختن
anchor chain	zanjir-e langar	زنجیر لنگر

port (harbour)	bandar	بندر
quay, wharf	eskele	اسکله
to berth (moor)	pahlu gereftan	پهلو گرفتن
to cast off	tark kardan	ترک کردن

trip, voyage	mosāferat	مسافرت
cruise (sea trip)	safar-e daryāyi	سفر دریایی
course (route)	masir	مسیر
route (itinerary)	masir	مسیر

fairway (safe water channel)	kešti-ye ru	کشتی رو
shallows	mahall-e kam omq	محل کم عمق
to run aground	be gel nešastan	به گل نشستن

storm	tufān	طوفان
signal	alāmat	علامت
to sink (vi)	qarq šodan	غرق شدن
Man overboard!	kas-i dar hāl-e qarq šodan-ast!	کسی در حال غرق شدن است!
SOS (distress signal)	sos	SOS
ring buoy	kamarband-e nejāt	کمربند نجات

172. Airport

airport	forudgāh	فرودگاه
aeroplane	havāpeymā	هواپیما
airline	šerkat-e havāpeymāyi	شرکت هواپیمایی
air traffic controller	ma'mur-e kontorol-e terāfik-e havāyi	مأمور کنترل ترافیک هوایی

departure	azimat	عزیمت
arrival	vorud	ورود
to arrive (by plane)	residan	رسیدن

| departure time | zamān-e parvāz | زمان پرواز |
| arrival time | zamān-e vorud | زمان ورود |

| to be delayed | ta'xir kardan | تأخیر کردن |
| flight delay | ta'xir-e parvāz | تأخیر پرواز |

| information board | tāblo-ye ettelā'āt | تابلوی اطلاعات |
| information | ettelā'āt | اطلاعات |

to announce (vt)	e'lām kardan	اعلام کردن
flight (e.g. next ~)	parvāz	پرواز
customs	gomrok	گمرک
customs officer	ma'mur-e gomrok	مأمور گمرک
customs declaration	ežhār-nāme	اظهارنامه
to fill in (vt)	por kardan	پر کردن
to fill in the declaration	ezhār-nāme rā por kardan	اظهارنامه را پر کردن
passport control	kontorol-e gozarnāme	کنترل گذرنامه
luggage	bār	بار
hand luggage	bār-e dasti	بار دستی
luggage trolley	čarx-e hamle bar	چرخ حمل بار
landing	forud	فرود
landing strip	bānd-e forudgāh	باند فرودگاه
to land (vi)	nešastan	نشستن
airstairs	pellekān	پلکان
check-in	ček in	چک این
check-in counter	bāje-ye kontorol	باجه کنترل
to check-in (vi)	čekin kardan	چکاین کردن
boarding card	kārt-e parvāz	کارت پرواز
departure gate	gi-yat xoruj	گیت خروج
transit	terānzit	ترانزیت
to wait (vt)	montazer budan	منتظر بودن
departure lounge	tālār-e entezār	تالار انتظار
to see off	badraqe kardan	بدرقه کردن
to say goodbye	xodāhāfezi kardan	خداحافظی کردن

173. Bicycle. Motorcycle

bicycle	dočarxe	دوچرخه
scooter	eskuter	اسکوتر
motorbike	motorsiklet	موتورسیکلت
to go by bicycle	bā dočarxe raftan	با دوچرخه رفتن
handlebars	farmān-e dočarxe	فرمان دوچرخه
pedal	pedāl	پدال
brakes	tormoz	ترمز
bicycle seat (saddle)	zin	زین
pump	pomp	پمپ
luggage rack	tarakband	ترکبند
front lamp	čerāq-e jelo	چراغ جلو
helmet	kolāh-e imeni	کلاه ایمنی
wheel	čarx	چرخ
mudguard	golgir	گلگیر
rim	towqe	طوقه
spoke	parre	پره

Cars

174. Types of cars

car	otomobil	اتومبيل
sports car	otomobil-e varzeši	اتومبيل ورزشی
limousine	limozin	ليموزين
off-road vehicle	jip	جيپ
drophead coupé (convertible)	kābriyole	كابريوليه
minibus	mini bus	مينی بوس
ambulance	āmbolāns	آمبولانس
snowplough	māšin-e barfrub	ماشين برف روب
lorry	kāmiyon	كاميون
road tanker	tānker	تانكر
van (small truck)	kāmiyon	كاميون
tractor unit	tereyler	تريلر
trailer	yadak	يدک
comfortable (adj)	rāhat	راحت
used (adj)	dast-e dovvom	دست دوم

175. Cars. Bodywork

bonnet	kāput	كاپوت
wing	golgir	گلگير
roof	saqf	سقف
windscreen	šiše-ye jelo	شيشه جلو
rear-view mirror	āyene-ye did-e aqab	آينه ديد عقب
windscreen washer	pak konande	پاک كننده
windscreen wipers	barf pāk kon	برف پاک كن
side window	šiše-ye baqal	شيشهٔ بغل
electric window	šiše bālābar	شيشه بالابر
aerial	ānten	آنتن
sunroof	sanrof	سانروف
bumper	separ	سپر
boot	sanduq-e aqab	صندوق عقب
roof luggage rack	bārband	باربند
door	darb	درب
door handle	dastgire-ye dar	دستگيرهٔ در
door lock	qofl	قفل
number plate	pelāk	پلاک
silencer	xafe kon	خفه كن

155

| petrol tank | bāk-e benzin | باک بنزین |
| exhaust pipe | lule-ye egzoz | لولۀ اگزوز |

accelerator	gāz	گاز
pedal	pedāl	پدال
accelerator pedal	pedāl-e gāz	پدال گاز

brake	tormoz	ترمز
brake pedal	pedāl-e tormoz	پدال ترمز
to brake (use the brake)	tormoz kardan	ترمز کردن
handbrake	tormoz-e dasti	ترمز دستی

clutch	kelāč	کلاچ
clutch pedal	pedāl-e kelāč	پدال کلاچ
clutch disc	disk-e kelāč	دیسک کلاچ
shock absorber	komak-e fanar	کمک فنر

wheel	čarx	چرخ
spare tyre	zāpās	زاپاس
wheel cover (hubcap)	qālpāq	قالپاق

driving wheels	čarxhā-ye moharrek	چرخ های محرک
front-wheel drive (as adj)	mehvarhā-ye jelo	محورهای جلو
rear-wheel drive (as adj)	mehvarhā-ye aqab	محورهای عقب
all-wheel drive (as adj)	tamām-e čarx	تمام چرخ

gearbox	ja'be-ye dande	جعبۀ دنده
automatic (adj)	otumātik	اتوماتیک
mechanical (adj)	mekāniki	مکانیکی
gear lever	ahrom-e ja'be dande	اهرم جعبه دنده

| headlamp | čerāq-e jelo | چراغ جلو |
| headlights | čerāq-hā | چراغ ها |

dipped headlights	nur-e pāin	نور پائین
full headlights	nur-e bālā	نور بالا
brake light	čerāq-e tormoz	چراغ ترمز

sidelights	čerāqhā-ye pārk	چراغ های پارک
hazard lights	čerāqha-ye xatar	چراغ های خطر
fog lights	čerāqhā-ye meh-e šekan	چراغ های مه شکن
turn indicator	čerāq-e rāhnamā	چراغ راهنما
reversing light	čerāq-e dande-ye aqab	چراغ دنده عقب

176. Cars. Passenger compartment

car inside (interior)	dāxel-e xodrow	داخل خودرو
leather (as adj)	čarmi	چرمی
velour (as adj)	maxmali	مخملی
upholstery	tuduzi	تودوزی

instrument (gage)	abzār	ابزار
dashboard	safhe-ye dāšbord	صفحه داشبورد
speedometer	sor'at sanj	سرعت سنج

needle (pointer)	aqrabe	عقربه
mileometer	kilumetr-e šomār	کیلومتر شمار
indicator (sensor)	nešāngar	نشانگر
level	sath	سطح
warning light	lāmp	لامپ

steering wheel	farmān	فرمان
horn	buq	بوق
button	dokme	دکمه
switch	kelid	کلید

seat	sandali	صندلی
backrest	pošti-ye sandali	پشتی صندلی
headrest	zir-e seri	زیر سری
seat belt	kamarband-e imeni	کمربند ایمنی
to fasten the belt	kamarband rā bastan	کمربند را بستن
adjustment (of seats)	tanzim	تنظیم

| airbag | kise-ye havā | کیسه هوا |
| air-conditioner | tahviye-ye matbu' | تهویه مطبوع |

radio	rādiyo	رادیو
CD player	paxš konande-ye si di	پخش کننده سی دی
to turn on	rowšan kardan	روشن کردن
aerial	ānten	آنتن
glove box	dāšbord	داشبورد
ashtray	zir-sigāri	زیرسیگاری

177. Cars. Engine

engine, motor	motor	موتور
diesel (as adj)	dizel	دیزل
petrol (as adj)	benzin	بنزین

engine volume	hajm-e motor	حجم موتور
power	niru	نیرو
horsepower	asb-e boxār	اسب بخار
piston	pistun	پیستون
cylinder	silandr	سیلندر
valve	supāp	سوپاپ

injector	anžektor	انژکتور
generator (alternator)	ženerātor	ژنراتور
carburettor	kārborātor	کاربراتور
motor oil	rowqan-e motor	روغن موتور

radiator	rādiyātor	رادیاتور
coolant	māye-'e sard konande	مایع سرد کننده
cooling fan	fan-e xonak konande	فن خنک کننده

battery (accumulator)	bātri-ye māšin	باتری ماشین
starter	estārt	استارت
ignition	ehterāq	احتراق
sparking plug	šam'-e motor	شمع موتور

terminal (of battery)	pāyāne	پایانه
positive terminal	mosbat	مثبت
negative terminal	manfi	منفی
fuse	fiyuz	فیوز
air filter	filter-e havā	فیلتر هوا
oil filter	filter-e rowqan	فیلتر روغن
fuel filter	filter-e suxt	فیلتر سوخت

178. Cars. Crash. Repair

car crash	tasādof	تصادف
traffic accident	tasādof	تصادف
to crash (into the wall, etc.)	barxord kardan	برخورد کردن
to get smashed up	tasādof kardan	تصادف کردن
damage	āsib	آسیب
intact (unscathed)	sālem	سالم
breakdown	xarābi	خرابی
to break down (vi)	xarāb šodan	خراب شدن
towrope	sim-e boksel	سیم بکسل
puncture	pančar	پنچر
to have a puncture	pančar šodan	پنچر شدن
to pump up	bād kardan	باد کردن
pressure	fešār	فشار
to check (to examine)	barresi kardan	بررسی کردن
repair	ta'mir	تعمیر
auto repair shop	ta'mirgāh-e xodro	تعمیرگاه خودرو
spare part	qet'e-ye yadaki	قطعه یدکی
part	qet'e	قطعه
bolt (with nut)	pič	پیچ
screw (fastener)	pič	پیچ
nut	mohre	مهره
washer	vāšer	واشر
bearing	yātāqān	یاتاقان
tube	lule	لوله
gasket (head ~)	vāšer	واشر
cable, wire	sim	سیم
jack	jak	جک
spanner	āčār	آچار
hammer	čakoš	چکش
pump	pomp	پمپ
screwdriver	pič gušti	پیچ گوشتی
fire extinguisher	kapsul-e ātašnešāni	کپسول آتش نشانی
warning triangle	alāmat-e ehtiyāt	علامت احتیاط
to stall (vi)	xāmuš šodan	خاموش شدن
stall (n)	tavaqqof	توقف

to be broken	xarāb budan	خراب بودن
to overheat (vi)	juš āvardan	جوش آوردن
to be clogged up	masdud šodan	مسدود شدن
to freeze up (pipes, etc.)	yax bastan	یخ بستن
to burst (vi, ab. tube)	tarakidan	ترکیدن

pressure	fešār	فشار
level	sath	سطح
slack (~ belt)	za'if	ضعیف

dent	foruraftegi	فرورفتگی
knocking noise (engine)	sedā	صدا
crack	tarak	ترک
scratch	xarāš	خراش

179. Cars. Road

road	rāh	راه
motorway	bozorgrāh	بزرگراه
highway	āzād-e rāh	آزاد راه
direction (way)	samt	سمت
distance	masāfat	مسافت

bridge	pol	پل
car park	pārking	پارکینگ
square	meydān	میدان
road junction	dowr bargardān	دوربرگردان
tunnel	tunel	تونل

petrol station	pomp-e benzin	پمپ بنزین
car park	pārking	پارکینگ
petrol pump	pomp-e benzin	پمپ بنزین
auto repair shop	ta'mirgāh-e xodro	تعمیرگاه خودرو
to fill up	benzin zadan	بنزین زدن
fuel	suxt	سوخت
jerrycan	dabbe	دبه

asphalt, tarmac	āsfālt	آسفالت
road markings	alāmat-e gozari	علامت گذاری
kerb	labe-ye jadval	لبه جدول
crash barrier	narde	نرده
ditch	juy	جوی
roadside (shoulder)	kenār rāh	کنار راه
lamppost	tir-e barq	تیر برق

to drive (a car)	rāndan	راندن
to turn (e.g., ~ left)	pičidan	پیچیدن
to make a U-turn	dowr zadan	دور زدن
reverse (~ gear)	dande aqab	دنده عقب

to honk (vi)	buq zadan	بوق زدن
honk (sound)	buq	بوق
to get stuck (in the mud, etc.)	gir kardan	گیر کردن
to spin the wheels	sor xordan	سر خوردن

to cut, to turn off (vt)	xāmuš kardan	خاموش کردن
speed	sor'at	سرعت
to exceed the speed limit	az sor'at-e mojāz gozāštan	ازسرعت مجاز گذشتن
to give a ticket	jarime kardan	جریمه کردن
traffic lights	čerāq-e rāhnamā	چراغ راهنما
driving licence	govāhi-nāme-ye rānandegi	گواهینامهٔ رانندگی
level crossing	taqāto'	تقاطع
crossroads	čahārrāh	چهارراه
zebra crossing	xatt-e āber-e piyāde	خط عابرپیاده
bend, curve	pič	پیچ
pedestrian precinct	mantaqe-ye āber-e piyāde	منطقهٔ عابر پیاده

180. Signs

Highway Code	āyinnāme-ye rāhnamāyi va rānandegi	آیین نامهٔ راهنمایی ورانندگی
road sign (traffic sign)	alāem-e rāhnamāyi-yo rānandegi	علائم راهنمایی ورانندگی
overtaking	sebqat	سبقت
curve	pič	پیچ
U-turn	dowr	دور
roundabout	harekat dar meydān	حرکت درمیدان
No entry	vorud-e mamnu'	ورود ممنوع
All vehicles prohibited	obur-e vasāyel-e naqliye mamnu'	عبور وسایل نقلیه ممنوع
No overtaking	sebqat mamnu'	سبقت ممنوع
No parking	pārk-e mamnu'	پارک ممنوع
No stopping	tavaqqof mamnu'	توقف ممنوع
dangerous curve	pič-e xatarnāk	پیچ خطرناک
steep descent	sarāšibi-ye tond	سراشیبی تند
one-way traffic	masir-e yektarafe	مسیر یک طرفه
zebra crossing	xatt-e āber-e piyāde	خط عابرپیاده
slippery road	jādde-ye laqzande	جاده لغزنده
GIVE WAY	re'āyat-e haq-e taqaddom	رعایت حق تقدم

PEOPLE. LIFE EVENTS

Life events

181. Holidays. Event

celebration, holiday	jašn	جشن
national day	eyd-e melli	عید ملی
public holiday	ruz-e jašn	روز جشن
to commemorate (vt)	jašn gereftan	جشن گرفتن

event (happening)	vāqe'e	واقعه
event (organized activity)	ruydād	رویداد
banquet (party)	ziyāfat	ضیافت
reception (formal party)	ziyāfat	ضیافت
feast	jašn	جشن

anniversary	sālgard	سالگرد
jubilee	sālgard	سالگرد
to celebrate (vt)	jašn gereftan	جشن گرفتن

New Year	sāl-e now	سال نو
Happy New Year!	sāl-e now mobārak	سال نو مبارک
Father Christmas	bābā noel	بابا نوئل

Christmas	kerismas	کریسمس
Merry Christmas!	kerismas mobārak!	کریسمس مبارک!
Christmas tree	kāj kerismas	کاج کریسمس
fireworks (fireworks show)	ātaš-e bāzi	آتش بازی

wedding	arusi	عروسی
groom	dāmād	داماد
bride	arus	عروس

to invite (vt)	da'vat kardan	دعوت کردن
invitation card	da'vatnāme	دعوتنامه

guest	mehmān	مهمان
to visit (~ your parents, etc.)	be mehmāni raftan	به مهمانی رفتن
to meet the guests	az mehmānān esteqbāl kardan	از مهمانان استقبال کردن

gift, present	hedye	هدیه
to give (sth as present)	hadye dādan	هدیه دادن
to receive gifts	hediye gereftan	هدیه گرفتن
bouquet (of flowers)	daste-ye gol	دسته گل

congratulations	tabrik	تبریک
to congratulate (vt)	tabrik goftan	تبریک گفتن

greetings card	kārt-e tabrik	کارت تبریک
to send a postcard	kārt-e tabrik ferestādan	کارت تبریک فرستادن
to get a postcard	kārt-e tabrik gereftan	کارت تبریک گرفتن

toast	be salāmati-ye kas-i nušidan	به سلامتی کسی نوشیدن
to offer (a drink, etc.)	pazirāyi kardan	پذیرایی کردن
champagne	šāmpāyn	شامپاین

to enjoy oneself	šādi kardan	شادی کردن
merriment (gaiety)	šādi	شادی
joy (emotion)	maserrat	مسرت

| dance | raqs | رقص |
| to dance (vi, vt) | raqsidan | رقصیدن |

| waltz | raqs-e vāls | رقص والس |
| tango | raqs tāngo | رقص تانگو |

182. Funerals. Burial

cemetery	qabrestān	قبرستان
grave, tomb	qabr	قبر
cross	salib	صلیب
gravestone	sang-e qabr	سنگ قبر
fence	hesār	حصار
chapel	kelisā-ye kučak	کلیسای کوچک

death	marg	مرگ
to die (vi)	mordan	مردن
the deceased	marhum	مرحوم
mourning	azā	عزا

to bury (vt)	dafn kardan	دفن کردن
undertakers	xadamat-e kafno dafn	خدمات کفن ودفن
funeral	tašyi-'e jenāze	تشییع جنازه
wreath	tāj-e gol	تاج گل
coffin	tābut	تابوت
hearse	na'š keš	نعش کش
shroud	kafan	کفن

funeral procession	tašyi-'e jenāze	تشییع جنازه
funerary urn	zarf-e xākestar-e morde	ظرف خاکستر مرده
crematorium	morde suz xāne	مرده سوز خانه

obituary	āgahi-ye tarhim	آگهی ترحیم
to cry (weep)	gerye kardan	گریه کردن
to sob (vi)	zār zār gerye kardan	زار زارگریه کردن

183. War. Soldiers

| platoon | daste | دسته |
| company | goruhān | گروهان |

regiment	hang	هنگ
army	arteš	ارتش
division	laškar	لشکر

section, squad	daste	دسته
host (army)	laškar	لشکر

soldier	sarbāz	سرباز
officer	afsar	افسر

private	sarbāz	سرباز
sergeant	goruhbān	گروهبان
lieutenant	sotvān	ستوان
captain	kāpitān	کاپیتان
major	sargord	سرگرد
colonel	sarhang	سرهنگ
general	ženerāl	ژنرال

sailor	malavān	ملوان
captain	kāpitān	کاپیتان
boatswain	sar malavān	سر ملوان

artilleryman	tupči	توپچی
paratrooper	sarbāz-e čatrbāz	سرباز چترباز
pilot	xalabān	خلبان
navigator	nāvbar	ناوبر
mechanic	mekānik	مکانیک

pioneer (sapper)	mohandes estehkāmāt	مهندس استحکامات
parachutist	čatr bāz	چترباز
reconnaissance scout	ettelā'āti	اطلاعاتی
sniper	tak tir andāz	تک تیر انداز

patrol (group)	gašt	گشت
to patrol (vt)	gašt zadan	گشت زدن
sentry, guard	negahbān	نگهبان

warrior	jangju	جنگجو
patriot	mihan parast	میهن پرست

hero	qahremān	قهرمان
heroine	qahremān-e zan	قهرمان زن

traitor	xāen	خائن
to betray (vt)	xiyānat kardan	خیانت کردن

deserter	farāri	فراری
to desert (vi)	farāri budan	فراری بودن

mercenary	mozdur	مزدور
recruit	sarbāz-e jadid	سرباز جدید
volunteer	dāvtalab	داوطلب

dead (n)	morde	مرده
wounded (n)	zaxmi	زخمی
prisoner of war	asir	اسیر

184. War. Military actions. Part 1

war	jang	جنگ
to be at war	jangidan	جنگیدن
civil war	jang-e dāxeli	جنگ داخلی
treacherously (adv)	xāenāne	خائنانه
declaration of war	e'lān-e jang	اعلان جنگ
to declare (~ war)	e'lān kardan	اعلان کردن
aggression	tajāvoz	تجاوز
to attack (invade)	hamle kardan	حمله کردن
to invade (vt)	tajāvoz kardan	تجاوز کردن
invader	tajāvozgar	تجاوزگر
conqueror	fāteh	فاتح
defence	defā'	دفاع
to defend (a country, etc.)	defā' kardan	دفاع کردن
to defend (against ...)	az xod defā' kardan	از خود دفاع کردن
enemy	došman	دشمن
foe, adversary	moxālef	مخالف
enemy (as adj)	došman	دشمن
strategy	rāhbord	راهبرد
tactics	tāktik	تاکتیک
order	farmān	فرمان
command (order)	dastur	دستور
to order (vt)	farmān dādan	فرمان دادن
mission	ma'muriyat	مأموریت
secret (adj)	mahramāne	محرمانه
battle	jang	جنگ
combat	nabard	نبرد
attack	hamle	حمله
charge (assault)	yureš	یورش
to storm (vt)	yureš bordan	یورش بردن
siege (to be under ~)	mohāsere	محاصره
offensive (n)	hamle	حمله
to go on the offensive	hamle kardan	حمله کردن
retreat	aqab nešini	عقب نشینی
to retreat (vi)	aqab nešini kardan	عقب نشینی کردن
encirclement	mohāsere	محاصره
to encircle (vt)	mohāsere kardan	محاصره کردن
bombing (by aircraft)	bombārān-e havāyi	بمباران هوایی
to drop a bomb	bomb āndaxtan	بمب انداختن
to bomb (vt)	bombārān kardan	بمباران کردن
explosion	enfejār	انفجار
shot	tirandāzi	تیراندازی

| to fire (~ a shot) | tirandāzi kardan | تیراندازی کردن |
| firing (burst of ~) | tirandāzi | تیراندازی |

to aim (to point a weapon)	nešāne raftan	نشانه رفتن
to point (a gun)	šhellik kardan	شلیک کردن
to hit (the target)	residan	رسیدن

to sink (~ a ship)	qarq šodan	غرق شدن
hole (in a ship)	surāx	سوراخ
to founder, to sink (vi)	qarq šodan	غرق شدن

front (war ~)	jebhe	جبهه
evacuation	taxliye	تخلیه
to evacuate (vt)	taxliye kardan	تخلیه کردن

trench	sangar	سنگر
barbed wire	sim-e xārdār	سیم خاردار
barrier (anti tank ~)	hesār	حصار
watchtower	borj	برج

military hospital	bimārestān-e nezāmi	بیمارستان نظامی
to wound (vt)	majruh kardan	مجروح کردن
wound	zaxm	زخم
wounded (n)	zaxmi	زخمی
to be wounded	zaxmi šodan	زخمی شدن
serious (wound)	zaxm-e saxt	زخم سخت

185. War. Military actions. Part 2

captivity	esārat	اسارت
to take captive	be esārat gereftan	به اسارت گرفتن
to be held captive	dar esārat budan	در اسارت بودن
to be taken captive	be esārat oftādan	به اسارت افتادن

concentration camp	ordugāh-e kār-e ejbāri	اردوگاه کار اجباری
prisoner of war	asir	اسیر
to escape (vi)	farār kardan	فرار کردن

to betray (vt)	xiyānat kardan	خیانت کردن
betrayer	xāen	خائن
betrayal	xiyānat	خیانت

| to execute (by firing squad) | tirbārān kardan | تیرباران کردن |
| execution (by firing squad) | tirbārān | تیرباران |

equipment (military gear)	uniform	یونیفرم
shoulder board	daraje-ye sarduši	درجه سردوشی
gas mask	māsk-e zedd-e gāz	ماسک ضد گاز

field radio	dastgāh-e bisim	دستگاه بی سیم
cipher, code	ramz	رمز
secrecy	mahramāne budan	محرمانه بودن
password	ramz	رمز
land mine	min	مین

| to mine (road, etc.) | min gozāštan | مین گذاشتن |
| minefield | meydān-e min | میدان مین |

air-raid warning	āžir-e havāyi	آژیر هوایی
alarm (alert signal)	āžir	آژیر
signal	alāmat	علامت
signal flare	monavvar	منور

headquarters	setād	ستاد
reconnaissance	šenāsāyi	شناسایی
situation	vaz'iyat	وضعیت
report	gozāreš	گزارش
ambush	kamin	کمین
reinforcement (of army)	taqviyat	تقویت

target	hadaf giri	هدف گیری
training area	meydān-e tir	میدان تیر
military exercise	mānovr	مانور

panic	vahšat	وحشت
devastation	xarābi	خرابی
destruction, ruins	xarābi-hā	خرابی ها
to destroy (vt)	xarāb kardan	خراب کردن

to survive (vi, vt)	zende māndan	زنده ماندن
to disarm (vt)	xal'-e selāh kardan	خلع سلاح کردن
to handle (~ a gun)	be kār bordan	به کار بردن

| Attention! | xabardār! | خبردار! |
| At ease! | āzād! | آزاد! |

act of courage	delāvari	دلاوری
oath (vow)	sowgand	سوگند
to swear (an oath)	sowgand xordan	سوگند خوردن

decoration (medal, etc.)	pādāš	پاداش
to award (give medal to)	medāl dādan	مدال دادن
medal	medāl	مدال
order (e.g. ~ of Merit)	nešān	نشان

victory	piruzi	پیروزی
defeat	šekast	شکست
armistice	ātaš bas	آتش بس

standard (battle flag)	parčam	پرچم
glory (honour, fame)	eftexār	افتخار
parade	reže	رژه
to march (on parade)	reže raftan	رژه رفتن

186. Weapons

weapons	selāh	سلاح
firearms	aslahe-ye garm	اسلحۀ گرم
cold weapons (knives, etc.)	aslahe-ye sard	اسلحۀ سرد

chemical weapons	taslihāt-e šimiyāyi	تسلیحات شیمیایی
nuclear (adj)	haste i	هسته ای
nuclear weapons	taslihāt-e hastei	تسلیحات هسته ای

| bomb | bomb | بمب |
| atomic bomb | bomb-e atomi | بمب اتمی |

pistol (gun)	kolt	کلت
rifle	tofang	تفنگ
submachine gun	mosalsal-e xodkār	مسلسل خودکار
machine gun	mosalsal	مسلسل

muzzle	sar-e lule-ye tofang	سر لوله تفنگ
barrel	lule-ye tofang	لوله تفنگ
calibre	kālibr	کالیبر

trigger	māše	ماشه
sight (aiming device)	nešāne ravi	نشانه روی
magazine	xešāb	خشاب
butt (shoulder stock)	qondāq	قنداق

| hand grenade | nārenjak | نارنجک |
| explosive | mādde-ye monfajere | مادۀ منفجره |

bullet	golule	گلوله
cartridge	fešang	فشنگ
charge	mohemmāt	مهمات
ammunition	mohemmāt	مهمات

bomber (aircraft)	bomb-afkan	بمبافکن
fighter	jangande	جنگنده
helicopter	helikopter	هلیکوپتر

anti-aircraft gun	tup-e zedd-e havāyi	توپ ضد هوایی
tank	tānk	تانک
tank gun	tup	توپ

artillery	tupxāne	توپخانه
gun (cannon, howitzer)	tofang	تفنگ
to lay (a gun)	šellik kardan	شلیک کردن

shell (projectile)	xompāre	خمپاره
mortar bomb	xompāre	خمپاره
mortar	xompāre andāz	خمپاره انداز
splinter (shell fragment)	tarkeš	ترکش

submarine	zirdaryāyi	زیردریایی
torpedo	eždar	اژدر
missile	mušak	موشک

to load (gun)	por kardan	پر کردن
to shoot (vi)	tirandāzi kardan	تیراندازی کردن
to point at (the cannon)	nešāne raftan	نشانه رفتن
bayonet	sarneyze	سرنیزه
rapier	šamšir	شمشیر
sabre (e.g. cavalry ~)	šamšir	شمشیر

spear (weapon)	neyze	نیزه
bow	kamān	کمان
arrow	tir	تیر
musket	tofang fetile-i	تفنگ فتیله‌ای
crossbow	kamān zanburak-i	کمان زنبورکی

187. Ancient people

primitive (prehistoric)	avvaliye	اولیه
prehistoric (adj)	piš az tārix	پیش از تاریخ
ancient (~ civilization)	qadimi	قدیمی

Stone Age	asr-e hajar	عصر حجر
Bronze Age	asr-e mafraq	عصر مفرغ
Ice Age	dowre-ye yaxbandān	دورهٔ یخبندان

tribe	qabile	قبیله
cannibal	ādam xār	آدم خوار
hunter	šekārči	شکارچی
to hunt (vi, vt)	šekār kardan	شکار کردن
mammoth	māmut	ماموت

cave	qār	غار
fire	ātaš	آتش
campfire	ātaš	آتش
cave painting	qār negāre	غار نگاره

tool (e.g. stone axe)	abzār-e kār	ابزار کار
spear	neyze	نیزه
stone axe	tabar-e sangi	تبر سنگی

| to be at war | jangidan | جنگیدن |
| to domesticate (vt) | rām kardan | رام کردن |

| idol | bot | بت |
| to worship (vt) | parastidan | پرستیدن |

| superstition | xorāfe | خرافه |
| rite | marāsem | مراسم |

| evolution | takāmol | تکامل |
| development | pišraft | پیشرفت |

| disappearance (extinction) | enqerāz | انقراض |
| to adapt oneself | sāzgār šodan | سازگار شدن |

archaeology	bāstān-šenāsi	باستان شناسی
archaeologist	bāstān-šenās	باستان شناس
archaeological (adj)	bāstān-šenāsi	باستان شناسی

excavation site	mahall-e haffārihā	محل حفاری ها
excavations	haffāri-hā	حفاری ها
find (object)	yāfteh	یافته
fragment	qet'e	قطعه

188. Middle Ages

people (ethnic group)	mellat	ملت
peoples	mellat-hā	ملت ها
tribe	qabile	قبیله
tribes	qabāyel	قبایل

barbarians	barbar-hā	بربر ها
Gauls	gul-hā	گول ها
Goths	gat-hā	گت ها
Slavs	eslāv-hā	اسلاو ها
Vikings	vāyking-hā	وایکینگ ها

| Romans | rumi-hā | رومی ها |
| Roman (adj) | rumi | رومی |

Byzantines	bizānsi-hā	بیزانسی ها
Byzantium	bizāns	بیزانس
Byzantine (adj)	bizānsi	بیزانسی

emperor	emperātur	امپراطور
leader, chief (tribal ~)	rahbar	رهبر
powerful (~ king)	moqtader	مقتدر
king	šāh	شاه
ruler (sovereign)	hākem	حاکم

knight	šovālie	شوالیه
feudal lord	feodāl	فئودال
feudal (adj)	feodāli	فئودالی
vassal	ra'yat	رعیت

duke	duk	دوک
earl	kont	کنت
baron	bāron	بارون
bishop	osqof	اسقف

armour	zereh	زره
shield	separ	سپر
sword	šamšir	شمشیر
visor	labe-ye kolāh	لبه کلاه
chainmail	jowšan	جوشن

| Crusade | jang-e salibi | جنگ صلیبی |
| crusader | jangju-ye salibi | جنگجوی صلیبی |

territory	qalamrow	قلمرو
to attack (invade)	hamle kardan	حمله کردن
to conquer (vt)	fath kardan	فتح کردن
to occupy (invade)	ešqāl kardan	اشغال کردن

siege (to be under ~)	mohāsere	محاصره
besieged (adj)	mahsur	محصور
to besiege (vt)	mohāsere kardan	محاصره کردن
inquisition	taftiš-e aqāyed	تفتیش عقاید
inquisitor	mofatteš	مفتش

torture	šekanje	شکنجه
cruel (adj)	bi rahm	بی رحم
heretic	molhed	ملحد
heresy	ertedād	ارتداد

seafaring	daryānavardi	دریانوردی
pirate	dozd-e daryāyi	دزد دریایی
piracy	dozdi-ye daryāyi	دزدی دریایی
boarding (attack)	hamle ruye arše	حمله روی عرشه
loot, booty	qanimat	غنیمت
treasures	ganj	گنج

discovery	kašf	کشف
to discover (new land, etc.)	kašf kardan	کشف کردن
expedition	safar	سفر

musketeer	tofangdār	تفنگدار
cardinal	kārdināl	کاردینال
heraldry	nešān-šenāsi	نشان شناسی
heraldic (adj)	manquš	منقوش

189. Leader. Chief. Authorities

king	šāh	شاه
queen	maleke	ملکه
royal (adj)	šāhi	شاهی
kingdom	pādšāhi	پادشاهی

| prince | šāhzāde | شاهزاده |
| princess | pranses | پرنسس |

president	ra'is jomhur	رئیس جمهور
vice-president	mo'āven-e rais-e jomhur	معاون رئیس جمهور
senator	senātor	سناتور

monarch	pādšāh	پادشاه
ruler (sovereign)	hākem	حاکم
dictator	diktātor	دیکتاتور
tyrant	zālem	ظالم
magnate	najib zāde	نجیب زاده

director	modir	مدیر
chief	ra'is	رئیس
manager (director)	modir	مدیر
boss	ra'is	رئیس
owner	sāheb	صاحب

leader	rahbar	رهبر
head (~ of delegation)	ra'is	رئیس
authorities	maqāmāt	مقامات
superiors	roasā	رؤسا

| governor | farmāndār | فرماندار |
| consul | konsul | کنسول |

diplomat	diplomāt	دیپلمات
mayor	šahrdār	شهردار
sheriff	kalāntar	کلانتر

emperor	emperātur	امپراطور
tsar, czar	tezār	تزار
pharaoh	fer'own	فرعون
khan	xān	خان

190. Road. Way. Directions

| road | rāh | راه |
| way (direction) | rāh | راه |

highway	āzād-e rāh	آزاد راه
motorway	bozorgrāh	بزرگراه
trunk road	rāh-e beyn-e eyālati	راه بین ایالتی

| main road | rāh-e asli | راه اصلی |
| dirt road | jādde-ye xāki | جاده خاکی |

| pathway | gozargāh | گذرگاه |
| footpath (troddenpath) | kure-ye rāh | کوره راه |

Where?	kojā?	کجا؟
Where (to)?	kojā?	کجا؟
From where?	az kojā?	از کجا؟

| direction (way) | samt | سمت |
| to point (~ the way) | nešān dādan | نشان دادن |

to the left	be čap	به چپ
to the right	be rāst	به راست
straight ahead (adv)	mostaqim be jelo	مستقیم به جلو
back (e.g. to turn ~)	be aqab	به عقب

bend, curve	pič	پیچ
to turn (e.g., ~ left)	pičidan	پیچیدن
to make a U-turn	dowr zadan	دور زدن

| to be visible (mountains, castle, etc.) | qābel-e mošāhede budan | قابل مشاهده بودن |
| to appear (come into view) | padidār šodan | پدیدار شدن |

stop, halt (e.g., during a trip)	tavaqqof	توقف
to rest, to pause (vi)	esterāhat kardan	استراحت کردن
rest (pause)	esterāhat	استراحت

to lose one's way	gom šodan	گم شدن
to lead to ... (ab. road)	be jā-yi bordan	به جایی بردن
to came out (e.g., on the highway)	residan be	رسیدن به
stretch (of road)	emtedād	امتداد
asphalt	āsfālt	آسفالت

kerb	labe-ye jadval	لبه جدول
ditch	juy	جوی
manhole	dariče	دریچه
roadside (shoulder)	kenār rāh	کنار راه
pit, pothole	gowdāl	گودال

| to go (on foot) | raftan | رفتن |
| to overtake (vt) | sebqat gereftan | سبقت گرفتن |

| step (footstep) | gām | گام |
| on foot (adv) | piyāde | پیاده |

to block (road)	masdud kardan	مسدود کردن
boom gate	māne'	مانع
dead end	bon bast	بن بست

191. Breaking the law. Criminals. Part 1

bandit	rāhzan	راهزن
crime	jenāyat	جنایت
criminal (person)	jenāyatkār	جنایتکار

thief	dozd	دزد
to steal (vi, vt)	dozdidan	دزدیدن
stealing (larceny)	dozdi	دزدی
theft	serqat	سرقت

to kidnap (vt)	ādam robudan	آدم ربودن
kidnapping	ādam robāyi	آدم ربایی
kidnapper	ādam robā	آدم ربا

| ransom | bāj | باج |
| to demand ransom | bāj xāstan | باج خواستن |

to rob (vt)	serqat kardan	سرقت کردن
robbery	serqat	سرقت
robber	qāratgar	غارتگر

to extort (vt)	axxāzi kardan	اخاذی کردن
extortionist	axxāz	اخاذ
extortion	axxāzi	اخاذی

to murder, to kill	koštan	کشتن
murder	qatl	قتل
murderer	qātel	قاتل

gunshot	tirandāzi	تیراندازی
to fire (~ a shot)	tirandāzi kardan	تیراندازی کردن
to shoot to death	bā tir zadan	با تیر زدن
to shoot (vi)	tirandāzi kardan	تیراندازی کردن
shooting	tirandāzi	تیراندازی

| incident (fight, etc.) | vāqe'e | واقعه |
| fight, brawl | zad-o xord | زد و خورد |

Help!	komak!	کمک!
victim	qorbāni	قربانی
to damage (vt)	xesārat resāndan	خسارت رساندن
damage	xesārat	خسارت
dead body, corpse	jasad	جسد
grave (~ crime)	vaxim	وخیم
to attack (vt)	hamle kardan	حمله کردن
to beat (to hit)	zadan	زدن
to beat up	kotak zadan	کتک زدن
to take (rob of sth)	bezur gereftan	به زور گرفتن
to stab to death	čāqu zadan	چاقو زدن
to maim (vt)	maʿyub kardan	معیوب کردن
to wound (vt)	majruh kardan	مجروح کردن
blackmail	šāntāž	شانتاژ
to blackmail (vt)	axxāzi kardan	اخاذی کردن
blackmailer	axxāz	اخاذ
protection racket	axxāzi	اخاذی
racketeer	axxāz	اخاذ
gangster	gāngester	گانگستر
mafia	māfiyā	مافیا
pickpocket	jib bor	جیب بر
burglar	sāreq	سارق
smuggling	qāčāq	قاچاق
smuggler	qāčāqči	قاچاقچی
forgery	qollābi	قلابی
to forge (counterfeit)	jaʿl kardan	جعل کردن
fake (forged)	jaʿli	جعلی

192. Breaking the law. Criminals. Part 2

rape	tajāvoz be nāmus	تجاوز به ناموس
to rape (vt)	tajāvoz kardan	تجاوز کردن
rapist	zenā konande	زنا کننده
maniac	majnun	مجنون
prostitute (fem.)	fāheše	فاحشه
prostitution	fāhešegi	فاحشگی
pimp	jākeš	جاکش
drug addict	moʿtād	معتاد
drug dealer	forušande-ye mavādd-e moxadder	فروشندهٔ مواد مخدر
to blow up (bomb)	monfajer kardan	منفجر کردن
explosion	enfejār	انفجار
to set fire	ātaš zadan	آتش زدن
arsonist	ātaš afruz	آتش افروز
terrorism	terorism	تروریسم

terrorist	terorist	تروریست
hostage	gerowgān	گروگان
to swindle (deceive)	farib dādan	فریب دادن
swindle, deception	farib	فریب
swindler	hoqqe bāz	حقه باز
to bribe (vt)	rešve dādan	رشوه دادن
bribery	rešve	رشوه
bribe	rešve	رشوه
poison	zahr	زهر
to poison (vt)	masmum kardan	مسموم کردن
to poison oneself	masmum šodan	مسموم شدن
suicide (act)	xod-koši	خودکشی
suicide (person)	xod-koši konande	خودکشی کننده
to threaten (vt)	tahdid kardan	تهدید کردن
threat	tahdid	تهدید
to make an attempt	su'-e qasd kardan	سوء قصد کردن
attempt (attack)	su'-e qasd	سوء قصد
to steal (a car)	robudan	ربودن
to hijack (a plane)	havāpeymā robāyi	هواپیما ربایی
revenge	enteqām	انتقام
to avenge (get revenge)	enteqām gereftan	انتقام گرفتن
to torture (vt)	šekanje dādan	شکنجه دادن
torture	šekanje	شکنجه
to torment (vt)	aziyat kardan	اذیت کردن
pirate	dozd-e daryāyi	دزد دریایی
hooligan	owbāš	اوباش
armed (adj)	mosallah	مسلح
violence	xošunat	خشونت
illegal (unlawful)	qeyr-e qānuni	غیر قانونی
spying (espionage)	jāsusi	جاسوسی
to spy (vi)	jāsusi kardan	جاسوسی کردن

193. Police. Law. Part 1

justice	edālat	عدالت
court (see you in ~)	dādgāh	دادگاه
judge	qāzi	قاضی
jurors	hey'at-e monsefe	هیئت منصفه
jury trial	hey'at-e monsefe	هیئت منصفه
to judge (vt)	mohākeme kardan	محاکمه کردن
lawyer, barrister	vakil	وکیل
defendant	mottaham	متهم

dock	jāygāh-e mottaham	جایگاه متهم
charge	ettehām	اتهام
accused	mottaham	متهم
sentence	hokm	حکم
to sentence (vt)	mahkum kardan	محکوم کردن
guilty (culprit)	moqasser	مقصر
to punish (vt)	mojāzāt kardan	مجازات کردن
punishment	mojāzāt	مجازات
fine (penalty)	jarime	جریمه
life imprisonment	habs-e abad	حبس ابد
death penalty	e'dām	اعدام
electric chair	sandali-ye barqi	صندلی برقی
gallows	čube-ye dār	چوبه دار
to execute (vt)	e'dām kardan	اعدام کردن
execution	e'dām	اعدام
prison	zendān	زندان
cell	sellul-e zendān	سلول زندان
escort	eskort	اسکورت
prison officer	negahbān zendān	نگهبان زندان
prisoner	zendāni	زندانی
handcuffs	dastband	دستبند
to handcuff (vt)	dastband zadan	دستبند زدن
prison break	farār	فرار
to break out (vi)	farār kardan	فرار کردن
to disappear (vi)	nāpadid šodan	ناپدید شدن
to release (from prison)	āzād kardan	آزاد کردن
amnesty	afv-e omumi	عفو عمومی
police	polis	پلیس
police officer	polis	پلیس
police station	kalāntari	کلانتری
truncheon	bātum	باتوم
megaphone (loudhailer)	bolandgu	بلندگو
patrol car	māšin-e gašt	ماشین گشت
siren	āžir-e xatar	آژیر خطر
to turn on the siren	āžir rā rowšan kardan	آژیررا روشن کردن
siren call	sedā-ye āžir	صدای آژیر
crime scene	mahall-e jenāyat	محل جنایت
witness	šāhed	شاهد
freedom	āzādi	آزادی
accomplice	hamdast	همدست
to flee (vi)	maxfi šodan	مخفی شدن
trace (to leave a ~)	rad	رد

194. Police. Law. Part 2

search (investigation)	jostoju	جستجو
to look for ...	jostoju kardan	جستجو کردن
suspicion	šok	شک
suspicious (e.g., ~ vehicle)	maškuk	مشکوک
to stop (cause to halt)	motevaghef kardan	متوقف کردن
to detain (keep in custody)	dastgir kardan	دستگیر کردن
case (lawsuit)	parvande	پرونده
investigation	tahqiq	تحقیق
detective	kārāgāh	کارآگاه
investigator	bāzpors	بازپرس
hypothesis	farziye	فرضیه
motive	angize	انگیزه
interrogation	bāzporsi	بازپرسی
to interrogate (vt)	bāzporsi kardan	بازپرسی کردن
to question	estentāq kardan	استنطاق کردن
(~ neighbors, etc.)		
check (identity ~)	taftiš	تفتیش
round-up	mohāsere	محاصره
search (~ warrant)	taftiš	تفتیش
chase (pursuit)	ta'qib	تعقیب
to pursue, to chase	ta'qib kardan	تعقیب کردن
to track (a criminal)	donbāl kardan	دنبال کردن
arrest	bāzdāšt	بازداشت
to arrest (sb)	bāzdāšt kardan	بازداشت کردن
to catch (thief, etc.)	dastgir kardan	دستگیر کردن
capture	dastgiri	دستگیری
document	sanad	سند
proof (evidence)	esbāt	اثبات
to prove (vt)	esbāt kardan	اثبات کردن
footprint	rad-e pā	رد پا
fingerprints	asar-e angošt	اثر انگشت
piece of evidence	šavāhed	شواهد
alibi	ozr-e qeybat	عذر غیبت
innocent (not guilty)	bi gonāh	بی گناه
injustice	bi edālati	بی عدالتی
unjust, unfair (adj)	qeyr-e ādelāne	غیر عادلانه
criminal (adj)	jenāyi	جنایی
to confiscate (vt)	mosādere kardan	مصادره کردن
drug (illegal substance)	mavādd-e moxadder	مواد مخدر
weapon, gun	selāh	سلاح
to disarm (vt)	xal'-e selāh kardan	خلع سلاح کردن
to order (command)	farmān dādan	فرمان دادن
to disappear (vi)	nāpadid šodan	ناپدید شدن
law	qānun	قانون
legal, lawful (adj)	qānuni	قانونی

illegal, illicit (adj)	qeyr-e qānuni	غیر قانونی
responsibility (blame)	mas'uliyat	مسئولیت
responsible (adj)	mas'ul	مسئول

NATURE

The Earth. Part 1

195. Outer space

space	fazā	فضا
space (as adj)	fazāyi	فضایی
outer space	fazā-ye keyhān	فضای کیهان
world	jahān	جهان
universe	giti	گیتی
galaxy	kahkešān	کهکشان
star	setāre	ستاره
constellation	surat-e falaki	صورت فلکی
planet	sayyāre	سیاره
satellite	māhvāre	ماهواره
meteorite	sang-e āsmāni	سنگ آسمانی
comet	setāre-ye donbāle dār	ستارهٔ دنباله دار
asteroid	šahāb	شهاب
orbit	madār	مدار
to revolve	gardidan	گردیدن
(~ around the Earth)		
atmosphere	jav	جو
the Sun	āftāb	آفتاب
solar system	manzume-ye šamsi	منظومه شمسی
solar eclipse	kosuf	کسوف
the Earth	zamin	زمین
the Moon	māh	ماه
Mars	merrix	مریخ
Venus	zahre	زهره
Jupiter	moštari	مشتری
Saturn	zohal	زحل
Mercury	atārod	عطارد
Uranus	orānus	اورانوس
Neptune	nepton	نپتون
Pluto	poloton	پلوتون
Milky Way	kahkešān rāh-e širi	کهکشان راه شیری
Great Bear (Ursa Major)	dobb-e akbar	دب اکبر
North Star	setāre-ye qotbi	ستاره قطبی
Martian	merrixi	مریخی

extraterrestrial (n)	farā zamini	فرا زمینی
alien	mowjud fazāyi	موجود فضایی
flying saucer	bošqāb-e parande	بشقاب پرنده

spaceship	fazā peymā	فضا پیما
space station	istgāh-e fazāyi	ایستگاه فضایی
blast-off	rāh andāzi	راه اندازی

engine	motor	موتور
nozzle	nāzel	نازل
fuel	suxt	سوخت

cockpit, flight deck	kābin	کابین
aerial	ānten	آنتن
porthole	panjere	پنجره
solar panel	bātri-ye xoršidi	باطری خورشیدی
spacesuit	lebās-e fazānavardi	لباس فضانوردی

| weightlessness | bi vazni | بی وزنی |
| oxygen | oksižen | اکسیژن |

| docking (in space) | vasl | وصل |
| to dock (vi, vt) | vasl kardan | وصل کردن |

observatory	rasadxāne	رصدخانه
telescope	teleskop	تلسکوپ
to observe (vt)	mošāhede kardan	مشاهده کردن
to explore (vt)	kašf kardan	کشف کردن

196. The Earth

the Earth	zamin	زمین
the globe (the Earth)	kare-ye zamin	کرۀ زمین
planet	sayyāre	سیاره

atmosphere	jav	جو
geography	joqrāfiyā	جغرافیا
nature	tabi'at	طبیعت

globe (table ~)	kare-ye joqrāfiyāyi	کرۀ جغرافیایی
map	naqše	نقشه
atlas	atlas	اطلس

Europe	orupā	اروپا
Asia	āsiyā	آسیا
Africa	āfriqā	آفریقا
Australia	ostorāliyā	استرالیا

America	emrikā	امریکا
North America	emrikā-ye šomāli	امریکای شمالی
South America	emrikā-ye jonubi	امریکای جنوبی

| Antarctica | qotb-e jonub | قطب جنوب |
| the Arctic | qotb-e šomāl | قطب شمال |

197. Cardinal directions

north	šomāl	شمال
to the north	be šomāl	به شمال
in the north	dar šomāl	در شمال
northern (adj)	šomāli	شمالی
south	jonub	جنوب
to the south	be jonub	به جنوب
in the south	dar jonub	در جنوب
southern (adj)	jonubi	جنوبی
west	qarb	غرب
to the west	be qarb	به غرب
in the west	dar qarb	در غرب
western (adj)	qarbi	غربی
east	šarq	شرق
to the east	be šarq	به شرق
in the east	dar šarq	در شرق
eastern (adj)	šarqi	شرقی

198. Sea. Ocean

sea	daryā	دریا
ocean	oqyānus	اقیانوس
gulf (bay)	xalij	خلیج
straits	tange	تنگه
land (solid ground)	zamin	زمین
continent (mainland)	qāre	قاره
island	jazire	جزیره
peninsula	šeb-e jazire	شبه جزیره
archipelago	majma'-ol-jazāyer	مجمع‌الجزایر
bay, cove	xalij-e kučak	خلیج کوچک
harbour	langargāh	لنگرگاه
lagoon	mordāb	مرداب
cape	damāqe	دماغه
atoll	jazire-ye marjāni	جزیره مرجانی
reef	tappe-ye daryāyi	تپه دریایی
coral	marjān	مرجان
coral reef	tappe-ye marjāni	تپه مرجانی
deep (adj)	amiq	عمیق
depth (deep water)	omq	عمق
abyss	partgāh	پرتگاه
trench (e.g. Mariana ~)	derāz godāl	درازگودال
current (Ocean ~)	jaryān	جریان
to surround (bathe)	ehāte kardan	احاطه کردن

| shore | sāhel | ساحل |
| coast | sāhel | ساحل |

flow (flood tide)	mod	مد
ebb (ebb tide)	jazr	جزر
shoal	sāhel-e šeni	ساحل شنی
bottom (~ of the sea)	qa'r	قعر

wave	mowj	موج
crest (~ of a wave)	nok	نوک
spume (sea foam)	kaf	کف

storm (sea storm)	tufān-e daryāyi	طوفان دریایی
hurricane	tufān	طوفان
tsunami	sonāmi	سونامی
calm (dead ~)	sokun-e daryā	سکون دریا
quiet, calm (adj)	ārām	آرام

| pole | qotb | قطب |
| polar (adj) | qotbi | قطبی |

latitude	arz-e joqrāfiyāyi	عرض جغرافیایی
longitude	tul-e joqrāfiyāyi	طول جغرافیایی
parallel	movāzi	موازی
equator	xatt-e ostavā	خط استوا

sky	āsemān	آسمان
horizon	ofoq	افق
air	havā	هوا

lighthouse	fānus-e daryāyi	فانوس دریایی
to dive (vi)	širje raftan	شیرجه رفتن
to sink (ab. boat)	qarq šodan	غرق شدن
treasures	ganj	گنج

199. Seas & Oceans names

Atlantic Ocean	oqyānus-e atlas	اقیانوس اطلس
Indian Ocean	oqyānus-e hend	اقیانوس هند
Pacific Ocean	oqyānus-e ārām	اقیانوس آرام
Arctic Ocean	oqyānus-e monjamed-e šomāli	اقیانوس منجمد شمالی

Black Sea	daryā-ye siyāh	دریای سیاه
Red Sea	daryā-ye sorx	دریای سرخ
Yellow Sea	daryā-ye zard	دریای زرد
White Sea	daryā-ye sefid	دریای سفید

Caspian Sea	daryā-ye xazar	دریای خزر
Dead Sea	daryā-ye morde	دریای مرده
Mediterranean Sea	daryā-ye meditarāne	دریای مدیترانه

| Aegean Sea | daryā-ye eže | دریای اژه |
| Adriatic Sea | daryā-ye ādriyātik | دریای آدریاتیک |

Arabian Sea	daryā-ye arab	دریای عرب
Sea of Japan	daryā-ye žāpon	دریای ژاپن
Bering Sea	daryā-ye brinq	دریای برینگ
South China Sea	daryā-ye čin-e jonubi	دریای چین جنوبی

Coral Sea	daryā-ye marjān	دریای مرجان
Tasman Sea	daryā-ye tās-emān	دریای تاسمان
Caribbean Sea	daryā-ye kārāib	دریای کارائیب

| Barents Sea | daryā-ye barntz | دریای بارنتز |
| Kara Sea | daryā-ye kārā | دریای کارا |

North Sea	daryā-ye šomāl	دریای شمال
Baltic Sea	daryā-ye bāltik	دریای بالتیک
Norwegian Sea	daryā-ye norvež	دریای نروژ

200. Mountains

mountain	kuh	کوه
mountain range	rešte-ye kuh	رشته کوه
mountain ridge	selsele-ye jebāl	سلسله جبال

summit, top	qolle	قله
peak	qolle	قله
foot (~ of the mountain)	dāmane-ye kuh	دامنهٔ کوه
slope (mountainside)	šib	شیب

volcano	ātaš-fešān	آتشفشان
active volcano	ātaš-fešān-e faʿāl	آتش فشان فعال
dormant volcano	ātaš-fešān-e xāmuš	آتش فشان خاموش

eruption	favarān	فوران
crater	dahāne-ye ātašfešān	دهانهٔ آتش فشان
magma	māgmā	ماگما
lava	godāze	گدازه
molten (~ lava)	godāxte	گداخته

canyon	tange	تنگه
gorge	darre-ye tang	دره تنگ
crevice	tange	تنگه
abyss (chasm)	partgāh	پرتگاه

pass, col	gozargāh	گذرگاه
plateau	falāt	فلات
cliff	saxre	صخره
hill	tappe	تپه

glacier	yaxčāl	یخچال
waterfall	ābšār	آبشار
geyser	češme-ye āb-e garm	چشمهٔ آب گرم
lake	daryāče	دریاچه

| plain | jolge | جلگه |
| landscape | manzare | منظره |

echo	en'ekās-e sowt	انعکاس صوت
alpinist	kuhnavard	کوهنورد
rock climber	saxre-ye navard	صخره نورد
to conquer (in climbing)	fath kardan	فتح کردن
climb (an easy ~)	so'ud	صعود

201. Mountains names

The Alps	ālp	آلپ
Mont Blanc	moan belān	مون بلان
The Pyrenees	pirene	پیرنه

The Carpathians	kuhhā-ye kārpāt	کوههای کارپات
The Ural Mountains	kuhe-i orāl	کوههای اورال
The Caucasus Mountains	qafqāz	قفقاز
Mount Elbrus	alborz	البرز

The Altai Mountains	āltāy	آلتای
The Tian Shan	tiyān šān	تیان شان
The Pamir Mountains	pāmir	پامیر
The Himalayas	himāliyā-vo	هیمالیا
Mount Everest	everest	اورست

| The Andes | ānd | آند |
| Mount Kilimanjaro | kelimānjāro | کلیمانجارو |

202. Rivers

river	rudxāne	رودخانه
spring (natural source)	češme	چشمه
riverbed (river channel)	bastar	بستر
basin (river valley)	howze	حوضه
to flow into ...	rixtan	ریختن

| tributary | enše'āb | انشعاب |
| bank (of river) | sāhel | ساحل |

current (stream)	jaryān	جریان
downstream (adv)	be samt-e pāin-e rudxāne	به سمت پائین رودخانه
upstream (adv)	be samt-e bālā-ye rudxāne	به سمت بالای رودخانه

inundation	seyl	سیل
flooding	toqyān	طغیان
to overflow (vi)	toqyān kardan	طغیان کردن
to flood (vt)	toqyān kardan	طغیان کردن

| shallow (shoal) | tangāb | تنگاب |
| rapids | tondāb | تندآب |

dam	sad	سد
canal	kānāl	کانال
reservoir (artificial lake)	maxzan-e āb	مخزن آب

sluice, lock	ābgir	آبگیر
water body (pond, etc.)	maxzan-e āb	مخزن آب
swamp (marshland)	bātlāq	باتلاق
bog, marsh	lajan zār	لجن زار
whirlpool	gerdāb	گرداب
stream (brook)	ravad	رود
drinking (ab. water)	āšāmidani	آشامیدنی
fresh (~ water)	širin	شیرین
ice	yax	یخ
to freeze over (ab. river, etc.)	yax bastan	یخ بستن

203. Rivers names

Seine	sen	سن
Loire	lavār	لوآر
Thames	timz	تیمز
Rhine	rāyn	راین
Danube	dānub	دانوب
Volga	volgā	ولگا
Don	don	دن
Lena	lenā	لنا
Yellow River	rud-e zard	رود زرد
Yangtze	yāng tese	یانگ تسه
Mekong	mekung	مکونگ
Ganges	gong	گنگ
Nile River	neyl	نیل
Congo River	kongo	کنگو
Okavango River	okavango	اوکاوانگو
Zambezi River	zāmbezi	زامبزی
Limpopo River	rud-e limpupu	رود لیمپوپو
Mississippi River	mi si si pi	می سی سی پی

204. Forest

forest, wood	jangal	جنگل
forest (as adj)	jangali	جنگلی
thick forest	jangal-e anbuh	جنگل انبوه
grove	biše	بیشه
forest clearing	marqzār	مرغزار
thicket	biše-hā	بیشه ها
scrubland	bute zār	بوته زار
footpath (troddenpath)	kure-ye rāh	کوره راه
gully	darre	دره

tree	deraxt	درخت
leaf	barg	برگ
leaves (foliage)	šāx-o barg	شاخ و برگ

fall of leaves	barg rizi	برگ ریزی
to fall (ab. leaves)	rixtan	ریختن
top (of the tree)	nok	نوک

branch	šāxe	شاخه
bough	šāxe	شاخه
bud (on shrub, tree)	šokufe	شکوفه
needle (of pine tree)	suzan	سوزن
fir cone	maxrut-e kāj	مخروط کاج

hollow (in a tree)	surāx	سوراخ
nest	lāne	لانه
burrow (animal hole)	lāne	لانه

trunk	tane	تنه
root	riše	ریشه
bark	pust	پوست
moss	xaze	خزه

to uproot (remove trees or tree stumps)	rišekan kardan	ریشه کن کردن
to chop down	boridan	بریدن
to deforest (vt)	boridan	بریدن
tree stump	kande-ye deraxt	کندۀ درخت

campfire	ātaš	آتش
forest fire	ātaš suzi	آتش سوزی
to extinguish (vt)	xāmuš kardan	خاموش کردن

forest ranger	jangal bān	جنگل بان
protection	mohāfezat	محافظت
to protect (~ nature)	mohāfezat kardan	محافظت کردن
poacher	šekārči-ye qeyr-e qānuni	شکارچی غیر قانونی
steel trap	tale	تله

| to gather, to pick (vt) | čidan | چیدن |
| to lose one's way | gom šodan | گم شدن |

205. Natural resources

natural resources	manābe-'e tabii	منابع طبیعی
minerals	mavādd-e ma'dani	مواد معدنی
deposits	tah nešast	ته نشست
field (e.g. oilfield)	meydān	میدان

to mine (extract)	estexrāj kardan	استخراج کردن
mining (extraction)	estexrāj	استخراج
ore	sang-e ma'dani	سنگ معدنی
mine (e.g. for coal)	ma'dan	معدن
shaft (mine ~)	ma'dan	معدن

miner	ma'danči	معدنچی
gas (natural ~)	gāz	گاز
gas pipeline	lule-ye gāz	لولهٔ گاز
oil (petroleum)	naft	نفت
oil pipeline	lule-ye naft	لولهٔ نفت
oil well	čāh-e naft	چاه نفت
derrick (tower)	dakal-e haffāri	دکل حفاری
tanker	tānker	تانکر
sand	šen	شن
limestone	sang-e āhak	سنگ آهک
gravel	sangrize	سنگریزه
peat	turb	تورب
clay	xāk-e ros	خاک رس
coal	zoqāl sang	زغال سنگ
iron (ore)	āhan	آهن
gold	talā	طلا
silver	noqre	نقره
nickel	nikel	نیکل
copper	mes	مس
zinc	ruy	روی
manganese	mangenez	منگنز
mercury	jive	جیوه
lead	sorb	سرب
mineral	mādde-ye ma'dani	مادهٔ معدنی
crystal	bolur	بلور
marble	marmar	مرمر
uranium	orāniyom	اورانیوم

The Earth. Part 2

206. Weather

weather	havā	هوا
weather forecast	piš bini havā	پیش بینی هوا
temperature	damā	دما
thermometer	damāsanj	دماسنج
barometer	havāsanj	هواسنج
humid (adj)	martub	مرطوب
humidity	rotubat	رطوبت
heat (extreme ~)	garmā	گرما
hot (torrid)	dāq	داغ
it's hot	havā xeyli garm ast	هوا خیلی گرم است
it's warm	havā garm ast	هوا گرم است
warm (moderately hot)	garm	گرم
it's cold	sard ast	سرد است
cold (adj)	sard	سرد
sun	āftāb	آفتاب
to shine (vi)	tābidan	تابیدن
sunny (day)	āftābi	آفتابی
to come up (vi)	tolu' kardan	طلوع کردن
to set (vi)	qorob kardan	غروب کردن
cloud	abr	ابر
cloudy (adj)	abri	ابری
rain cloud	abr-e bārānzā	ابر باران زا
somber (gloomy)	tire	تیره
rain	bārān	باران
it's raining	bārān mibārad	باران می بارد
rainy (~ day, weather)	bārāni	بارانی
to drizzle (vi)	nam-nam bāridan	نم نم باریدن
pouring rain	bārān šodid	باران شدید
downpour	ragbār	رگبار
heavy (e.g. ~ rain)	šadid	شدید
puddle	čāle	چاله
to get wet (in rain)	xis šodan	خیس شدن
fog (mist)	meh	مه
foggy	meh ālud	مه آلود
snow	barf	برف
it's snowing	barf mibārad	برف می بارد

207. Severe weather. Natural disasters

thunderstorm	tufān	طوفان
lightning (~ strike)	barq	برق
to flash (vi)	barq zadan	برق زدن
thunder	ra'd	رعد
to thunder (vi)	qorridan	غریدن
it's thundering	ra'd mizanad	رعد می زند
hail	tagarg	تگرگ
it's hailing	tagarg mibārad	تگرگ می بارد
to flood (vt)	toqyān kardan	طغیان کردن
flood, inundation	seyl	سیل
earthquake	zamin-larze	زمین لرزه
tremor, quake	tekān	تکان
epicentre	kānun-e zaminlarze	کانون زمین لرزه
eruption	favarān	فوران
lava	godāze	گدازه
twister, tornado	gerdbād	گردباد
typhoon	tufān	طوفان
hurricane	tufān	طوفان
storm	tufān	طوفان
tsunami	sonāmi	سونامی
cyclone	gerdbād	گردباد
bad weather	havā-ye bad	هوای بد
fire (accident)	ātaš suzi	آتش سوزی
disaster	balā-ye tabi'i	بلای طبیعی
meteorite	sang-e āsmāni	سنگ آسمانی
avalanche	bahman	بهمن
snowslide	bahman	بهمن
blizzard	kulāk	کولاک
snowstorm	barf-o burān	برف و بوران

208. Noises. Sounds

silence (quiet)	sokut	سکوت
sound	sedā	صدا
noise	sar-o sedā	سر و صدا
to make noise	sar-o sedā kardan	سر و صدا کردن
noisy (adj)	por sar-o sedā	پر سر و صدا
loudly (to speak, etc.)	boland	بلند
loud (voice, etc.)	boland	بلند
constant (e.g., ~ noise)	dāemi	دائمی
cry, shout (n)	faryād	فریاد

to cry, to shout (vi)	faryād zadan	فریاد زدن
whisper	najvā	نجوا
to whisper (vi, vt)	najvā kardan	نجوا کردن
barking (dog's ~)	vāq vāq	واق واق
to bark (vi)	vāq-vāq kardan	واق واق کردن
groan (of pain, etc.)	nāle	ناله
to groan (vi)	nāle kardan	ناله کردن
cough	sorfe	سرفه
to cough (vi)	sorfe kardan	سرفه کردن
whistle	sut	سوت
to whistle (vi)	sut zadan	سوت زدن
knock (at the door)	dar zadan	درزدن
to knock (at the door)	dar zadan	درزدن
to crack (vi)	šekastan	شکستن
crack (cracking sound)	tarak	ترک
siren	āžir-e xatar	آژیر خطر
whistle (factory ~, etc.)	buq	بوق
to whistle (ab. train)	buq zadan	بوق زدن
honk (car horn sound)	buq	بوق
to honk (vi)	buq zadan	بوق زدن

209. Winter

winter (n)	zemestān	زمستان
winter (as adj)	zemestāni	زمستانی
in winter	dar zemestān	در زمستان
snow	barf	برف
it's snowing	barf mibārad	برف می بارد
snowfall	bāreš-e barf	بارش برف
snowdrift	tappe-ye barf	تپۀ برف
snowflake	barf-e rize	برف ریزه
snowball	golule-ye barf	گلولۀ برف
snowman	ādam-e barfi	آدم برفی
icicle	qandil	قندیل
December	desāmr	دسامبر
January	žānvie	ژانویه
February	fevriye	فوریه
frost (severe ~, freezing cold)	yaxbandān	یخبندان
frosty (weather, air)	sard	سرد
below zero (adv)	zir-e sefr	زیر صفر
first frost	avalin moje sarmā	اولین موج سرما
hoarfrost	barf-e rize	برف ریزه
cold (cold weather)	sarmā	سرما
it's cold	sard ast	سرد است

fur coat	pālto-ye pustin	پالتوی پوستین
mittens	dastkeš-e yek angošti	دستکش یک انگشتی
to fall ill	bimār šodan	بیمار شدن
cold (illness)	sarmā xordegi	سرما خوردگی
to catch a cold	sarmā xordan	سرما خوردن
ice	yax	یخ
black ice	lāye-ye yax	لایه یخ
to freeze over (ab. river, etc.)	yax bastan	یخ بستن
ice floe	tekke-ye yax-e šenāvar	تکه یخ شناور
skis	eski	اسکی
skier	eski bāz	اسکی باز
to ski (vi)	eski kardan	اسکی کردن
to skate (vi)	eskeyt bāzi kardan	اسکیت بازی کردن

Fauna

210. Mammals. Predators

English	Persian (transliteration)	Persian
predator	heyvān-e darande	حیوان درنده
tiger	bebar	ببر
lion	šir	شیر
wolf	gorg	گرگ
fox	rubāh	روباه
jaguar	jagvār	جگوار
leopard	palang	پلنگ
cheetah	yuzpalang	یوزپلنگ
black panther	palang-e siyāh	پلنگ سیاه
puma	yuzpalang	یوزپلنگ
snow leopard	palang-e barfi	پلنگ برفی
lynx	siyāh guš	سیاه گوش
coyote	gorg-e sahrāyi	گرگ صحرایی
jackal	šoqāl	شغال
hyena	kaftār	کفتار

211. Wild animals

English	Persian (transliteration)	Persian
animal	heyvān	حیوان
beast (animal)	heyvān	حیوان
squirrel	sanjāb	سنجاب
hedgehog	xārpošt	خارپشت
hare	xarguš	خرگوش
rabbit	xarguš	خرگوش
badger	gurkan	گورکن
raccoon	rākon	راکون
hamster	muš-e bozorg	موش بزرگ
marmot	muš-e xormā-ye kuhi	موش خرمای کوهی
mole	muš-e kur	موش کور
mouse	muš	موش
rat	muš-e sahrāyi	موش صحرایی
bat	xoffāš	خفاش
ermine	qāqom	قاقم
sable	samur	سمور
marten	samur	سمور
weasel	rāsu	راسو
mink	tire-ye rāsu	تیره راسو

| beaver | sag-e ābi | سگ آبی |
| otter | samur ābi | سمور آبی |

horse	asb	اسب
moose	gavazn	گوزن
deer	āhu	آهو
camel	šotor	شتر

bison	gāvmiš	گاومیش
aurochs	gāv miš	گاو میش
buffalo	bufālo	بوفالو

zebra	gurexar	گورخر
antelope	boz-e kuhi	بز کوهی
roe deer	šukā	شوکا
fallow deer	qazāl	غزال
chamois	boz-e kuhi	بز کوهی
wild boar	gorāz	گراز

whale	nahang	نهنگ
seal	fak	فک
walrus	širmāhi	شیرماهی
fur seal	gorbe-ye ābi	گربۀ آبی
dolphin	delfin	دلفین

bear	xers	خرس
polar bear	xers-e sefid	خرس سفید
panda	pāndā	پاندا

monkey	meymun	میمون
chimpanzee	šampānze	شمپانزه
orangutan	orāngutān	اورانگوتان
gorilla	guril	گوریل
macaque	mākāk	ماکاک
gibbon	gibon	گیبون

elephant	fil	فیل
rhinoceros	kargadan	کرگدن
giraffe	zarrāfe	زرافه
hippopotamus	asb-e ābi	اسب آبی

| kangaroo | kāngoro | کانگورو |
| koala (bear) | kovālā | کوالا |

mongoose	xadang	خدنگ
chinchilla	čin čila	چین چیلا
skunk	rāsu-ye badbu	راسوی بدبو
porcupine	taši	تشی

212. Domestic animals

cat	gorbe	گربه
tomcat	gorbe-ye nar	گربۀ نر
dog	sag	سگ

horse	asb	اسب
stallion (male horse)	asb-e nar	اسب نر
mare	mādiyān	مادیان
cow	gāv	گاو
bull	gāv-e nar	گاو نر
ox	gāv-e axte	گاو اخته
sheep (ewe)	gusfand	گوسفند
ram	gusfand-e nar	گوسفند نر
goat	boz-e mādde	بز ماده
billy goat, he-goat	boz-e nar	بز نر
donkey	xar	خر
mule	qāter	قاطر
pig	xuk	خوک
piglet	bače-ye xuk	بچهٔ خوک
rabbit	xarguš	خرگوش
hen (chicken)	morq	مرغ
cock	xorus	خروس
duck	ordak	اردک
drake	ordak-e nar	اردک نر
goose	qāz	غاز
tom turkey, gobbler	buqalamun-e nar	بوقلمون نر
turkey (hen)	buqalamun-e māde	بوقلمون ماده
domestic animals	heyvānāt-e ahli	حیوانات اهلی
tame (e.g. ~ hamster)	ahli	اهلی
to tame (vt)	rām kardan	رام کردن
to breed (vt)	parvareš dādan	پرورش دادن
farm	mazrae	مزرعه
poultry	morq-e xānegi	مرغ خانگی
cattle	dām	دام
herd (cattle)	galle	گله
stable	establ	اصطبل
pigsty	āqol xuk	آغل خوک
cowshed	āqol gāv	آغل گاو
rabbit hutch	lanye xarguš	لانه خرگوش
hen house	morq dāni	مرغ دانی

213. Dogs. Dog breeds

dog	sag	سگ
sheepdog	sag-e gele	سگ گله
German shepherd	sag-e jerman šeperd	سگ ژرمن شپرد
poodle	pudel	پودل
dachshund	sag-e pākutāh	سگ پاکوتاه
bulldog	buldāg	بولداگ

boxer	boksor	بوكسور
mastiff	mâstif	ماستيف
Rottweiler	rotveylir	روتويلر
Doberman	dobermen	دوبرمن

basset	ba's-at	باسيت
bobtail	dam čatri	دم چترى
Dalmatian	dâlmâsi	دالماسى
cocker spaniel	kâkir spâniyel	كاكير سپانيیل

| Newfoundland | nyufâundland | نيوفاوندلند |
| Saint Bernard | sant bernârd | سنت برنارد |

husky	sag-e surtme	سگ سورتمه
Chow Chow	čâu-čâu	چاو-چاو
spitz	espitz	اسپيتز
pug	pâg	پاگ

214. Sounds made by animals

barking (n)	vâq vâq	واق واق
to bark (vi)	vâq-vâq kardan	واق واق كردن
to miaow (vi)	miyu-miyu kardan	ميو ميو كردن
to purr (vi)	xor-xor kardan	خرخر كردن

to moo (vi)	mu-mu kardan	مو مو كردن
to bellow (bull)	na're kešidan	نعره كشيدن
to growl (vi)	qorqor kardan	غرغر كردن

howl (n)	zuze	زوزه
to howl (vi)	zuze kešidan	زوزه كشيدن
to whine (vi)	zuze kešidan	زوزه كشيدن

to bleat (sheep)	ba'ba' kardan	بع بع كردن
to oink, to grunt (pig)	xor-xor kardan	خرخر كردن
to squeal (vi)	jiq zadan	جيغ زدن

to croak (vi)	qur-qur kardan	قورقور كردن
to buzz (insect)	vez-vez kardan	وزوز كردن
to chirp (crickets, grasshopper)	jir-jir kardan	جير جير كردن

215. Young animals

cub	tule	توله
kitten	bačče gorbe	بچه گربه
baby mouse	bače-ye muš	بچهٔ موش
puppy	tule-ye sag	تولهٔ سگ

leveret	bače-ye xarguš	بچهٔ خرگوش
baby rabbit	bače-ye xarguš	بچهٔ خرگوش
wolf cub	bače-ye gorg	بچهٔ گرگ

fox cub	bače-ye rubāh	بچۀ روباه
bear cub	bače-ye xers	بچۀ خرس
lion cub	bače-ye šir	بچۀ شیر
tiger cub	bače-ye bebar	بچۀ ببر
elephant calf	bače-ye fil	بچۀ فیل
piglet	bače-ye xuk	بچۀ خوک
calf (young cow, bull)	gusāle	گوساله
kid (young goat)	bozqāle	بزغاله
lamb	barre	بره
fawn (young deer)	bače-ye gavazn	بچۀ گوزن
young camel	bače-ye šotor	بچۀ شتر
snakelet (baby snake)	bače-ye mār	بچۀ مار
froglet (baby frog)	bače-ye qurbāqe	بچۀ قرباغه
baby bird	juje	جوجه
chick (of chicken)	juje	جوجه
duckling	juje-ye ordak	جوجۀ اردک

216. Birds

bird	parande	پرنده
pigeon	kabutar	کبوتر
sparrow	gonješk	گنجشک
tit (great tit)	morq-e zanburxār	مرغ زنبورخوار
magpie	zāqi	زاغی
raven	kalāq-e siyāh	کلاغ سیاه
crow	kalāq	کلاغ
jackdaw	zāq	زاغ
rook	kalāq-e siyāh	کلاغ سیاه
duck	ordak	اردک
goose	qāz	غاز
pheasant	qarqāvol	قرقاول
eagle	oqāb	عقاب
hawk	qerqi	قرقی
falcon	šāhin	شاهین
vulture	karkas	کرکس
condor (Andean ~)	karkas-e emrikāyi	کرکس امریکایی
swan	qu	قو
crane	dornā	درنا
stork	lak lak	لک لک
parrot	tuti	طوطی
hummingbird	morq-e magas-e xār	مرغ مگس خوار
peacock	tāvus	طاووس
ostrich	šotormorq	شترمرغ
heron	havāsil	حواصیل

| flamingo | felāmingo | فلامینگو |
| pelican | pelikān | پلیکان |

| nightingale | bolbol | بلبل |
| swallow | parastu | پرستو |

thrush	bāstarak	باسترک
song thrush	torqe	طرقه
blackbird	tukā-ye siyāh	توکای سیاه

swift	bādxorak	بادخورک
lark	čakāvak	چکاوک
quail	belderčin	بلدرچین

woodpecker	dārkub	دارکوب
cuckoo	fāxte	فاخته
owl	joqd	جغد
eagle owl	šāh buf	شاه بوف
wood grouse	siāh xorus	سیاه خروس
black grouse	siāh xorus-e jangali	سیاه خروس جنگلی
partridge	kabk	کبک

starling	sār	سار
canary	qanāri	قناری
hazel grouse	siyāh xorus-e fandoqi	سیاه خروس فندقی
chaffinch	sehre-ye jangali	سهره جنگلی
bullfinch	sohre sar-e siyāh	سهره سر سیاه

seagull	morq-e daryāyi	مرغ دریایی
albatross	morq-e daryāyi	مرغ دریایی
penguin	pangoan	پنگوئن

217. Birds. Singing and sounds

to sing (vi)	xāndan	خواندن
to call (animal, bird)	faryād kardan	فریاد کردن
to crow (cock)	ququli ququ kardan	قوقولی قوقو کردن
cock-a-doodle-doo	ququli ququ	قوقولی قوقو

to cluck (hen)	qodqod kardan	قدقد کردن
to caw (vi)	qār-qār kardan	قارقار کردن
to quack (duck)	qāt-qāt kardan	قات قات کردن
to cheep (vi)	jir-jir kardan	جیر جیر کردن
to chirp, to twitter	jik-jik kardan	جیک جیک کردن

218. Fish. Marine animals

bream	māhi-ye sim	ماهی سیم
carp	kapur	کپور
perch	māhi-e luti	ماهی لوتی
catfish	gorbe-ye māhi	گربه ماهی
pike	ordak māhi	اردک ماهی

salmon	māhi-ye salemon	ماهی سالمون
sturgeon	māhi-ye xāviār	ماهی خاویار
herring	māhi-ye šur	ماهی شور
Atlantic salmon	sālmon-e atlāntik	سالمون اتلانتیک
mackerel	māhi-ye esqumeri	ماهی اسقومری
flatfish	sofre māhi	سفره ماهی
zander, pike perch	suf	سوف
cod	māhi-ye rowqan	ماهی روغن
tuna	tan māhi	تن ماهی
trout	māhi-ye qezelālā	ماهی قزل آلا
eel	mārmāhi	مارماهی
electric ray	partomahiye barqi	پرتوماهی برقی
moray eel	mārmāhi	مارماهی
piranha	pirānā	پیرانا
shark	kuse-ye māhi	کوسه ماهی
dolphin	delfin	دلفین
whale	nahang	نهنگ
crab	xarčang	خرچنگ
jellyfish	arus-e daryāyi	عروس دریایی
octopus	hašt pā	هشت پا
starfish	setāre-ye daryāyi	ستاره دریایی
sea urchin	xārpošt-e daryāyi	خارپشت دریایی
seahorse	asb-e daryāyi	اسب دریایی
oyster	sadaf-e xorāki	صدف خوراکی
prawn	meygu	میگو
lobster	xarčang-e daryāyi	خرچنگ دریایی
spiny lobster	xarčang-e xārdār	خرچنگ خاردار

219. Amphibians. Reptiles

snake	mār	مار
venomous (snake)	sammi	سمی
viper	af'i	افعی
cobra	kobrā	کبرا
python	mār-e pinton	مار پیتون
boa	mār-e bwa	مار بوا
grass snake	mār-e čaman	مار چمن
rattle snake	mār-e zangi	مار زنگی
anaconda	mār-e ānākondā	مار آناکوندا
lizard	susmār	سوسمار
iguana	susmār-e deraxti	سوسمار درختی
monitor lizard	bozmajje	بزمجه
salamander	samandar	سمندر
chameleon	āftāb-parast	آفتاب پرست

scorpion	aqrab	عقرب
turtle	lāk pošt	لاک پشت
frog	qurbāqe	قورباغه
toad	vazaq	وزغ
crocodile	temsāh	تمساح

220. Insects

insect	hašare	حشره
butterfly	parvāne	پروانه
ant	murče	مورچه
fly	magas	مگس
mosquito	paše	پشه
beetle	susk	سوسک

wasp	zanbur	زنبور
bee	zanbur-e asal	زنبور عسل
bumblebee	xar zanbur	خرزنبور
gadfly (botfly)	xarmagas	خرمگس

| spider | ankabut | عنکبوت |
| spider's web | tār-e ankabut | تارعنکبوت |

dragonfly	sanjāqak	سنجاقک
grasshopper	malax	ملخ
moth (night butterfly)	bid	بید

cockroach	susk	سوسک
tick	kane	کنه
flea	kak	کک
midge	paše-ye rize	پشه ریزه

locust	malax	ملخ
snail	halazun	حلزون
cricket	jirjirak	جیرجیرک
firefly	kerm-e šab-tāb	کرم شب تاب
ladybird	kafšduzak	کفشدوزک
cockchafer	susk bāldār	سوسک بالدار

leech	zālu	زالو
caterpillar	kerm-e abrišam	کرم ابریشم
earthworm	kerm	کرم
larva	lārv	لارو

221. Animals. Body parts

beak	nok	نوک
wings	bāl-hā	بال ها
foot (of bird)	panje	پنجه
feathers (plumage)	por-o bāl	پر و بال
feather	por	پر
crest	kākol	کاکل

gills	ābšoš	آبشش
spawn	toxme mahi	تخم ماهی
larva	lārv	لارو
fin	bāle-ye māhi	باله ماهی
scales (of fish, reptile)	fals	فلس

fang (canine)	niš	نیش
paw (e.g. cat's ~)	panje	پنجه
muzzle (snout)	puze	پوزه
mouth (of cat, dog)	dahān	دهان
tail	dam	دم
whiskers	sebil	سبیل

| hoof | sam | سم |
| horn | šāx | شاخ |

carapace	lāk	لاک
shell (of mollusc)	sadaf	صدف
eggshell	puste	پوسته

| animal's hair (pelage) | pašm | پشم |
| pelt (hide) | pust | پوست |

222. Actions of animals

to fly (vi)	parvāz kardan	پرواز کردن
to fly in circles	dowr zadan	دور زدن
to fly away	parvāz kardan	پرواز کردن
to flap (~ the wings)	bāl zadan	بال زدن

to peck (vi)	nok zadan	نوک زدن
to sit on eggs	ru-ye toxm xābidan	روی تخم خوابیدن
to hatch out (vi)	az toxm birun āmadan	از تخم بیرون آمدن
to build a nest	lāne sāxtan	لانه ساختن

to slither, to crawl	xazidan	خزیدن
to sting, to bite (insect)	gozidan	گزیدن
to bite (ab. animal)	gāz gereftan	گاز گرفتن

to sniff (vt)	buyidan	بوییدن
to bark (vi)	vāq-vāq kardan	واق واق کردن
to hiss (snake)	his kardan	هیس کردن

| to scare (vt) | tarsāndan | ترساندن |
| to attack (vt) | hamle kardan | حمله کردن |

to gnaw (bone, etc.)	javidan	جویدن
to scratch (with claws)	čang zadan	چنگ زدن
to hide (vi)	penhān šodan	پنهان شدن

to play (kittens, etc.)	bāzi kardan	بازی کردن
to hunt (vi, vt)	šekār kardan	شکار کردن
to hibernate (vi)	dar xāb-e zemestāni budan	درخواب زمستانی بودن
to go extinct	monqarez šodan	منقرض شدن

223. Animals. Habitats

habitat	zistgāh	زیستگاه
migration	mohājerat	مهاجرت
mountain	kuh	کوه
reef	tappe-ye daryāyi	تپه دریایی
cliff	saxre	صخره
forest	jangal	جنگل
jungle	jangal	جنگل
savanna	sāvānā	ساوانا
tundra	tondrā	توندرا
steppe	estep	استپ
desert	biyābān	بیابان
oasis	vāhe	واحه
sea	daryā	دریا
lake	daryāče	دریاچه
ocean	oqyānus	اقیانوس
swamp (marshland)	bātlāq	باتلاق
freshwater (adj)	ab-e širin	آب شیرین
pond	tālāb	تالاب
river	rudxāne	رودخانه
den (bear's ~)	lāne-ye xers	لانه خرس
nest	lāne	لانه
hollow (in a tree)	surāx	سوراخ
burrow (animal hole)	lāne	لانه
anthill	lāne-ye murče	لانه مورچه

224. Animal care

zoo	bāq-e vahš	باغ وحش
nature reserve	mantaqe hefāzat šode	منطقه حفاظت شده
breeder (cattery, kennel, etc.)	zaxire-ye gāh	ذخیره گاه
open-air cage	lāne	لانه
cage	qafas	قفس
kennel	lāne-ye sag	لانه سگ
dovecot	lāne-ye kabutar	لانه کبوتر
aquarium (fish tank)	ākvāriyom	آکواریوم
dolphinarium	delfin xane	دلفین خانه
to breed (animals)	parvareš dādan	پرورش دادن
brood, litter	juje, tule	جوجه، توله
to tame (vt)	rām kardan	رام کردن
to train (animals)	tarbiyat kardan	تربیت کردن
feed (fodder, etc.)	xorāk	خوراک
to feed (vt)	xorāk dādan	خوراک دادن

pet shop	forušgāh-e heyvānāt-e ahli	فروشگاه حیوانات اهلی
muzzle (for dog)	puze band	پوزه بند
collar (e.g., dog ~)	qallāde	قلاده
name (of animal)	laqab	لقب
pedigree (of dog)	nežād	نژاد

225. Animals. Miscellaneous

pack (wolves)	daste	دسته
flock (birds)	daste	دسته
shoal, school (fish)	daste	دسته
herd (horses)	galle	گله
male (n)	nar	نر
female (n)	mādde	ماده
hungry (adj)	gorosne	گرسنه
wild (adj)	vahši	وحشی
dangerous (adj)	xatarnāk	خطرناک

226. Horses

horse	asb	اسب
breed (race)	nežād	نژاد
foal	korre asb	کره اسب
mare	mādiyān	ماديان
mustang	asb-e vahš-i	اسب وحشی
pony	asbče	اسبچه
draught horse	asb-e bārkeš	اسب بارکش
mane	yāl	يال
tail	dam	دم
hoof	sam	سم
horseshoe	na'l	نعل
to shoe (vt)	na'l zadan	نعل زدن
blacksmith	āhangar	آهنگر
saddle	zin	زين
stirrup	rekāb	رکاب
bridle	lejām	لجام
reins	afsār	افسار
whip (for riding)	tāziyāne	تازيانه
rider	savārkār	سواركار
to saddle up (vt)	zin kardan	زين کردن
to mount a horse	ruy-ye zin nešastan	روی زين نشستن
gallop	čāhārna'l	چهارنعل
to gallop (vi)	čāhārna'l tāxtan	چهارنعل تاختن

trot (n)	yurtme	یورتمه
at a trot (adv)	yurtme	یورتمه
to go at a trot	yurtme raftan	یورتمه رفتن
racehorse	asb-e mosābeqe	اسب مسابقه
horse racing	asb-e davāni	اسب دوانی
stable	establ	اصطبل
to feed (vt)	xorāk dādan	خوراک دادن
hay	alaf-e xošk	علف خشک
to water (animals)	āb dādan	آب دادن
to wash (horse)	pāk kardan	پاک کردن
horse-drawn cart	gāri	گاری
to graze (vi)	čaridan	چریدن
to neigh (vi)	šeyhe kešidan	شیهه کشیدن
to kick (about horse)	lagad zadan	لگد زدن

Flora

227. Trees

tree	deraxt	درخت
deciduous (adj)	barg riz	برگ ریز
coniferous (adj)	maxrutiyān	مخروطیان
evergreen (adj)	hamiše sabz	همیشه سبز
apple tree	deraxt-e sib	درخت سیب
pear tree	golābi	گلابی
sweet cherry tree	gilās	گیلاس
sour cherry tree	ālbālu	آلبالو
plum tree	ālu	آلو
birch	tus	توس
oak	balut	بلوط
linden tree	zirfun	زیرفون
aspen	senowbar-e larzān	صنوبر لرزان
maple	afrā	افرا
spruce	senowbar	صنوبر
pine	kāj	کاج
larch	senowbar-e ārāste	صنوبر آراسته
fir tree	šāh deraxt	شاه درخت
cedar	sedr	سدر
poplar	sepidār	سپیدار
rowan	zabān gonješk-e kuhi	زبان گنجشک کوهی
willow	bid	بید
alder	tuskā	توسکا
beech	rāš	راش
elm	nārvan-e qermez	نارون قرمز
ash (tree)	zabān-e gonješk	زبان گنجشک
chestnut	šāh balut	شاه بلوط
magnolia	māgnoliyā	ماگنولیا
palm tree	naxl	نخل
cypress	sarv	سرو
mangrove	karnā	کرنا
baobab	bāobāb	بائوباب
eucalyptus	okaliptus	اوکالیپتوس
sequoia	sorx-e čub	سرخ چوب

228. Shrubs

bush	bute	بوته
shrub	bute zār	بوته زار

| grapevine | angur | انگور |
| vineyard | tākestān | تاکستان |

raspberry bush	tamešk	تمشک
blackcurrant bush	angur-e farangi-ye siyāh	انگور فرنگی سیاه
redcurrant bush	angur-e farangi-ye sorx	انگور فرنگی سرخ
gooseberry bush	angur-e farangi	انگور فرنگی

acacia	aqāqiyā	اقاقیا
barberry	zerešk	زرشک
jasmine	yāsaman	یاسمن

juniper	ardaj	اردج
rosebush	bute-ye gol-e mohammadi	بوتهٔ گل محمدی
dog rose	nastaran	نسترن

229. Mushrooms

mushroom	qārč	قارچ
edible mushroom	qārč-e xorāki	قارچ خوراکی
poisonous mushroom	qārč-e sammi	قارچ سمی
cap (of mushroom)	kolāhak-e qārč	کلاهک قارچ
stipe (of mushroom)	pāye	پایه

cep, penny bun	qārč-e sefid	قارچ سفید
orange-cap boletus	samāruq	سماروغ
birch bolete	qārč-e bulet	قارچ بولت
chanterelle	qārč-e zard	قارچ زرد
russula	qārč-e tiqe-ye tord	قارچ تیغه ترد

morel	qārč-e morkelā	قارچ مورکلا
fly agaric	qārč-e magas	قارچ مگس
death cap	kolāhak-e marg	کلاهک مرگ

230. Fruits. Berries

| fruit | mive | میوه |
| fruits | mive jāt | میوه جات |

apple	sib	سیب
pear	golābi	گلابی
plum	ālu	آلو

strawberry (garden ~)	tut-e farangi	توت فرنگی
sour cherry	ālbālu	آلبالو
sweet cherry	gilās	گیلاس
grape	angur	انگور

raspberry	tamešk	تمشک
blackcurrant	angur-e farangi-ye siyāh	انگور فرنگی سیاه
redcurrant	angur-e farangi-ye sorx	انگور فرنگی سرخ
gooseberry	angur-e farangi	انگور فرنگی

cranberry	nārdānak-e vahši	ناردانک وحشی
orange	porteqāl	پرتقال
tangerine	nārengi	نارنگی
pineapple	ānānās	آناناس
banana	mowz	موز
date	xormā	خرما
lemon	limu	لیمو
apricot	zardālu	زردآلو
peach	holu	هلو
kiwi	kivi	کیوی
grapefruit	gerip forut	گریپ فوروت
berry	mive-ye butei	میوهٔ بوته ای
berries	mivehā-ye butei	میوه های بوته ای
cowberry	tut-e farangi-ye jangali	توت فرنگی جنگلی
wild strawberry	zoqāl axte	زغال اخته
bilberry	zoqāl axte	زغال اخته

231. Flowers. Plants

flower	gol	گل
bouquet (of flowers)	daste-ye gol	دسته گل
rose (flower)	gol-e sorx	گل سرخ
tulip	lāle	لاله
carnation	mixak	میخک
gladiolus	susan-e sefid	سوسن سفید
cornflower	gol-e gandom	گل گندم
harebell	gol-e estekāni	گل استکانی
dandelion	gol-e qāsedak	گل قاصدک
camomile	bābune	بابونه
aloe	oloviye	آلوئه
cactus	kāktus	کاکتوس
rubber plant, ficus	fikus	فیکوس
lily	susan	سوسن
geranium	gol-e šam'dāni	گل شمعدانی
hyacinth	sonbol	سنبل
mimosa	mimosā	میموسا
narcissus	narges	نرگس
nasturtium	gol-e lādan	گل لادن
orchid	orkide	ارکیده
peony	gol-e ašrafi	گل اشرفی
violet	banafše	بنفشه
pansy	banafše-ye farangi	بنفشه فرنگی
forget-me-not	gol-e farāmuš-am makon	گل فراموشم مکن
daisy	gol-e morvārid	گل مروارید
poppy	xašxāš	خشخاش

| hemp | šāh dāne | شاه دانه |
| mint | na'nā' | نعناع |

| lily of the valley | muge | موگه |
| snowdrop | gol-e barfi | گل برفی |

nettle	gazane	گزنه
sorrel	toršak	ترشک
water lily	nilufar-e abi	نیلوفر آبی
fern	saraxs	سرخس
lichen	golesang	گلسنگ

greenhouse (tropical ~)	golxāne	گلخانه
lawn	čaman	چمن
flowerbed	baqče-ye gol	باغچه گل

plant	giyāh	گیاه
grass	alaf	علف
blade of grass	alaf	علف

leaf	barg	برگ
petal	golbarg	گلبرگ
stem	sāqe	ساقه
tuber	riše	ریشه

| young plant (shoot) | javāne | جوانه |
| thorn | xār | خار |

to blossom (vi)	gol kardan	گل کردن
to fade, to wither	pažmorde šodan	پژمرده شدن
smell (odour)	bu	بو
to cut (flowers)	boridan	بریدن
to pick (a flower)	kandan	کندن

232. Cereals, grains

grain	dāne	دانه
cereal crops	qallāt	غلات
ear (of barley, etc.)	xuše	خوشه

wheat	gandom	گندم
rye	čāvdār	چاودار
oats	jow-e sahrāyi	جو صحرایی
millet	arzan	ارزن
barley	jow	جو
maize	zorrat	ذرت
rice	berenj	برنج
buckwheat	gandom-e siyāh	گندم سیاه

pea plant	noxod	نخود
kidney bean	lubiyā qermez	لوبیا قرمز
soya	sowyā	سویا
lentil	adas	عدس
beans (pulse crops)	lubiyā	لوبیا

233. Vegetables. Greens

vegetables	sabzijāt	سبزیجات
greens	sabzi	سبزی
tomato	gowje farangi	گوجه فرنگی
cucumber	xiyār	خیار
carrot	havij	هویج
potato	sib zamini	سیب زمینی
onion	piyāz	پیاز
garlic	sir	سیر
cabbage	kalam	کلم
cauliflower	gol kalam	گل کلم
Brussels sprouts	koll-am boruksel	کلم بروکسل
broccoli	kalam borokli	کلم بروکلی
beetroot	čoqondar	چغندر
aubergine	bādenjān	بادنجان
marrow	kadu sabz	کدو سبز
pumpkin	kadu tanbal	کدو تنبل
turnip	šalqam	شلغم
parsley	ja'fari	جعفری
dill	šavid	شوید
lettuce	kāhu	کاهو
celery	karafs	کرفس
asparagus	mārčube	مارچوبه
spinach	esfenāj	اسفناج
pea	noxod	نخود
beans	lubiyā	لوبیا
maize	zorrat	ذرت
kidney bean	lubiyā qermez	لوبیا قرمز
pepper	felfel	فلفل
radish	torobče	تربچه
artichoke	kangar farangi	کنگرفرنگی

REGIONAL GEOGRAPHY

Countries. Nationalities

234. Western Europe

Europe	orupā	اروپا
European Union	ettehādiye-ye orupā	اتحادیه اروپا
European (n)	orupāyi	اروپایی
European (adj)	orupāyi	اروپایی

Austria	otriš	اتریش
Austrian (masc.)	mard-e otriši	مرد اتریشی
Austrian (fem.)	zan-e otriši	زن اتریشی
Austrian (adj)	otriši	اتریشی

Great Britain	beritāniyā-ye kabir	بریتانیای کبیر
England	engelestān	انگلستان
British (masc.)	mard-e engelisi	مرد انگلیسی
British (fem.)	zan-e engelisi	زن انگلیسی
English, British (adj)	engelisi	انگلیسی

Belgium	belžik	بلژیک
Belgian (masc.)	mard-e belžiki	مرد بلژیکی
Belgian (fem.)	zan-e belžiki	زن بلژیکی
Belgian (adj)	belžiki	بلژیکی

Germany	ālmān	آلمان
German (masc.)	mard-e ālmāni	مرد آلمانی
German (fem.)	zan-e ālmāni	زن آلمانی
German (adj)	ālmāni	آلمانی

Netherlands	holand	هلند
Holland	holand	هلند
Dutch (masc.)	mard-e holandi	مرد هلندی
Dutch (fem.)	zan-e holandi	زن هلندی
Dutch (adj)	holandi	هلندی

Greece	yunān	یونان
Greek (masc.)	mard-e yunāni	مرد یونانی
Greek (fem.)	zan-e yunāni	زن یونانی
Greek (adj)	yunāni	یونانی

Denmark	dānmārk	دانمارک
Dane (masc.)	mard-e dānmārki	مرد دانمارکی
Dane (fem.)	zan-e dānmārki	زن دانمارکی
Danish (adj)	dānmārki	دانمارکی
Ireland	irland	ایرلند
Irish (masc.)	mard-e irlandi	مرد ایرلندی

Irish (fem.)	zan-e irlandi	زن ایرلندی
Irish (adj)	irlandi	ایرلندی
Iceland	island	ایسلند
Icelander (masc.)	mard-e island-i	مرد ایسلندی
Icelander (fem.)	zan-e island-i	زن ایسلندی
Icelandic (adj)	island-i	ایسلندی
Spain	espāniyā	اسپانیا
Spaniard (masc.)	mard-e espāniyāyi	مرد اسپانیایی
Spaniard (fem.)	zan-e espāniyāyi	زن اسپانیایی
Spanish (adj)	espāniyāyi	اسپانیایی
Italy	itāliyā	ایتالیا
Italian (masc.)	mard-e itāliyāyi	مرد ایتالیایی
Italian (fem.)	zan-e itāliyāyi	زن ایتالیایی
Italian (adj)	itāliyāyi	ایتالیایی
Cyprus	qebres	قبرس
Cypriot (masc.)	mard-e qebresi	مرد قبرسی
Cypriot (fem.)	zan-e qebresi	زن قبرسی
Cypriot (adj)	qebresi	قبرسی
Malta	mālt	مالت
Maltese (masc.)	mard-e mālti	مرد مالتی
Maltese (fem.)	zan-e mālti	زن مالتی
Maltese (adj)	mālti	مالتی
Norway	norvež	نروژ
Norwegian (masc.)	mard-e norveži	مرد نروژی
Norwegian (fem.)	zan-e norveži	زن نروژی
Norwegian (adj)	norveži	نروژی
Portugal	porteqāl	پرتغال
Portuguese (masc.)	mard-e porteqāli	مرد پرتغالی
Portuguese (fem.)	zan-e porteqāli	زن پرتغالی
Portuguese (adj)	porteqāli	پرتغالی
Finland	fanlānd	فنلاند
Finn (masc.)	mard-e fanlāndi	مرد فنلاندی
Finn (fem.)	zan-e fanlāndi	زن فنلاندی
Finnish (adj)	fanlāndi	فنلاندی
France	farānse	فرانسه
French (masc.)	mard-e farānsavi	مرد فرانسوی
French (fem.)	zan-e farānsavi	زن فرانسوی
French (adj)	farānsavi	فرانسوی
Sweden	sued	سوئد
Swede (masc.)	mard-e suedi	مرد سوئدی
Swede (fem.)	zan-e suedi	زن سوئدی
Swedish (adj)	suedi	سوئدی
Switzerland	suis	سوئیس
Swiss (masc.)	mard-e suisi	مرد سوئیسی
Swiss (fem.)	zan-e suisi	زن سوئیسی

Swiss (adj)	suisi	سوئیسی
Scotland	eskätland	اسکاتلند
Scottish (masc.)	mard-e eskätlandi	مرد اسکاتلندی
Scottish (fem.)	zan-e eskätlandi	زن اسکاتلندی
Scottish (adj)	eskätlandi	اسکاتلندی

Vatican	vätikän	واتیکان
Liechtenstein	lixteneštäyn	لیختن‌اشتاین
Luxembourg	lokzämborg	لوکزامبورگ
Monaco	monäko	موناکو

235. Central and Eastern Europe

Albania	älbäni	آلبانی
Albanian (masc.)	mard-e älbäniyäyi	مرد آلبانیایی
Albanian (fem.)	zan-e älbäniyäyi	زن آلبانیایی
Albanian (adj)	älbäniyäyi	آلبانیایی

Bulgaria	bolqärestän	بلغارستان
Bulgarian (masc.)	mard-e bolqäri	مرد بلغاری
Bulgarian (fem.)	zan-e bolqäri	زن بلغاری
Bulgarian (adj)	bolqäri	بلغاری

Hungary	majärestän	مجارستان
Hungarian (masc.)	mard-e majäri	مرد مجاری
Hungarian (fem.)	zan-e majäri	زن مجاری
Hungarian (adj)	majäri	مجاری

Latvia	letuni	لتونی
Latvian (masc.)	mard-e letoniyäyi	مرد لتونیایی
Latvian (fem.)	zan-e letoniyäyi	زن لتونیایی
Latvian (adj)	letuniyäyi	لتونیایی

Lithuania	litväni	لیتوانی
Lithuanian (masc.)	mard-e litväniyäyi	مرد لیتوانیایی
Lithuanian (fem.)	zan-e litväniyäyi	زن لیتوانیایی
Lithuanian (adj)	litväniyäyi	لیتوانیایی

Poland	lahestän	لهستان
Pole (masc.)	mard-e lahestäni	مرد لهستانی
Pole (fem.)	zan-e lahestäni	زن لهستانی
Polish (adj)	lahestäni	لهستانی

Romania	romäni	رومانی
Romanian (masc.)	mard-e romäniyäyi	مرد رومانیایی
Romanian (fem.)	zan-e romäniyäyi	زن رومانیایی
Romanian (adj)	romäniyäyi	رومانیایی

Serbia	serbestän	صربستان
Serbian (masc.)	mard-e serb	مرد صرب
Serbian (fem.)	zan-e serb	زن صرب
Serbian (adj)	serb	صرب
Slovakia	eslowäki	اسلواکی
Slovak (masc.)	mard-e eslowäk	مرد اسلواک

| Slovak (fem.) | zan-e eslovāk | زن اسلواک |
| Slovak (adj) | eslovāk | اسلواک |

Croatia	korovāsi	کرواسی
Croatian (masc.)	mard-e korovāt	مرد کروات
Croatian (fem.)	zan-e korovāt	زن کروات
Croatian (adj)	korovāt	کروات

Czech Republic	jomhuri-ye ček	جمهوری چک
Czech (masc.)	mard-e ček	مرد چک
Czech (fem.)	zan-e ček	زن چک
Czech (adj)	ček	چک

Estonia	estoni	استونی
Estonian (masc.)	mard-e estuniyāyi	مرد استونیایی
Estonian (fem.)	zan-e estuniyāyi	زن استونیایی
Estonian (adj)	estuniyāyi	استونیایی

Bosnia and Herzegovina	bosni-yo herzogovin	بوسنی وهرزگوین
Macedonia (Republic of ~)	jomhuri-ye maqduniye	جمهوری مقدونیه
Slovenia	eslovoni	اسلوونی
Montenegro	montenegro	مونته‌نگرو

236. Former USSR countries

Azerbaijan	āzarbāyjān	آذربایجان
Azerbaijani (masc.)	mard-e āzarbāyejāni	مرد آذربایجانی
Azerbaijani (fem.)	zan-e āzarbāyejāni	زن آذربایجانی
Azerbaijani, Azeri (adj)	āzarbāyejāni	آذربایجانی

Armenia	armanestān	ارمنستان
Armenian (masc.)	mard-e armani	مرد ارمنی
Armenian (fem.)	zan-e armani	زن ارمنی
Armenian (adj)	armani	ارمنی

Belarus	belārus	بلاروس
Belarusian (masc.)	mard belārus-i	مرد بلاروسی
Belarusian (fem.)	zan belārus-i	زن بلاروسی
Belarusian (adj)	belārus-i	بلاروسی

Georgia	gorjestān	گرجستان
Georgian (masc.)	mard-e gorji	مرد گرجی
Georgian (fem.)	zan-e gorji	زن گرجی
Georgian (adj)	gorji	گرجی

Kazakhstan	qazzāqestān	قزاقستان
Kazakh (masc.)	mard-e qazzāq	مرد قزاق
Kazakh (fem.)	zan-e qazzāq	زن قزاق
Kazakh (adj)	qazzāqi	قزاقی

Kirghizia	qerqizestān	قرقیزستان
Kirghiz (masc.)	mard-e qerqiz	مرد قرقیز
Kirghiz (fem.)	zan-e qerqiz	زن قرقیز
Kirghiz (adj)	qerqiz	قرقیز

Moldova, Moldavia	moldāvi	مولداوی
Moldavian (masc.)	mard-e moldāv	مرد مولداو
Moldavian (fem.)	zan-e moldāv	زن مولداو
Moldavian (adj)	moldāv	مولداو

Russia	rusiye	روسیه
Russian (masc.)	mard-e rusi	مرد روسی
Russian (fem.)	zan-e rusi	زن روسی
Russian (adj)	rusi	روسی

Tajikistan	tājikestān	تاجیکستان
Tajik (masc.)	mard-e tājik	مرد تاجیک
Tajik (fem.)	zan-e tājik	زن تاجیک
Tajik (adj)	tājik	تاجیک

Turkmenistan	torkamanestān	ترکمنستان
Turkmen (masc.)	mard-e torkaman	مرد ترکمن
Turkmen (fem.)	zan-e torkaman	زن ترکمن
Turkmenian (adj)	torkaman	ترکمن

Uzbekistan	ozbakestān	ازبکستان
Uzbek (masc.)	mard-e ozbak	مرد ازبک
Uzbek (fem.)	zan-e ozbak	زن ازبک
Uzbek (adj)	ozbak	ازبک

Ukraine	okrāyn	اوکراین
Ukrainian (masc.)	mard-e okrāyni	مرد اوکراینی
Ukrainian (fem.)	zan-e okrāyni	زن اوکراینی
Ukrainian (adj)	okrāyni	اوکراینی

237. Asia

| Asia | āsiyā | آسیا |
| Asian (adj) | āsiyāyi | آسیایی |

Vietnam	viyetnām	ویتنام
Vietnamese (masc.)	mard-e viyetnāmi	مرد ویتنامی
Vietnamese (fem.)	zan-e viyetnāmi	زن ویتنامی
Vietnamese (adj)	viyetnāmi	ویتنامی

India	hendustān	هندوستان
Indian (masc.)	mard-e hendi	مرد هندی
Indian (fem.)	zan-e hendi	زن هندی
Indian (adj)	hendi	هندی

Israel	esrāil	اسرائیل
Israeli (masc.)	mard-e esrāili	مرد اسرائیلی
Israeli (fem.)	zan-e esrāili	زن اسرائیلی
Israeli (adj)	esrāili	اسرائیلی

Jew (n)	mard-e yahudi	مرد یهودی
Jewess (n)	zan-e yahudi	زن یهودی
Jewish (adj)	yahudi	یهودی
China	čin	چین

Chinese (masc.)	mard-e čini	مرد چینی
Chinese (fem.)	zan-e čini	زن چینی
Chinese (adj)	čini	چینی

Korean (masc.)	mard-e karei	مرد کره ای
Korean (fem.)	zan-e karei	زن کره ای
Korean (adj)	kare i	کره ای

Lebanon	lobnān	لبنان
Lebanese (masc.)	mard-e lobnāni	مرد لبنانی
Lebanese (fem.)	zan-e lobnāni	زن لبنانی
Lebanese (adj)	lobnāni	لبنانی

Mongolia	moqolestān	مغولستان
Mongolian (masc.)	mard-e moqol	مرد مغول
Mongolian (fem.)	zan-e moqol	زن مغول
Mongolian (adj)	moqol	مغول

Malaysia	mālezi	مالزی
Malaysian (masc.)	mard-e māleziāyi	مرد مالزیایی
Malaysian (fem.)	zan-e māleziāyi	زن مالزیایی
Malaysian (adj)	māleziāyi	مالزیایی

Pakistan	pākestān	پاکستان
Pakistani (masc.)	mard-e pākestāni	مرد پاکستانی
Pakistani (fem.)	zan-e pākestāni	زن پاکستانی
Pakistani (adj)	pākestāni	پاکستانی

Saudi Arabia	arabestān-e soʻudi	عربستان سعودی
Arab (masc.)	mard-e arab	مرد عرب
Arab (fem.)	zan-e arab	زن عرب
Arab, Arabic (adj)	arab	عرب

Thailand	tāyland	تایلند
Thai (masc.)	mard-e tāylandi	مرد تایلندی
Thai (fem.)	zan-e tāylandi	زن تایلندی
Thai (adj)	tāylandi	تایلندی

Taiwan	tāyvān	تایوان
Taiwanese (masc.)	mard-e tāyvāni	مرد تایوانی
Taiwanese (fem.)	zan-e tāyvāni	زن تایوانی
Taiwanese (adj)	tāyvāni	تایوانی

Turkey	torkiye	ترکیه
Turk (masc.)	mard-e tork	مرد ترک
Turk (fem.)	zan-e tork	زن ترک
Turkish (adj)	tork	ترک

Japan	žāpon	ژاپن
Japanese (masc.)	mard-e žāponi	مرد ژاپنی
Japanese (fem.)	zan-e žāponi	زن ژاپنی
Japanese (adj)	žāponi	ژاپنی

Afghanistan	afqānestān	افغانستان
Bangladesh	bangelādeš	بنگلادش
Indonesia	andonezi	اندونزی

Jordan	ordon	اردن
Iraq	arāq	عراق
Iran	irān	ایران
Cambodia	kāmboj	کامبوج
Kuwait	koveyt	کویت
Laos	lāus	لائوس
Myanmar	miyānmār	میانمار
Nepal	nepāl	نپال
United Arab Emirates	emārāt-e mottahede-ye arabi	امارات متحده عربی
Syria	suriye	سوریه
Palestine	felestin	فلسطین
South Korea	kare-ye jonubi	کرۀ جنوبی
North Korea	kare-ye šomāli	کرۀ شمالی

238. North America

United States of America	eyālāt-e mottahede-ye emrikā	ایالات متحدۀ امریکا
American (masc.)	mard-e emrikāyi	مرد امریکایی
American (fem.)	zan-e emrikāyi	زن امریکایی
American (adj)	emrikāyi	امریکایی
Canada	kānādā	کانادا
Canadian (masc.)	mard-e kānādāyi	مرد کانادایی
Canadian (fem.)	zan-e kānādāyi	زن کانادایی
Canadian (adj)	kānādāyi	کانادایی
Mexico	mekzik	مکزیک
Mexican (masc.)	mard-e mekziki	مرد مکزیکی
Mexican (fem.)	zan-e mekziki	زن مکزیکی
Mexican (adj)	mekziki	مکزیکی

239. Central and South America

Argentina	āržāntin	آرژانتین
Argentinian (masc.)	mard-e āržāntini	مرد آرژانتینی
Argentinian (fem.)	zan-e āržāntini	زن آرژانتینی
Argentinian (adj)	āržāntini	آرژانتینی
Brazil	berezil	برزیل
Brazilian (masc.)	mard-e berezili	مرد برزیلی
Brazilian (fem.)	zan-e berezili	زن برزیلی
Brazilian (adj)	berezili	برزیلی
Colombia	kolombiyā	کلمبیا
Colombian (masc.)	mard-e kolombiyāyi	مرد کلمبیایی
Colombian (fem.)	zan-e kolombiyāyi	زن کلمبیایی
Colombian (adj)	kolombiyāyi	کلمبیایی
Cuba	kubā	کوبا
Cuban (masc.)	mard-e kubāyi	مرد کوبایی

Cuban (fem.)	zan-e kubāyi	زن کوبایی
Cuban (adj)	kubāyi	کوبایی
Chile	šhili	شیلی
Chilean (masc.)	mard-e šhiliyāyi	مرد شیلیایی
Chilean (fem.)	zan-e šhiliyāyi	زن شیلیایی
Chilean (adj)	šhiliyāyi	شیلیایی
Bolivia	bulivi	بولیوی
Venezuela	venezuelā	ونزوئلا
Paraguay	pārāgue	پاراگوئه
Peru	porov	پرو
Suriname	surinām	سورینام
Uruguay	orogue	اوروگوئه
Ecuador	ekvādor	اکوادور
The Bahamas	bāhāmā	باهاما
Haiti	hāiti	هائیتی
Dominican Republic	jomhuri-ye dominikan	جمهوری دومینیکن
Panama	pānāmā	پاناما
Jamaica	jāmāikā	جامائیکا

240. Africa

Egypt	mesr	مصر
Egyptian (masc.)	mard-e mesri	مرد مصری
Egyptian (fem.)	zan-e mesri	زن مصری
Egyptian (adj)	mesri	مصری
Morocco	marākeš	مراکش
Moroccan (masc.)	mard-e marākeši	مرد مراکشی
Moroccan (fem.)	zan-e marākeši	زن مراکشی
Moroccan (adj)	marākeši	مراکشی
Tunisia	tunes	تونس
Tunisian (masc.)	mard-e tunesi	مرد تونسی
Tunisian (fem.)	zan-e tunesi	زن تونسی
Tunisian (adj)	tunesi	تونسی
Ghana	qanā	غنا
Zanzibar	zangbār	زنگبار
Kenya	keniyā	کنیا
Libya	libi	لیبی
Madagascar	mādāgāskār	ماداگاسکار
Namibia	nāmibiyā	نامیبیا
Senegal	senegāl	سنگال
Tanzania	tānzāniyā	تانزانیا
South Africa	jomhuri-ye āfriqā-ye jonubi	جمهوری آفریقای جنوبی
African (masc.)	mard-e āfriqāyi	مرد آفریقایی
African (fem.)	zan-e āfriqāyi	زن آفریقایی
African (adj)	āfriqāyi	آفریقایی

241. Australia. Oceania

Australia	ostorāliyā	استرالیا
Australian (masc.)	mard-e ostorāliyāyi	مرد استرالیایی
Australian (fem.)	zan-e ostorāliyāyi	زن استرالیایی
Australian (adj)	ostorāliyāyi	استرالیایی
New Zealand	niyuzland	نیوزلند
New Zealander (masc.)	mard-e niyuzlandi	مرد نیوزلندی
New Zealander (fem.)	zan-e niyuzlandi	زن نیوزلندی
New Zealand (as adj)	niyuzlandi	نیوزلندی
Tasmania	tāsmāni	تاسمانی
French Polynesia	polinezi-ye farānse	پلینزی فرانسه

242. Cities

Amsterdam	āmesterdām	آمستردام
Ankara	ānkārā	آنکارا
Athens	āten	آتن
Baghdad	baqdād	بغداد
Bangkok	bānkok	بانکوک
Barcelona	bārselon	بارسلون
Beijing	pekan	پکن
Beirut	beyrut	بیروت
Berlin	berlin	برلین
Mumbai (Bombay)	bombai	بمبئی
Bonn	bon	بن
Bordeaux	bordo	بوردو
Bratislava	bratislav	براتیسلاو
Brussels	boruksel	بروکسل
Bucharest	boxārest	بخارست
Budapest	budāpest	بوداپست
Cairo	qāhere	قاهره
Kolkata (Calcutta)	kalkate	کلکته
Chicago	šikāgo	شیکاگو
Copenhagen	kopenhāk	کپنهاک
Dar-es-Salaam	dārossalām	دارالسلام
Delhi	dehli	دهلی
Dubai	debi	دبی
Dublin	dublin	دوبلین
Düsseldorf	duseldorf	دوسلدورف
Florence	felorāns	فلورانس
Frankfurt	ferānkfort	فرانکفورت
Geneva	ženev	ژنو
The Hague	lāhe	لاهه
Hamburg	hāmborg	هامبورگ

Hanoi	hānoy	هانوی
Havana	hāvānā	هاوانا
Helsinki	helsinki	هلسینکی
Hiroshima	hirošimā	هیروشیما
Hong Kong	hong kong	هنگ کنگ

Istanbul	estānbol	استامبول
Jerusalem	beytolmoqaddas	بیت المقدس
Kyiv	keyf	کیف
Kuala Lumpur	kuālālāmpur	کوالالامپور
Lisbon	lisbun	لیسبون
London	landan	لندن
Los Angeles	losānjeles	لس آنجلس
Lyons	liyon	لیون

Madrid	mādrid	مادرید
Marseille	mārsey	مارسی
Mexico City	mekziko	مکزیکو
Miami	mayāmey	میامی
Montreal	montreāl	مونترآل
Moscow	moskow	مسکو
Munich	munix	مونیخ

Nairobi	nāyrubi	نایروبی
Naples	nāpl	ناپل
New York	niyuyork	نیویورک
Nice	nis	نیس
Oslo	oslo	اسلو
Ottawa	otāvā	اتاوا

Paris	pāris	پاریس
Prague	perāg	پراگ
Rio de Janeiro	riyo-do-žāniro	ریو دو ژانیرو
Rome	ram	رم

Saint Petersburg	sān peterzburg	سن پترزبورگ
Seoul	seul	سئول
Shanghai	šānghāy	شانگهای
Singapore	sangāpur	سنگاپور
Stockholm	āstokholm	استکهلم
Sydney	sidni	سیدنی

Taipei	tāype	تایپه
Tokyo	tokiyo	توکیو
Toronto	torento	تورنتو
Venice	veniz	ونیز
Vienna	viyan	وین
Warsaw	varšow	ورشو
Washington	vāšangton	واشنگتن

243. Politics. Government. Part 1

| politics | siyāsat | سیاست |
| political (adj) | siyāsi | سیاسی |

politician	siyāsatmadār	سیاستمدار
state (country)	dowlat	دولت
citizen	šahrvand	شهروند
citizenship	šahrvandi	شهروندی

| national emblem | nešān melli | نشان ملی |
| national anthem | sorud-e melli | سرود ملی |

government	hokumat	حکومت
head of state	rahbar-e dowlat	رهبر دولت
parliament	pārlemān	پارلمان
party	hezb	حزب

| capitalism | sarmāye dāri | سرمایه داری |
| capitalist (adj) | kāpitālisti | کاپیتالیستی |

| socialism | sosiyālism | سوسیالیسم |
| socialist (adj) | sosiyālisti | سوسیالیستی |

communism	komonism	کمونیسم
communist (adj)	komonisti	کمونیستی
communist (n)	komonist	کمونیست

democracy	demokrāsi	دموکراسی
democrat	demokrāt	دموکرات
democratic (adj)	demokrātik	دموکراتیک
Democratic party	hezb-e demokrāt	حزب دموکرات

| liberal (n) | liberāl | لیبرال |
| Liberal (adj) | liberāli | لیبرالی |

| conservative (n) | mohāfeze kār | محافظه کار |
| conservative (adj) | mohāfeze kāri | محافظه کاری |

republic (n)	jomhuri	جمهوری
republican (n)	jomhuri xāh	جمهوری خواه
Republican party	hezb-e jomhurixāh	حزب جمهوری خواه

elections	entexābāt	انتخابات
to elect (vt)	entexāb kardan	انتخاب کردن
elector, voter	entexāb konande	انتخاب کننده
election campaign	kampeyn-e entexābāti	کمپین انتخاباتی

voting (n)	axz-e ra'y	اخذ رأی
to vote (vi)	ra'y dādan	رأی دادن
suffrage, right to vote	haqq-e ra'y	حق رأی

candidate	nāmzad	نامزد
to be a candidate	nāmzad šodan	نامزد شدن
campaign	kampeyn	کمپین

| opposition (as adj) | moxālef | مخالف |
| opposition (n) | opozisyon | اپوزیسیون |

| visit | vizit | ویزیت |
| official visit | vizit-e rasmi | ویزیت رسمی |

international (adj)	beynolmelali	بین المللی
negotiations	mozākerāt	مذاکرات
to negotiate (vi)	mozākere kardan	مذاکره کردن

244. Politics. Government. Part 2

society	jam'iyat	جمعیت
constitution	qānun-e asāsi	قانون اساسی
power (political control)	hākemiyat	حاکمیت
corruption	fesād	فساد

| law (justice) | qānun | قانون |
| legal (legitimate) | qānuni | قانونی |

| justice (fairness) | edālat | عدالت |
| just (fair) | ādel | عادل |

committee	komite	کمیته
bill (draft law)	lāyehe-ye qānun	لایحهٔ قانون
budget	budje	بودجه
policy	siyāsat	سیاست
reform	eslāhāt	اصلاحات
radical (adj)	efrāti	افراطی

power (strength, force)	niru	نیرو
powerful (adj)	moqtader	مقتدر
supporter	tarafdār	طرفدار
influence	ta'sir	تأثیر

regime (e.g. military ~)	nezām	نظام
conflict	dargiri	درگیری
conspiracy (plot)	towtee	توطئه
provocation	tahrik	تحریک

to overthrow (regime, etc.)	sarnegun kardan	سرنگون کردن
overthrow (of government)	sarneguni	سرنگونی
revolution	enqelāb	انقلاب

| coup d'état | kudetā | کودتا |
| military coup | kudetā-ye nezāmi | کودتای نظامی |

crisis	bohrān	بحران
economic recession	rokud-e eqtesādi	رکود اقتصادی
demonstrator (protester)	tazāhorāt konande	تظاهرات کننده
demonstration	tazāhorāt	تظاهرات
martial law	hālat-e nezāmi	حالت نظامی
military base	pāygāh-e nezāmi	پایگاه نظامی

| stability | sobāt | ثبات |
| stable (adj) | bāsobāt | باثبات |

exploitation	bahre bardār-i	بهره برداری
to exploit (workers)	bahre bardār-i kardan	بهره برداری کردن
racism	nežādparasti	نژادپرستی

racist	nežādparast	نژادپرست
fascism	fāšizm	فاشیزم
fascist	fāšist	فاشیست

245. Countries. Miscellaneous

foreigner	xāreji	خارجی
foreign (adj)	xāreji	خارجی
abroad (in a foreign country)	dar xārej	در خارج

emigrant	mohājer	مهاجر
emigration	mohājerat	مهاجرت
to emigrate (vi)	mohājerat kardan	مهاجرت کردن

the West	qarb	غرب
the East	xāvar	خاور
the Far East	xāvar-e-dur	خاوردور
civilization	tamaddon	تمدن
humanity (mankind)	ensāniyat	انسانیت
the world (earth)	jahān	جهان
peace	solh	صلح
worldwide (adj)	jahāni	جهانی

homeland	vatan	وطن
people (population)	mellat	ملت
population	mardom	مردم
people (a lot of ~)	afrād	افراد
nation (people)	mellat	ملت
generation	nasl	نسل
territory (area)	qalamrow	قلمرو
region	mantaqe	منطقه
state (part of a country)	eyālat	ایالت

tradition	sonnat	سنت
custom (tradition)	ādat	عادت
ecology	mohit-e zist	محیط زیست

Indian (Native American)	hendi	هندی
Gypsy (masc.)	mard-e kowli	مرد کولی
Gypsy (fem.)	zan-e kowli	زن کولی
Gypsy (adj)	kowli	کولی

empire	emperāturi	امپراطوری
colony	mosta'mere	مستعمره
slavery	bardegi	بردگی
invasion	tahājom	تهاجم
famine	gorosnegi	گرسنگی

246. Major religious groups. Confessions

| religion | din | دین |
| religious (adj) | dini | دینی |

faith, belief	e'teqād	اعتقاد
to believe (in God)	e'teqād dāštan	اعتقاد داشتن
believer	mo'men	مؤمن
atheism	bi dini	بی دینی
atheist	molhed	ملحد
Christianity	masihiyat	مسیحیت
Christian (n)	masihi	مسیحی
Christian (adj)	masihi	مسیحی
Catholicism	mazhab-e kātolik	مذهب کاتولیک
Catholic (n)	kātolik	کاتولیک
Catholic (adj)	kātolik	کاتولیک
Protestantism	āin-e porotestān	آئین پروتستان
Protestant Church	kelisā-ye porotestān	کلیسای پروتستان
Protestant (n)	porotestān	پروتستان
Orthodoxy	mazhab-e ortodoks	مذهب ارتدوکس
Orthodox Church	kelisā-ye ortodoks	کلیسای ارتدوکس
Orthodox (n)	ortodoks	ارتدوکس
Presbyterianism	persbiterinism	پرسبیترینیسم
Presbyterian Church	kelisā-ye persbiteri	کلیسای پرسبیتری
Presbyterian (n)	persbiteri	پرسبیتری
Lutheranism	kelisā-ye lutrān	کلیسای لوتران
Lutheran (n)	lutrān	لوتران
Baptist Church	kelisā-ye baptist	کلیسای باپتیست
Baptist (n)	baptist	باپتیست
Anglican Church	kelisā-ye anglikān	کلیسای انگلیکان
Anglican (n)	anglikān	انگلیکان
Mormonism	ferqe-ye mormon	فرقه مورمون
Mormon (n)	mormon	مورمون
Judaism	yahudiyat	یهودیت
Jew (n)	yahudi	یهودی
Buddhism	budism	بودیسم
Buddhist (n)	budāyi	بودایی
Hinduism	hendi	هندی
Hindu (n)	hendu	هندو
Islam	eslām	اسلام
Muslim (n)	mosalmān	مسلمان
Muslim (adj)	mosalmāni	مسلمانی
Shiah Islam	ši'e	شیعه
Shiite (n)	ši'e	شیعه
Sunni Islam	senni	سنی
Sunnite (n)	senni	سنی

247. Religions. Priests

priest	kešiš	کشیش
the Pope	pāp	پاپ
monk, friar	rāheb	راهب
nun	rāhebe	راهبه
pastor	pišvā-ye ruhān-i	پیشوای روحانی
abbot	rāheb-e bozorg	راهب بزرگ
vicar (parish priest)	keš-yaš baxš	کشیش بخش
bishop	osqof	اسقف
cardinal	kārdināl	کاردینال
preacher	vā'ez	واعظ
preaching	mo'eze	موعظه
parishioners	kešiš tabār	کشیش تبار
believer	mo'men	مؤمن
atheist	molhed	ملحد

248. Faith. Christianity. Islam

Adam	ādam	آدم
Eve	havvā	حوا
God	xodā	خدا
the Lord	xodā	خدا
the Almighty	xodā	خدا
sin	gonāh	گناه
to sin (vi)	gonāh kardan	گناه کردن
sinner (masc.)	gonāhkār	گناهکار
sinner (fem.)	gonāhkār	گناهکار
hell	jahannam	جهنم
paradise	behešt	بهشت
Jesus	isā	عیسی
Jesus Christ	isā masih	عیسی مسیح
the Holy Spirit	ruh olqodos	روح القدس
the Saviour	monji	منجی
the Virgin Mary	maryam bākere	مریم باکره
the Devil	šeytān	شیطان
devil's (adj)	šeytāni	شیطانی
Satan	šeytān	شیطان
satanic (adj)	šeytāni	شیطانی
angel	ferešte	فرشته
guardian angel	ferešte-ye negahbān	فرشتهٔ نگهبان
angelic (adj)	ferešte i	فرشته ای

apostle	havāri	حواری
archangel	ferešte-ye moqarrab	فرشتهٔ مقرب
the Antichrist	dajjāl	دجال

Church	kelisā	کلیسا
Bible	enjil	انجیل
biblical (adj)	enjili	انجیلی

Old Testament	ahd-e atiq	عهد عتیق
New Testament	ahd-e jadid	عهد جدید
Gospel	enjil	انجیل
Holy Scripture	ketāb-e moqaddas	کتاب مقدس
Heaven	behešt	بهشت

Commandment	farmān	فرمان
prophet	payāmbar	پیامبر
prophecy	payāmbari	پیامبری

Allah	allāh	الله
Mohammed	mohammad	محمد
the Koran	qor'ān	قرآن

mosque	masjed	مسجد
mullah	mala'	ملا
prayer	namāz	نماز
to pray (vi, vt)	do'ā kardan	دعا کردن

pilgrimage	ziyārat	زیارت
pilgrim	zāer	زائر
Mecca	makke	مکه

church	kelisā	کلیسا
temple	haram	حرم
cathedral	kelisā-ye jāme'	کلیسای جامع
Gothic (adj)	gotik	گوتیک
synagogue	kenešt	کنشت
mosque	masjed	مسجد

chapel	kelisā-ye kučak	کلیسای کوچک
abbey	sowme'e	صومعه
convent	sowme'e	صومعه
monastery	deyr	دیر

bell (church ~s)	nāqus	ناقوس
bell tower	borj-e nāqus	برج ناقوس
to ring (ab. bells)	sedā kardan	صدا کردن

cross	salib	صلیب
cupola (roof)	gonbad	گنبد
icon	šamāyel-e moqaddas	شمایل مقدس

soul	jān	جان
fate (destiny)	sarnevešt	سرنوشت
evil (n)	badi	بدی
good (n)	niki	نیکی
vampire	xun āšām	خون آشام

witch (evil ~)	jādugar	جادوگر
demon	div	دیو
spirit	ruh	روح

| redemption (giving us ~) | talab-e afv | طلب عفو |
| to redeem (vt) | talab-e afv kardan | طلب عفو کردن |

church service, mass	ebādat	عبادت
to say mass	ebādat kardan	عبادت کردن
confession	marāsem-e towbe	مراسم توبه
to confess (vi)	towbe kardan	توبه کردن

saint (n)	qeddis	قدیس
sacred (holy)	moqaddas	مقدس
holy water	āb-e moqaddas	آب مقدس

ritual (n)	marāsem	مراسم
ritual (adj)	āyini	آیینی
sacrifice	qorbāni	قربانی

superstition	xorāfe	خرافه
superstitious (adj)	xorāfāti	خرافاتی
afterlife	zendegi pas az marg	زندگی پس ازمرگ
eternal life	zendegi-ye jāvid	زندگی جاوید

MISCELLANEOUS

249. Various useful words

background (green ~)	zamine	زمینه
balance (of situation)	ta'ādol	تعادل
barrier (obstacle)	hesār	حصار
base (basis)	pāye	پایه
beginning	šoru'	شروع
category	tabaqe	طبقه
cause (reason)	sabab	سبب
choice	entexāb	انتخاب
coincidence	tatāboq	تطابق
comfortable (~ chair)	rāhat	راحت
comparison	qiyās	قیاس
compensation	jobrān	جبران
degree (extent, amount)	daraje	درجه
development	pišraft	پیشرفت
difference	farq	فرق
effect (e.g. of drugs)	asar	اثر
effort (exertion)	kušeš	کوشش
element	onsor	عنصر
end (finish)	etmām	اتمام
example (illustration)	mesāl	مثال
fact	haqiqat	حقیقت
frequent (adj)	mokarrar	مکرر
growth (development)	rošd	رشد
help	komak	کمک
ideal	ide āl	ایده آل
kind (sort, type)	no'	نوع
labyrinth	hezār tuy	هزارتوی
mistake, error	eštebāh	اشتباه
moment	lahze	لحظه
object (thing)	mabhas	مبحث
obstacle	māne'	مانع
original (original copy)	asli	اصلی
part (~ of sth)	joz	جزء
particle, small part	zarre	ذره
pause (break)	maks	مکث
position	vaz'	وضع
principle	asl	اصل
problem	moškel	مشکل
process	ravand	روند

progress	taraqqi	ترقی
property (quality)	xāsiyat	خاصیت
reaction	vākoneš	واکنش
risk	risk	ریسک

secret	rāz	راز
series	seri	سری
shape (outer form)	šekl	شکل
situation	vaz'iyat	وضعیت
solution	hal	حل

standard (adj)	estāndārd	استاندارد
standard (level of quality)	estāndārd	استاندارد
stop (pause)	tavaqqof	توقف
style	sabok	سبک

system	sistem	سیستم
table (chart)	jadval	جدول
tempo, rate	sor'at	سرعت
term (word, expression)	estelāh	اصطلاح
thing (object, item)	čiz	چیز

truth (e.g. moment of ~)	haqiqat	حقیقت
turn (please wait your ~)	nowbat	نوبت
type (sort, kind)	no'	نوع
urgent (adj)	fowri	فوری
urgently	foran	فوراً

utility (usefulness)	fāyede	فایده
variant (alternative)	moteqayyer	متغیر
way (means, method)	tariq	طریق
zone	mantaqe	منطقه

250. Modifiers. Adjectives. Part 1

additional (adj)	ezāfi	اضافی
ancient (~ civilization)	qadimi	قدیمی
artificial (adj)	masnu'i	مصنوعی
back, rear (adj)	aqab	عقب
bad (adj)	bad	بد

beautiful (~ palace)	zibā	زیبا
beautiful (person)	zibā	زیبا
big (in size)	bozorg	بزرگ
bitter (taste)	talx	تلخ
blind (sightless)	kur	کور

calm, quiet (adj)	ārām	آرام
careless (negligent)	bi mas'uliyyat	بی مسئولیت
caring (~ father)	ba molāheze	با ملاحظه
central (adj)	markazi	مرکزی

| cheap (low-priced) | arzān | ارزان |
| cheerful (adj) | šād | شاد |

children's (adj)	kudakāne	کودکانه
civil (~ law)	madani	مدنی
clandestine (secret)	maxfi	مخفی
clean (free from dirt)	pāk	پاک
clear (explanation, etc.)	vāzeh	واضح
clever (intelligent)	bāhuš	باهوش
close (near in space)	nazdik	نزدیک
closed (adj)	baste	بسته
cloudless (sky)	sāf	صاف
cold (drink, weather)	sard	سرد
compatible (adj)	sāzgār	سازگار
contented (satisfied)	rāzi	راضی
continuous (uninterrupted)	modāvem	مداوم
cool (weather)	xonak	خنک
dangerous (adj)	xatarnāk	خطرناک
dark (room)	tārik	تاریک
dead (not alive)	morde	مرده
dense (fog, smoke)	qaliz	غلیظ
destitute (extremely poor)	faqir	فقیر
different (not the same)	motefāvet	متفاوت
difficult (decision)	moškel	مشکل
difficult (problem, task)	saxt	سخت
dim, faint (light)	kam nur	کم نور
dirty (not clean)	kasif	کثیف
distant (in space)	dur	دور
dry (clothes, etc.)	xošk	خشک
easy (not difficult)	āsān	آسان
empty (glass, room)	xāli	خالی
even (e.g. ~ surface)	hamvār	هموار
exact (amount)	daqiq	دقیق
excellent (adj)	āli	عالی
excessive (adj)	ziyād az had	زیاد ازحد
expensive (adj)	gerān	گران
exterior (adj)	xāreji	خارجی
far (the ~ East)	dur	دور
fast (quick)	sari'	سریع
fatty (food)	čarb	چرب
fertile (land, soil)	hāzer	حاصلخیز
flat (~ panel display)	hamvār	هموار
foreign (adj)	xāreji	خارجی
fragile (china, glass)	šekanande	شکننده
free (at no cost)	majjāni	مجانی
free (unrestricted)	āzād	آزاد
fresh (~ water)	širin	شیرین
fresh (e.g. ~ bread)	tāze	تازه
frozen (food)	yax zade	یخ زده
full (completely filled)	por	پر

gloomy (house, forecast)	tārik	تاریک
good (book, etc.)	xub	خوب
good, kind (kindhearted)	mehrbān	مهربان
grateful (adj)	sepāsgozār	سپاسگزار
happy (adj)	xošbaxt	خوشبخت
hard (not soft)	soft	سفت
heavy (in weight)	sangin	سنگین
hostile (adj)	xasmāne	خصمانه
hot (adj)	dāq	داغ
huge (adj)	bozorg	بزرگ
humid (adj)	martub	مرطوب
hungry (adj)	gorosne	گرسنه
ill (sick, unwell)	bimār	بیمار
immobile (adj)	bi harekat	بی حرکت
important (adj)	mohem	مهم
impossible (adj)	qeyr-e momken	غیر ممکن
incomprehensible	nāmafhum	نامفهوم
indispensable (adj)	zaruri	ضروری
inexperienced (adj)	bi tajrobe	بی تجربه
insignificant (adj)	nāčiz	ناچیز
interior (adj)	dāxeli	داخلی
joint (~ decision)	moštarek	مشترک
last (e.g. ~ week)	piš	پیش
last (final)	āxarin	آخرین
left (e.g. ~ side)	čap	چپ
legal (legitimate)	qānuni	قانونی
light (in weight)	sabok	سبک
light (pale color)	rowšan	روشن
limited (adj)	mahdud	محدود
liquid (fluid)	māye'	مایع
long (e.g. ~ hair)	derāz	دراز
loud (voice, etc.)	boland	بلند
low (voice)	āheste	آهسته

251. Modifiers. Adjectives. Part 2

main (principal)	asli	اصلی
matt, matte	tār	تار
meticulous (job)	daqiq	دقیق
mysterious (adj)	asrār āmiz	اسرارآرمیز
narrow (street, etc.)	bārik	باریک
native (~ country)	bumi	بومی
nearby (adj)	nazdik	نزدیک
needed (necessary)	lāzem	لازم
negative (~ response)	manfi	منفی
neighbouring (adj)	hamsāye	همسایه
nervous (adj)	asabi	عصبی

new (adj)	jadid	جدید
next (e.g. ~ week)	digar	دیگر
nice (kind)	xub	خوب
nice (voice)	delpasand	دلپسند
normal (adj)	ma'muli	معمولی
not big (adj)	nesbatan kučak	نسبتاً کوچک
not difficult (adj)	āsān	آسان
obligatory (adj)	ejbāri	اجباری
old (house)	qadimi	قدیمی
open (adj)	bāz	باز
opposite (adj)	moqābel	مقابل
ordinary (usual)	ādi	عادی
original (unusual)	orijināl	اوریژینال
past (recent)	gozašte	گذشته
permanent (adj)	dāemi	دائمی
personal (adj)	xosusi	خصوصی
polite (adj)	moaddab	مؤدب
poor (not rich)	faqir	فقیر
possible (adj)	ehtemāli	احتمالی
present (current)	hāzer nabudan	حاضر
previous (adj)	qabli	قبلی
principal (main)	asāsi	اساسی
private (~ jet)	xosusi	خصوصی
probable (adj)	mohtamel	محتمل
prolonged (e.g. ~ applause)	tulāni	طولانی
public (open to all)	omumi	عمومی
punctual (person)	vaqt šenās	وقت شناس
quiet (tranquil)	ārām	آرام
rare (adj)	nāder	نادر
raw (uncooked)	xām	خام
right (not left)	rāst	راست
right, correct (adj)	dorost	درست
ripe (fruit)	reside	رسیده
risky (adj)	xatarnāk	خطرناک
sad (~ look)	anduhgin	اندوهگین
sad (depressing)	qamgin	غمگین
safe (not dangerous)	amn	امن
salty (food)	šur	شور
satisfied (customer)	rāzi	راضی
second hand (adj)	dast-e dovvom	دست دوم
shallow (water)	kam omq	کم عمق
sharp (blade, etc.)	tiz	تیز
short (in length)	kutāh	کوتاه
short, short-lived (adj)	kutāh moddat	کوتاه مدت
short-sighted (adj)	nazdik bin	نزدیک بین
significant (notable)	mohem	مهم

| similar (adj) | šabih | شبيه |
| simple (easy) | ādi | عادى |

skinny	lāqar	لاغر
small (in size)	kučak	كوچک
smooth (surface)	hamvār	هموار
soft (~ toys)	narm	نرم
solid (~ wall)	mohkam	محكم

sour (flavour, taste)	torš	ترش
spacious (house, etc.)	vasiʿ	وسيع
special (adj)	maxsus	مخصوص
straight (line, road)	rāst	راست
strong (person)	nirumand	نيرومند

stupid (foolish)	ahmaq	احمق
suitable (e.g. ~ for drinking)	monāseb	مناسب
sunny (day)	āftābi	آفتابى
superb, perfect (adj)	āli	عالى
swarthy (adj)	sabze ru	سبزه رو

sweet (sugary)	širin	شيرين
tanned (adj)	boronze	برنزه
tasty (delicious)	xoš mazze	خوش مزه
tender (affectionate)	mehrbān	مهربان

the highest (adj)	āli	عالى
the most important	mohemmtarin	مهمترين
the nearest	nazdik tarin	نزديک ترين
the same, equal (adj)	yeksān	يكسان

thick (e.g. ~ fog)	zaxim	ضخيم
thick (wall, slice)	koloft	كلفت
thin (person)	lāqar	لاغر
tight (~ shoes)	tang	تنگ
tired (exhausted)	xaste	خسته

tiring (adj)	xaste konande	خسته كننده
transparent (adj)	šaffāf	شفاف
unclear (adj)	nāmoʿayyan	نامعين
unique (exceptional)	kamyāb	كمياب
various (adj)	moxtalef	مختلف

warm (moderately hot)	garm	گرم
wet (e.g. ~ clothes)	xis	خيس
whole (entire, complete)	kāmel	كامل
wide (e.g. ~ road)	vasiʿ	وسيع
young (adj)	javān	جوان

MAIN 500 VERBS

252. Verbs A-C

to accompany (vt)	ham-rāhi kardan	همراهی کردن
to accuse (vt)	mottaham kardan	متهم کردن
to acknowledge (admit)	e'terāf kardan	اعتراف کردن
to act (take action)	amal kardan	عمل کردن
to add (supplement)	afzudan	افزودن
to address (speak to)	morāje'e kardan	مراجعه کردن
to admire (vi)	tahsin kardan	تحسین کردن
to advertise (vt)	tabliq kardan	تبلیغ کردن
to advise (vt)	nasihat kardan	نصیحت کردن
to affirm (assert)	ta'kid kardan	تأکید کردن
to agree (say yes)	movāfeqat kardan	موافقت کردن
to aim (to point a weapon)	nešāne raftan	نشانه رفتن
to allow (sb to do sth)	ejāze dādan	اجازه دادن
to amputate (vt)	qat' kardan	قطع کردن
to answer (vi, vt)	javāb dādan	جواب دادن
to apologize (vi)	ozr xāstan	عذر خواستن
to appear (come into view)	padidār šodan	پدیدار شدن
to applaud (vi, vt)	dast zadan	دست زدن
to appoint (assign)	ta'yin kardan	تعیین کردن
to approach (come closer)	nazdik šodan	نزدیک شدن
to arrive (ab. train)	residan	رسیدن
to ask (~ sb to do sth)	xāstan	خواستن
to aspire to …	eštiyāq dāštan	اشتیاق داشتن
to assist (help)	mo'āvenat kardan	معاونت کردن
to attack (mil.)	hamle kardan	حمله کردن
to attain (objectives)	be natije residan	به نتیجه رسیدن
to avenge (get revenge)	enteqām gereftan	انتقام گرفتن
to avoid (danger, task)	duri jostan	دوری جستن
to award (give medal to)	medāl dādan	مدال دادن
to battle (vi)	jangidan	جنگیدن
to be (vi)	budan	بودن
to be a cause of …	sabab budan	سبب بودن
to be afraid	tarsidan	ترسیدن
to be angry (with …)	baxš-am āmadan	بخشم آمدن
to be at war	jangidan	جنگیدن
to be based (on …)	mottaki budan	متکی بودن
to be bored	hosele sar raftan	حوصله سررفتن

to be convinced	mo'taqed šodan	معتقد شدن
to be enough	kāfi budan	کافی بودن
to be envious	hasad bordan	حسد بردن
to be indignant	xašmgin šodan	خشمگین شدن
to be interested in ...	alāqe dāštan	علاقه داشتن
to be lost in thought	be fekr foru raftan	به فکر فرو رفتن
to be lying (~ on the table)	qarār dāštan	قرار داشتن
to be needed	hāmi budan	حامی بودن
to be perplexed (puzzled)	heyrat kardan	حیرت کردن
to be preserved	mahfuz māndan	محفوظ ماندن
to be required	zaruri budan	ضروری بودن
to be surprised	mote'ajjeb šodan	متعجب شدن
to be worried	negarān šodan	نگران شدن
to beat (to hit)	zadan	زدن
to become (e.g. ~ old)	šodan	شدن
to behave (vi)	raftār kardan	رفتار کردن
to believe (think)	bāvar kardan	باور کردن
to belong to ...	ta'alloq dāštan	تعلق داشتن
to berth (moor)	pahlu gereftan	پهلو گرفتن
to blind (other drivers)	kur kardan	کور کردن
to blow (wind)	vazidan	وزیدن
to blush (vi)	sorx šodan	سرخ شدن
to boast (vi)	be rox kešidan	به رخ کشیدن
to borrow (money)	qarz gereftan	قرض گرفتن
to break (branch, toy, etc.)	šekastan	شکستن
to breathe (vi)	nafas kešidan	نفس کشیدن
to bring (sth)	āvardan	آوردن
to burn (paper, logs)	suzāndan	سوزاندن
to buy (purchase)	xarid kardan	خرید کردن
to call (~ for help)	komak xāstan	کمک خواستن
to call (yell for sb)	sedā kardan	صدا کردن
to calm down (vt)	ārām kardan	آرام کردن
can (v aux)	tavānestan	توانستن
to cancel (call off)	laqv kardan	لغو کردن
to cast off (of a boat or ship)	tark kardan	ترک کردن
to catch (e.g. ~ a ball)	gereftan	گرفتن
to change (~ one's opinion)	avaz kardan	عوض کردن
to change (exchange)	avaz kardan	عوض کردن
to charm (vt)	del bordan	دل بردن
to choose (select)	entexāb kardan	انتخاب کردن
to chop off (with an axe)	boridan	بریدن
to clean (e.g. kettle from scale)	pāk kardan	پاک کردن
to clean (shoes, etc.)	tamiz kardan	تمیز کردن
to clean up (tidy)	jam-o jur kardan	جمع و جورکردن
to close (vt)	bastan	بستن

to comb one's hair	sar xod rā šāne kardan	سر خود را شانه کردن
to come down (the stairs)	pāyin āmadan	پایین آمدن
to come out (book)	montašer šodan	منتشر شدن
to compare (vt)	moqāyse kardan	مقایسه کردن
to compensate (vt)	jobrān kardan	جبران کردن
to compete (vi)	reqābat kardan	رقابت کردن
to compile (~ a list)	tanzim kardan	تنظیم کردن
to complain (vi, vt)	šekāyat kardan	شکایت کردن
to complicate (vt)	pičide kardan	پیچیده کردن
to compose (music, etc.)	tasnif kardan	تصنیف کردن
to compromise (reputation)	badnām kardan	بدنام کردن
to concentrate (vi)	motemarkez šodan	متمرکز شدن
to confess (criminal)	e'terāf kardan	اعتراف کردن
to confuse (mix up)	qāti kardan	قاطی کردن
to congratulate (vt)	tabrik goftan	تبریک گفتن
to consult (doctor, expert)	mošāvere šodan	مشاوره شدن
to continue (~ to do sth)	edāme dādan	ادامه دادن
to control (vt)	kontorol kardan	کنترل کردن
to convince (vt)	moteqā'ed kardan	متقاعد کردن
to cooperate (vi)	ham-kāri kardan	همکاری کردن
to coordinate (vt)	hamāhang kardan	هماهنگ کردن
to correct (an error)	eslāh kardan	اصلاح کردن
to cost (vt)	qeymat dāštan	قیمت داشتن
to count (money, etc.)	hesāb kardan	حساب کردن
to count on ...	hesāb kardan	حساب کردن
to crack (ceiling, wall)	tarak xordan	ترک خوردن
to create (vt)	ijād kardan	ایجاد کردن
to crush, to squash (~ a bug)	lah kardan	له کردن
to cry (weep)	gerye kardan	گریه کردن
to cut off (with a knife)	boridan	بریدن

253. Verbs D-G

to dare (~ to do sth)	jor'at kardan	جرأت کردن
to date from ...	tārix gozāri šodan	تاریخ گذاری شدن
to deceive (vi, vt)	farib dādan	فریب دادن
to decide (~ to do sth)	tasmim gereftan	تصمیم گرفتن
to decorate (tree, street)	tazyin kardan	تزیین کردن
to dedicate (book, etc.)	ehdā kardan	اهدا کردن
to defend (a country, etc.)	defā' kardan	دفاع کردن
to defend oneself	az xod defā' kardan	از خود دفاع کردن
to demand (request firmly)	darxāst kardan	درخواست کردن
to denounce (vt)	lo dādan	لو دادن
to deny (vt)	enkār kardan	انکار کردن
to depend on ...	vābaste budan	وابسته بودن
to deprive (vt)	mahrum kardan	محروم کردن

to deserve (vt)	šāyeste budan	شایسته بودن
to design (machine, etc.)	tarh rizi kardan	طرح ریزی کردن
to desire (want, wish)	xāstan	خواستن
to despise (vt)	tahqir kardan	تحقیر کردن
to destroy (documents, etc.)	az beyn bordan	از بین بردن
to differ (from sth)	farq dāštan	فرق داشتن
to dig (tunnel, etc.)	kandan	کندن
to direct (point the way)	hedāyat kardan	هدایت کردن
to disappear (vi)	nāpadid šodan	ناپدید شدن
to discover (new land, etc.)	kašf kardan	کشف کردن
to discuss (vt)	bahs kardan	بحث کردن
to distribute (leaflets, etc.)	towzi' kardan	توزیع کردن
to disturb (vt)	mozāhem šodan	مزاحم شدن
to dive (vi)	širje raftan	شیرجه رفتن
to divide (math)	taqsim kardan	تقسیم کردن
to do (vt)	anjām dādan	انجام دادن
to do the laundry	šostan-e lebās	شستن لباس
to double (increase)	do barābar kardan	دو برابر کردن
to doubt (have doubts)	šok dāštan	شک داشتن
to draw a conclusion	estenbāt kardan	استنباط کردن
to dream (daydream)	ārezu kardan	آرزو کردن
to dream (in sleep)	xāb didan	خواب دیدن
to drink (vi, vt)	nušidan	نوشیدن
to drive a car	rāndan	راندن
to drive away (scare away)	rāndan	راندن
to drop (let fall)	andāxtan	انداختن
to drown (ab. person)	qarq šodan	غرق شدن
to dry (clothes, hair)	xošk kardan	خشک کردن
to eat (vi, vt)	xordan	خوردن
to eavesdrop (vi)	esterāq-e sam' kardan	استراق سمع کردن
to emit (diffuse - odor, etc.)	paxš kardan	پخش کردن
to enjoy oneself	šādi kardan	شادی کردن
to enter (on the list)	darj kardan	درج کردن
to enter (room, house, etc.)	vāred šodan	وارد شدن
to entertain (amuse)	sargarm kardan	سرگرم کردن
to equip (fit out)	mojahhaz kardan	مجهز کردن
to examine (proposal)	barresi kardan	بررسی کردن
to exchange (sth)	avaz kardan	عوض کردن
to excuse (forgive)	baxšidan	بخشیدن
to exist (vi)	vojud dāštan	وجود داشتن
to expect (anticipate)	montazer budan	منتظر بودن
to expect (foresee)	pišbini kardan	پیش بینی کردن
to expel (from school, etc.)	exrāj kardan	اخراج کردن
to explain (vt)	touzih dādan	توضیح دادن
to express (vt)	bayān kardan	بیان کردن
to extinguish (a fire)	xāmuš kardan	خاموش کردن

to fall in love (with ...)	āšeq šodan	عاشق شدن
to fancy (vt)	dust dāštan	دوست داشتن
to feed (provide food)	xorāk dādan	خوراک دادن
to fight (against the enemy)	mobāreze kardan	مبارزه کردن
to fight (vi)	zad-o-xord kardan	زد و خورد کردن
to fill (glass, bottle)	por kardan	پر کردن
to find (~ lost items)	peydā kardan	پیدا کردن
to finish (vt)	be pāyān resāndan	به پایان رساندن
to fish (angle)	māhi gereftan	ماهی گرفتن
to fit (ab. dress, etc.)	monāseb budan	مناسب بودن
to flatter (vt)	tamalloq goftan	تملق گفتن
to fly (bird, plane)	parvāz kardan	پرواز کردن
to follow ... (come after)	donbāl kardan	دنبال کردن
to forbid (vt)	mamnu' kardan	ممنوع کردن
to force (compel)	majbur kardan	مجبور کردن
to forget (vi, vt)	farāmuš kardan	فراموش کردن
to forgive (pardon)	baxšidan	بخشیدن
to form (constitute)	bevojud āvardan	بوجود آوردن
to get dirty (vi)	kasif šodan	کثیف شدن
to get infected (with ...)	mobtalā šodan	مبتلا شدن
to get irritated	xašmgin šodan	خشمگین شدن
to get married	ezdevāj kardan	ازدواج کردن
to get rid of ...	xalās šodan az	خلاص شدن از
to get tired	xaste šodan	خسته شدن
to get up (arise from bed)	boland šodan	بلند شدن
to give (vt)	dādan	دادن
to give a bath (to bath)	hamām kardan	حمام کردن
to give a hug, to hug (vt)	dar āquš gereftan	در آغوش گرفتن
to give in (yield to)	taslim šodan	تسلیم شدن
to glimpse (vt)	didan	دیدن
to go (by car, etc.)	raftan	رفتن
to go (on foot)	raftan	رفتن
to go for a swim	ābtani kardan	آبتنی کردن
to go out (for dinner, etc.)	birun raftan	بیرون رفتن
to go to bed (go to sleep)	be raxtexāb raftan	به رختخواب رفتن
to greet (vt)	salām kardan	سلام کردن
to grow (plants)	kāštan	کاشتن
to guarantee (vt)	tazmin kardan	تضمین کردن
to guess (the answer)	hads zadan	حدس زدن

254. Verbs H-M

to hand out (distribute)	paxš kardan	پخش کردن
to hang (curtains, etc.)	āvizān kardan	آویزان کردن
to have (vt)	dāštan	داشتن

to have a bath	hamām kardan	حمام کردن
to have a try	kušidan	کوشیدن
to have breakfast	sobhāne xordan	صبحانه خوردن
to have dinner	šām xordan	شام خوردن
to have lunch	nāhār xordan	ناهار خوردن
to head (group, etc.)	rahbari kardan	رهبری کردن
to hear (vt)	šenidan	شنیدن
to heat (vt)	garm kardan	گرم کردن
to help (vt)	komak kardan	کمک کردن
to hide (vt)	penhān kardan	پنهان کردن
to hire (e.g. ~ a boat)	kerāye kardan	کرایه کردن
to hire (staff)	estexdām kardan	استخدام کردن
to hope (vi, vt)	omid dāštan	امید داشتن
to hunt (for food, sport)	šekār kardan	شکار کردن
to hurry (vi)	ajale kardan	عجله کردن
to imagine (to picture)	tasavvor kardan	تصور کردن
to imitate (vt)	taqlid kardan	تقلید کردن
to implore (vt)	eltemās kardan	التماس کردن
to import (vt)	vāred kardan	وارد کردن
to increase (vi)	afzāyeš yāftan	افزایش یافتن
to increase (vt)	afzudan	افزودن
to infect (vt)	mobtalā kardan	مبتلا کردن
to influence (vt)	ta'sir gozāštan	تأثیر گذاشتن
to inform (e.g. ~ the police about …)	xabar dādan	خبر دادن
to inform (vt)	āgah kardan	آگاه کردن
to inherit (vt)	be ers bordan	به ارث بردن
to inquire (about …)	bāxabar šodan	باخبر شدن
to insert (put in)	qarār dādan	قرار دادن
to insinuate (imply)	kenāye zadan	کنایه زدن
to insist (vi, vt)	esrār kardan	اصرار کردن
to inspire (vt)	elhām baxšidan	الهام بخشیدن
to instruct (teach)	yād dādan	یاد دادن
to insult (offend)	towhin kardan	توهین کردن
to interest (vt)	jāleb budan	جالب بودن
to intervene (vi)	modāxele kardan	مداخله کردن
to introduce (sb to sb)	mo'arrefi kardan	معرفی کردن
to invent (machine, etc.)	exterā' kardan	اختراع کردن
to invite (vt)	da'vat kardan	دعوت کردن
to iron (clothes)	oto kardan	اتو کردن
to irritate (annoy)	xašmgin kardan	خشمگین کردن
to isolate (vt)	jodā kardan	جدا کردن
to join (political party, etc.)	peyvastan	پیوستن
to joke (be kidding)	šuxi kardan	شوخی کردن
to keep (old letters, etc.)	negāh dāštan	نگاه داشتن
to keep silent	sāket māndan	ساکت ماندن
to kill (vt)	koštan	کشتن

to knock (at the door)	dar zadan	در زدن
to know (sb)	šenāxtan	شناختن
to know (sth)	dānestan	دانستن
to laugh (vi)	xandidan	خندیدن
to launch (start up)	šoru' kardan	شروع کردن

to leave (~ for Mexico)	raftan	رفتن
to leave (forget sth)	jā gozāštan	جا گذاشتن
to leave (spouse)	rahā kardan	رها کردن
to liberate (city, etc.)	āzād kardan	آزاد کردن
to lie (~ on the floor)	derāz kešidan	دراز کشیدن

to lie (tell untruth)	doruq goftan	دروغ گفتن
to light (campfire, etc.)	rowšan kardan	روشن کردن
to light up (illuminate)	rowšan kardan	روشن کردن
to limit (vt)	mahdud kardan	محدود کردن

to listen (vi)	guš dādan	گوش دادن
to live (~ in France)	zendegi kardan	زندگی کردن
to live (exist)	zendegi kardan	زندگی کردن
to load (gun)	por kardan	پر کردن
to load (vehicle, etc.)	bār kardan	بار کردن

to look (I'm just ~ing)	negāh kardan	نگاه کردن
to look for ... (search)	jostoju kardan	جستجو کردن
to look like (resemble)	šabih budan	شبیه بودن

| to lose (umbrella, etc.) | gom kardan | گم کردن |
| to love (e.g. ~ dancing) | dust dāštan | دوست داشتن |

to love (sb)	dust dāštan	دوست داشتن
to lower (blind, head)	pāin āvardan	پائین آوردن
to make (~ dinner)	hāzer kardan	حاضر کردن

| to make a mistake | eštebāh kardan | اشتباه کردن |
| to make angry | xašmgin kardan | خشمگین کردن |

to make easier	āsān kardan	آسان کردن
to make multiple copies	kopi gereftan	کپی گرفتن
to make the acquaintance	āšnā šodan	آشنا شدن

| to make use (of ...) | estefāde kardan | استفاده کردن |
| to manage, to run | edāre kardan | اداره کردن |

to mark (make a mark)	nešāne gozāštan	نشانه گذاشتن
to mean (signify)	ma'ni dāštan	معنی داشتن
to memorize (vt)	be xāter sepordan	به خاطر سپردن

| to mention (talk about) | zekr kardan | ذکر کردن |
| to miss (school, etc.) | qāyeb budan | غایب بودن |

to mix (combine, blend)	maxlut kardan	مخلوط کردن
to mock (make fun of)	masxare kardan	مسخره کردن
to move (to shift)	jābejā kardan	جابه جا کردن
to multiply (math)	zarb kardan	ضرب کردن
must (v aux)	bāyad	باید

255. Verbs N-R

to name, to call (vt)	nāmidan	نامیدن
to negotiate (vi)	mozākere kardan	مذاکره کردن
to note (write down)	yāddāšt kardan	یادداشت کردن
to notice (see)	motevajjeh šodan	متوجه شدن
to obey (vi, vt)	etā'at kardan	اطاعت کردن
to object (vi, vt)	moxalefat kardan	مخالفت کردن
to observe (see)	mošāhede kardan	مشاهده کردن
to offend (vt)	ranjāndan	رنجاندن
to omit (word, phrase)	az qalam andāxtan	از قلم انداختن
to open (vt)	bāz kardan	باز کردن
to order (in restaurant)	sefāreš dādan	سفارش دادن
to order (mil.)	farmān dādan	فرمان دادن
to organize (concert, party)	taškil dādan	تشکیل دادن
to overestimate (vt)	mobāleqe kardan	مبالغه کردن
to own (possess)	sāheb budan	صاحب بودن
to participate (vi)	šerekat kardan	شرکت کردن
to pass through (by car, etc.)	gozāštan	گذشتن
to pay (vi, vt)	pardāxtan	پرداختن
to peep, to spy on	pāyidan	پاییدن
to penetrate (vt)	nofuz kardan	نفوذ کردن
to permit (vt)	ejāze dādan	اجازه دادن
to pick (flowers)	kandan	کندن
to place (put, set)	qarār dādan	قرار دادن
to plan (~ to do sth)	barnāmerizi kardan	برنامه ریزی کردن
to play (actor)	bāzi kardan	بازی کردن
to play (children)	bāzi kardan	بازی کردن
to point (~ the way)	nešān dādan	نشان دادن
to pour (liquid)	rixtan	ریختن
to pray (vi, vt)	do'ā kardan	دعا کردن
to prefer (vt)	tarjih dādan	ترجیح دادن
to prepare (~ a plan)	āmāde kardan	آماده کردن
to present (sb to sb)	mo'arrefi kardan	معرفی کردن
to preserve (peace, life)	hefz kardan	حفظ کردن
to prevail (vt)	bartari dāštan	برتری داشتن
to progress (move forward)	piš raftan	پیش رفتن
to promise (vt)	qowl dādan	قول دادن
to pronounce (vt)	talaffoz kardan	تلفظ کردن
to propose (vt)	pišnahād dādan	پیشنهاد دادن
to protect (e.g. ~ nature)	mohāfezat kardan	محافظت کردن
to protest (vi)	e'terāz kardan	اعتراض کردن
to prove (vt)	esbāt kardan	اثبات کردن
to provoke (vt)	tahrik kardan	تحریک کردن
to pull (~ the rope)	kešidan	کشیدن
to punish (vt)	tanbih kardan	تنبیه کردن

to push (~ the door)	hel dādan	هل دادن
to put away (vt)	morattab kardan	مرتب کردن
to put in order	morattab kardan	مرتب کردن
to put, to place	gozāštan	گذاشتن
to quote (cite)	naql-e qowl kardan	نقل قول کردن
to reach (arrive at)	residan	رسیدن
to read (vi, vt)	xāndan	خواندن
to realize (a dream)	amali kardan	عملی کردن
to recognize (identify sb)	šenāxtan	شناختن
to recommend (vt)	towsie kardan	توصیه کردن
to recover (~ from flu)	behbud yāftan	بهبود یافتن
to redo (do again)	dobāre anjām dādan	دوباره انجام دادن
to reduce (speed, etc.)	kam kardan	کم کردن
to refuse (~ sb)	rad kardan	رد کردن
to regret (be sorry)	afsus xordan	افسوس خوردن
to reinforce (vt)	tahkim kardan	تحکیم کردن
to remember (Do you ~ me?)	be xāter āvardan	به خاطر آوردن
to remember (I can't ~ her name)	be xāter āvardan	به خاطر آوردن
to remind of ...	yād-āvari kardan	یادآوری کردن
to remove (~ a stain)	bardāštan	برداشتن
to remove (~ an obstacle)	raf' kardan	رفع کردن
to rent (sth from sb)	ejāre kardan	اجاره کردن
to repair (mend)	dorost kardan	درست کردن
to repeat (say again)	tekrār kardan	تکرار کردن
to report (make a report)	gozāreš dādan	گزارش دادن
to reproach (vt)	sarzaneš kardan	سرزنش کردن
to reserve, to book	rezerv kardan	رزرو کردن
to restrain (hold back)	māne' šodan	مانع شدن
to return (come back)	bargaštan	برگشتن
to risk, to take a risk	risk kardan	ریسک کردن
to rub out (erase)	pāk kardan	پاک کردن
to run (move fast)	davidan	دویدن
to rush (hurry sb)	be ajale vā dāštan	به عجله وا داشتن

256. Verbs S-W

to satisfy (please)	qāne' kardan	قانع کردن
to save (rescue)	najāt dādan	نجات دادن
to say (~ thank you)	goftan	گفتن
to scold (vt)	da'vā kardan	دعوا کردن
to scratch (with claws)	čang zadan	چنگ زدن
to select (to pick)	entexāb kardan	انتخاب کردن
to sell (goods)	foruxtan	فروختن
to send (a letter)	ferestādan	فرستادن
to send back (vt)	pas ferestādan	پس فرستادن

to sense (~ danger)	hess kardan	حس کردن
to sentence (vt)	mahkum kardan	محکوم کردن
to serve (in restaurant)	serv kardan	سرو کردن
to settle (a conflict)	hal-o-fasl kardan	حل و فصل کردن
to shake (vt)	tekān dādan	تکان دادن
to shave (vi)	riš tarāšidan	ریش تراشیدن
to shine (gleam)	deraxšidan	درخشیدن
to shiver (with cold)	larzidan	لرزیدن
to shoot (vi)	tirandāzi kardan	تیراندازی کردن
to shout (vi)	faryād zadan	فریاد زدن
to show (to display)	nešān dādan	نشان دادن
to shudder (vi)	larzidan	لرزیدن
to sigh (vi)	āh kešidan	آه کشیدن
to sign (document)	emzā kardan	امضا کردن
to signify (mean)	ma'ni dādan	معنی دادن
to simplify (vt)	sāde kardan	ساده کردن
to sin (vi)	gonāh kardan	گناه کردن
to sit (be sitting)	nešastan	نشستن
to sit down (vi)	nešastan	نشستن
to smell (emit an odor)	bu dādan	بو دادن
to smell (inhale the odor)	buidan	بوئیدن
to smile (vi)	labxand zadan	لبخند زدن
to snap (vi, ab. rope)	pāre šodan	پاره شدن
to solve (problem)	hal kardan	حل کردن
to sow (seed, crop)	kāštan	کاشتن
to spill (liquid)	rixtan	ریختن
to spill out, scatter (flour, etc.)	rixtan	ریختن
to spit (vi)	tof kardan	تف کردن
to stand (toothache, cold)	tāqat āvordan	طاقت آوردن
to start (begin)	šoru' kardan	شروع کردن
to steal (money, etc.)	dozdidan	دزدیدن
to stop (for pause, etc.)	motevaghef šhodan	متوقف شدن
to stop (please ~ calling me)	bas kardan	بس کردن
to stop talking	sāket šodan	ساکت شدن
to stroke (caress)	navāzeš kardan	نوازش کردن
to study (vt)	dars xāndan	درس خواندن
to suffer (feel pain)	ranj didan	رنج دیدن
to support (cause, idea)	poštibāni kardan	پشتیبانی کردن
to suppose (assume)	farz kardan	فرض کردن
to surface (ab. submarine)	bālā-ye āb āmadan	بالای آب آمدن
to surprise (amaze)	mote'ajjeb kardan	متعجب کردن
to suspect (vt)	su'-e zann-e dāštan	سوء ظن داشتن
to swim (vi)	šenā kardan	شنا کردن
to take (get hold of)	bardāštan	برداشتن
to take a rest	esterāhat kardan	استراحت کردن

to take away (e.g. about waiter)	bā xod bordan	با خود بردن
to take off (aeroplane)	parvāz kardan	پرواز کردن
to take off (painting, curtains, etc.)	bardāštan	برداشتن
to take pictures	aks gereftan	عکس گرفتن
to talk to ...	harf zadan bā	حرف زدن با
to teach (give lessons)	āmuxtan	آموختن
to tear off, to rip off (vt)	kandan	کندن
to tell (story, joke)	hekāyat kardan	حکایت کردن
to thank (vt)	tašakkor kardan	تشکر کردن
to think (believe)	fekr kardan	فکر کردن
to think (vi, vt)	fekr kardan	فکر کردن
to threaten (vt)	tahdid kardan	تهدید کردن
to throw (stone, etc.)	andāxtan	انداختن
to tie to ...	bastan	بستن
to tie up (prisoner)	bastan	بستن
to tire (make tired)	xaste kardan	خسته کردن
to touch (one's arm, etc.)	lams kardan	لمس کردن
to tower (over ...)	sar be āsmān kešidan	سر به آسمان کشیدن
to train (animals)	tarbiyat kardan	تربیت کردن
to train (sb)	tamrin dādan	تمرین دادن
to train (vi)	tamrin kardan	تمرین کردن
to transform (vt)	taqyir dādan	تغییر دادن
to translate (vt)	tarjome kardan	ترجمه کردن
to treat (illness)	mo'āleje kardan	معالجه کردن
to trust (vt)	etminān kardan	اطمینان کردن
to try (attempt)	talāš kardan	تلاش کردن
to turn (e.g., ~ left)	pičidan	پیچیدن
to turn away (vi)	ru bargardāndan	رو برگرداندن
to turn off (the light)	xāmuš kardan	خاموش کردن
to turn on (computer, etc.)	rowšan kardan	روشن کردن
to turn over (stone, etc.)	qaltāndan	غلتاندن
to underestimate (vt)	dast-e kam gereftan	دست کم گرفتن
to underline (vt)	xatt kešidan	خط کشیدن
to understand (vt)	fahmidan	فهمیدن
to undertake (vt)	mobāderat kardan	مبادرت کردن
to unite (vt)	mottahed kardan	متحد کردن
to untie (vt)	bāz kardan	باز کردن
to use (phrase, word)	este'māl kardan	استعمال کردن
to vaccinate (vt)	vāksine kardan	واکسینه کردن
to vote (vi)	ra'y dādan	رأی دادن
to wait (vt)	montazer budan	منتظر بودن
to wake (sb)	bidār kardan	بیدار کردن
to want (wish, desire)	xāstan	خواستن
to warn (of the danger)	hošdār dādan	هشدار دادن

to wash (clean)	šostan	شستن
to water (plants)	āb dādan	آب دادن
to wave (the hand)	tekān dādan	تکان دادن

to weigh (have weight)	vazn dāštan	وزن داشتن
to work (vi)	kār kardan	کار کردن
to worry (make anxious)	negarān kardan	نگران کردن
to worry (vi)	negarān šodan	نگران شدن

to wrap (parcel, etc.)	baste bandi kardan	بسته بندی کردن
to wrestle (sport)	košti gereftan	کشتی گرفتن
to write (vt)	neveštan	نوشتن
to write down	neveštan	نوشتن

Made in the USA
Middletown, DE
06 March 2022

62229881R00137